HUNGRY GHOSTS

TO THE READER

Hungry Ghosts presents the story of a brutal world in which profanity is commonplace—even often the *essence* of that environment. To delete, or substitute less shocking language—to avoid offending sensibilities—would detract from the courage, the conviction, and the compassion that the author, whose credentials as a Christian are impeccable, brings to her work in a hell that few of us outside the penal system could ever know or imagine. Therefore, we are making an exception to our longstanding policy of deleting such language. We do not recommend this book for children under eighteen or for adults who would be offended by reading strong language.

We make this exception because Mary Previte has graphically depicted the hungry ghosts, the wounded spirits she has ministered to, as they *are*—not to shock but to accurately depict the woeful degradation to which they have been relegated.

We thank you for your understanding of the need for our decision. Names of all Youth Center residents have been changed.

Drugs, Murder, and Abuse
Turned These Children Into...

HUNGRY GHOSTS

One Woman's Mission to
Change Their World

Mary Taylor Previte

ZondervanPublishingHouse
Grand Rapids, Michigan

A Division of HarperCollins*Publishers*

Hungry Ghosts
Copyright © 1994 by Mary Taylor Previte
All rights reserved

Published by Zondervan Publishing House
Grand Rapids, Michigan 49530

Library of Congress Cataloging-in-Publication Data

Previte, Mary Taylor.
    Hungry ghosts : one woman's mission to change their world / Mary Taylor Previte.
       p. cm.
    ISBN 0-310-20665-0 (Softcover)
    1. Camden County Youth Center—Case studies. 2. Juvenile detention Centers—
New Jersey—Blackwood—Case studies. 3. Juvenile delinquents—New Jersey—Blackwood—Case studies. 4. Camden County Youth Center. I. Title.
    HV9105.N52C367   1993
    365'.42'092—dc20   94-1994
    [B]   CIP

All Scripture quotations, unless otherwise indicated, are taken from the Holy Bible,
New International Version®. NIV®. Copyright © 1973, 1978, 1984 by International
Bible Society. Used by permission of Zondervan Publishing House. All rights reserved.

Printed in the United States of America

Edited by Mary McCormick and Lyn Cryderman
Cover designed by John M. Lucas

96 97 98 99 00 01 02 /❖DH/ 10 9 8 7 6 5 4 3 2 1

CONTENTS

To my parents,
James and Alice Taylor,
with immeasurable love

ACKNOWLEDGMENTS

This book would never have been written without the patience of my Youth Center officers, teachers, and social workers, who let me camp out in their space to watch and listen. My thanks to all of these who have shaped this book: John Wiggins, Leo Gold, Bernice Bose, Johann Arnold, Edward Deitrick, Greg Lyons, Robert Reid, Vernon Boyd, Mark Johnson, John Golaszewski, Ray Ruiz, Robert Ranjo, Juan Colon, Ernest Sheppard, William Mapp, Al Thomas, Sonnie DeCencio, Mary Ann Zeiser, and Signe Solem-Stubits.

The Reverend and Mrs. Winsor Cooper and Renee and Mario Pinardo, volunteers at the Youth Center, have been a constant source of inspiration. So has Detective Lenny Hall of the Camden Police Department.

I owe not only thanks but apologies to my cousins, Herbert and Peg Taylor, and to Robert McGee, who gave unstintingly of their time in my search for Camden's past and present. They are not represented in this book in fair proportion to their generosity.

Barbara Seger, Greg and Liz Lyons, and John V. R. Bull have helped with intelligent and ruthless commentary—and bravos when I needed them most. I have been coached by the best: Donald Barlett, Jim Steel, and Gloria Hochman have guided me in turning a dream into a successful book. Editor Charles Layton shaped the stories on Weihsien Concentration Camp and the Youth Center student newspaper when they were first featured in the *Inquirer Magazine*.

Thanks to my former Camden High School student Lewis Katz, who launched me in the career about which this book is written.

I never would have undertaken this book without two friends who have preached to me—for years—that I could do it: Jim Buick, president of Zondervan, college classmate, and lifetime friend; and Joe Hann. They never stop cheering.

My thanks to the Zondervan team who have helped me produce this book: Lyn Cryderman, Mary McCormick, and Scott Bolinder.

No one has lived through the highs and lows of this book more than Alice Previte, my daughter. I only hope *Hungry Ghosts* justifies her faith and her love.

THE LEADEN-EYED

Let not young souls be smothered out
Before they do quaint deeds and fully flaunt their pride.
It is the world's one crime its babes grow dull,
Its poor are ox-like, limp and leaden-eyed.

Not that they starve, but that they starve so dreamlessly;
Not that they sow, but that they seldom reap;
Not that they serve but have no gods to serve;
Not that they die, but that they die like sheep.

—VACHEL LINDSAY

1

MIRACLES

Miss Pyle made us learn it by heart—
the verse about moving mountains. There, right in sight of the barbed
wire atop the concentration camp wall that closed us in. I was eleven
years old that year. I can't remember now how many feet or inches
separated the metal rods that strung the electrified wire across the
barrier walls. Or exactly how many turreted guard boxes dotted the
walls. I remember the jagged glass buried in the concrete. How many
Japanese soldiers. I remember the Bible verse:

"Remember this: If you have faith as big as a mustard seed, you can
say to this mountain, 'Go from here to there!' and it will go. You can
do anything."

You could stand anyplace in that concentration camp and see the
barrier wall, but our teachers kept saying it: Look *inside* you—that's
what matters.

>—<>—O—<>—<

The building was haunted with death. The insulated room at the far
end of the moldering basement had once been the morgue for the
hospital next door. In March, a year before I came, fourteen-year-old
George Dunbar hanged himself upstairs on a pipe in Room 205. A poor
black youngster. Alive and well and waiting for his breakfast at 7:00
A.M. shift change. Hanging dead, with a sheet around his neck at 7:12
A.M.

Few people noticed. Maybe Officers Ed Deitrick and Greg Lyons,
who found him there. The prosecutor.

A delegation from the National Council of Jewish Women who
came to investigate sat stunned in their cars. They said that the
building spoke to them: the Children's Shelter, a place where floors
sparkled but where children never smiled.

>—<>—O—<>—<

The memories exist now only like shadowy ghosts in cobwebby
corners of my mind. Through the telephone I could hear fists crashing

in the background. They blurred the panic I was hearing from the voice on the phone.

"Riot here on the North Side, Ma'am. Lockdown's in progress."

Horror was wheezing through Monahan's emphysema. His gasps made an unlikely duet with the muffled thuds shaking the crumbling plaster of the Children's Shelter.

"Pretty bad, Ma'am." Monahan was afraid I wasn't picking up his alarm. "You better come."

I was being summoned from hosting a dinner party on a Saturday night in March—oak logs burning in my fireplace, china and crystal and candlelight—to put down a riot in an exploding lockup. That's what the Children's Shelter was—a lockup for young teenage criminals and children with family problems. It was a dot on the 684 leafy acres of the county's crumbling human-service campus that also served the forgotten elderly, young drug addicts, the mentally ill. Up on a hilltop hidden behind a grove of oaks the county buried its penniless dead, abandoned babies buried in cardboard boxes. Tucked away under rows of giant sycamore trees at the end of the county, this was Camden County's hideaway for misfits and discards. Camden County, New Jersey.

It was my first weekend on the job. Nine miles later, my car crunched into the parking space marked: ADMINISTRATOR.

Behind security screens rusted to lacework on the second-floor windows I could hear the cursing. Angry teenage boys with bodies as grown-up as men's—with livelier hormones—were being held at bay behind steel doors. Clamoring. Spitting. Assaulting the locks with bruised fists.

This was supposed to be the future spreading invitingly before me? New challenge? New career? With every thud—more like new doubts.

I knew their history: John was there for murder, Stevie for aggravated assault. My mind ran down the daily custody list: armed robbery, rape, looting, stabbing, mayhem of every kind. These were teenage hell-raisers, every one—the dropouts who were rallying frightened citizens to neighborhood watch groups, keeping America at siege behind dead-bolt locks and security alarms.

I had taught Sunday school. Mothered a Brownie troop. Organized block parties in my neighborhood. Taught English in a ghetto high school. Lobbied on children's issues in the state Assembly.

I was the new administrator. Five feet four-and-a-half inches, 125 pounds of clean-scrubbed Middle America. American-Wholesome— walking into the maw of a riot.

The lines were being drawn for a very uneven battle on this cold March night. Sober-faced sheriff's officers stood by, armed with riot gear and Mace.

Standing at the top of the stairs on the second floor were my officers, most of them riot-weary veterans with no reason to be patient. Deitrick had almost bitten his tongue off in a blow to the jaw by one of the boys a few months before. Cerrone had been slashed with a razor blade. DiSeveria had been punched in the face. Several officers had started making paybacks: Talbot and Jobe had taken to sneaking live mice into the shoes of sleeping boys, draping themselves in sheets Ku Klux Klan-like to spook the black boys from Camden's inner city.

It was hard to ignore race. Most of the officers were white. Most of the boys were black. Carpenter had been newly hired that week, untrained—they were all untrained—then handed a fistful of keys and told to start.

When I arrived on the North Side, I found combat in progress against the boy in Room 205. No way the security screen on his window—now badly rusted from urine—was going to withstand the fury of those kicks. To prevent an escape from the now-buckling steel screen in this second-floor bedroom, the officers were unlocking the door to face him down.

It was uglier than anything I'd ever seen: Grown men were using flameproof mattresses to charge 170 pounds of grunting, spitting, yowling, fighting fury. The idea was to sandwich him—pin him—to the wall with mattresses—brute force—until they could capture a flailing arm or leg to handcuff it to the bed. Beds throughout the Youth Center were bolted solidly to the floor, a precaution against angry boys' using beds for battering rams against locks and windows. Up and down the corridor the rest of the boys were pounding steel doors in unison. The building shook with an ominous tom-tom beat of battle. This was the unison beat of a single-purpose mob.

Somewhere deep inside me, I shuddered—they could kill if the locks gave way. This was the North Side, housing twenty older boys. Boys by age, perhaps, but there was nothing boyish about their bodies. These were men. Tonight they were gorillas. I had never heard such language. It was mixed with the Banshee howls from the locked-down bodies straining to see into Room 205.

I suddenly believed every rumor I had heard that week about officers' calling in sick everytime there was a hint of trouble. "Blue flu" they called it. I wasn't sure that my own voice would come out steady tonight. My heart faltered. I struggled to keep something from coming undone inside me. I needed time. A deep-breath pause to think. I felt myself standing tall—and little—both at once. There was something instinctive about this needing to appear in control—yet also vulnerable—to these boys.

My father—very British, every inch a gentleman—had taught me chivalry from the minute I was born. Bold knights always rescued maidens from dragons. Courtesy. Respect for women and mothers. Protecting the vulnerable. There was something visceral about believing that chivalry, respect for women, were lessons these boys knew, too. I did not believe that these boys would hit me.

My officers knew better. Their weapons often were Mace, mattresses, and untrained hands. They stood watching now—I felt their gaze—on a slender young mother in a hostess dress moving onto their battlefield.

This would be a make-or-break stand for me. I knew it. My officers knew it. If I expected these men to rally around me in the months to come, I had to win that night. It was a matter of earned respect. Trust. If I was going to turn upside down this crazy place, I had to start with a win. To the very core I knew it: My men would never rally around a loser.

Nor would I.

I picked my starting point carefully. It would be Stevie, sixteen years old. Room 221. Stevie had already been an eager volunteer, working on a project for me. Could he create a plan, I had asked him earlier that week, a plan for us to reward good behavior instead of always punishing bad?

Punishment was legendary at the Shelter. Teenagers locked in their rooms for day added to unending days. Solitary confinements for any infraction. Isolation had become so boldfaced, the judge had stretched out his angry judicial hand, reaching across the whole length of the county, to issue a court order stopping the seventy-two-hour "medical isolation" imposed at every admission. These youth were waiting for trial. Accused, he said, but not proven guilty. Three days of "solitary"—under the euphemistic name of "medical isolation"—was used to soften up a kid. If locking a grown-up in solitary confinement for no good reason in a jail was against the law, then teenagers would get the same rights. The judge was angry and firm.

Rewards were what I wanted for these boys—not punishments. Little, bite-sized pieces of praise. Something to work for. In this building everyone—old and young—was being punished.

In round, penciled letters in his room, Stevie had sketched some crude rewards. The boys could earn coupons for being cooperative. He listed the prize behaviors: *Get up and go to bed on time; attend school; clean your room; clean the bathrooms.*

They would exchange the coupons for candy bars and chips in a snack room. We could call it "Mary's Market," Stevie had told me. "The 'Mary' is for you," he had said, looking hopefully for my response to see if I was as charmed as he had hoped I'd be. This boy, I would discover, never gave up. Maybe that was the moment when I fell in love with Stevie and this houseful of bad boys.

Mary's Market. The Mary is for you. The Market is for us. He was leaving nothing to chance. For the market, couldn't they use the cobwebby storage room in the basement, across from the morgue?

Someone had left a draft of Stevie's plan on my desk, the beginnings of a masterpiece. I tracked him down—he was playing basketball outside. "It's wonderful," I told him. "Just wonderful!"

"I know," he said, smiling "I'm 'A.T.'"

"A.T.?"

"Academically talented."

Tonight, Stevie would be my starting point—my first point of battle.

I stepped up to the metal door marked Room 221, Stevie's room. Stevie's face pressed waffled to the grate, straining to see through the dimness of the night lights across the hallway into Room 205. The noise was bedlam, bouncing off the glazed yellow brick of the north corridor.

"Stevie," I said softly. They would have to quit banging in order to hear. "Can you tell me what this is all about?" The boy knew that every boy would be listening to see whose side he was on. I was standing close. That in itself said something. I was easily within spitting range.

Stevie began listing the grievances. No recreation. No fresh air. The rec staff never showed up. I felt a flicker of hope. We could do something about these problems.

Brian in Room 222 hushed so he could hear, a brown nose flat against the grille. Rasheed hushed in Room 223.

"That dress looks nice." Quiet. Soft.

Friendly, ordinary words. He was moving the talk off his dangerous turf onto mine. My hand rested unthreateningly on my skirt. "Comfortable," I said, moving closer to the steel door that separated us. "Come on, you guys! I was having a dinner party when they called me."

I thought I saw a smirk. In my book, a boyish smirk is a cue for mischief and pranks, not death threats.

I didn't know why, but suddenly in the midst of a riot I was listening to eager questions from curious boys, up and down the hall.

"How many people be at your party?"

"You drinkin' anything?"

"Wuch y'all bin eatin'?"

"You cook?"

"What town you live in?"

"How much that dress cost?"

"How old's your daughter?"

Could these rugged felons really be asking such ordinary questions? I would think about that moment for years to come. It launched a new battle strategy: a tone of voice and boy talk. Talk to them as though they were ordinary boys, and perhaps ordinary boys would respond. From five years of teaching in an inner-city high school I knew too well: Talk to them as though they are teenage hell-raisers, and teenage hell-raisers respond. Two approaches. I could take my pick. Tonight, these sounded like ordinary boys asking me ordinary questions. I had a gut feeling: Ordinary boys would not go into combat against a lady in a floor-length hostess dress.

Into the night I listened and talked. We talked about boys and parties and recreation, my voice a sleepy, good-night tone. One by one—the excitement gone—they fell asleep.

It was the boys themselves who had calmed the riot, hooked by their boyish curiosity about a slender young mother in a floor-length hostess dress, talking softly to them at each door.

After that convulsive night I never underestimated their potential for savagery. I had seen them angry enough to kill. I had been a player in a drama of mortal danger. We all were. We are still.

It would take a miracle, but the Children's Shelter would have to change.

My mountain.

But I had lived miracles before.

2

WEIHSIEN CONCENTRATION CAMP

They were spilling from the guts of the low-flying plane, dangling from parachutes that looked like giant silk poppies, dropping into the fields outside the concentration camp. I dashed to the window in time to see the American red, white, and blue emblazoned on the plane's vulnerable belly. The Americans had come. It was August 1945.

"Weihsien Civilian Assembly Center," the Japanese called our concentration camp in China. I was twelve years old. For the past three years, my sister, two brothers, and I had been captives of the Japanese. For five-and-one-half years we had been separated from our missionary parents by warring armies.

But now the Americans were spilling from the skies. I raced for the forbidden gates, which were now awash with cheering, weeping, disbelieving prisoners, surging beyond those barrier walls into the open fields. Americans, British, men, women, and children—dressed in proud patches and emaciated by hunger—we made a mad welcoming committee. Our Japanese guards put down their guns and let us go. The war was over.

Kathleen, Jamie, Johnny, and I were the children of Free Methodist missionaries. We and all our classmates and teachers had been taken prisoner in the early days of World War II when Japanese soldiers commandeered our boarding school in Chefoo, on the east coast of China. As the Japanese army advanced, my parents, James and Alice Taylor, escaped to China's vast northwest, where for the remainder of the war, they continued their missionary work. Before the war came, the fabled land of my childhood had been a country of ancient Buddhas, gentle temple bells, and simple peasants harnessed to their plows. But across the China Sea in Japan, land-hungry soldiers were pushing for expansion.

As the Japanese continued to eat away at China, Dad and Mother were finding it increasingly difficult to continue their work in Henan province in central China. The Japanese soldiers were cocky. *When you pass through the city gate, you dismount and bow to us*—that was the order. Twice when Mother hadn't dismounted fast enough from her bicycle, soldiers struck her across the head with a stick. So Dad and Mother took Johnny and me and headed for a breather in Chefoo, where the two older children, Kathleen and Jamie, were already enrolled in school.

The Chefoo School was, more than anything else, a British school. Its purpose was to serve the many children of Protestant missionaries in a vast, foreign continent—to be a tiny outpost where we could learn English and get a Western-style education. The original school had been ten rooms and an outhouse, but by our time it had grown into a modern campus, a schoolmaster's dream, just a few steps off the beach. When the Japanese armies reached Chefoo, Latin master, Gordon Martin, was teaching a Latin noun to the Fourth Form. "So," he said softly, "here are our new rulers."

Wearing steel helmets, bemedaled khaki uniforms, highly-polished knee-high boots, and carrying bayonets, Japanese soldiers took up duty on the road in front of the school. Swords swaggered at their waists. From an aircraft carrier in the harbor, a plane dropped leaflets in Chinese about "The New Order in East Asia." There was no effective resistance. "The New Order in East Asia" had arrived.

It was the schoolteacher in her, I think, but Mother believed in learning things "by heart." With so much turmoil around us—wars, starvation, anxiety, distrust—she was determined to fill us with faith and trust and God's promises. The best way to do this, she decided, was to put the Psalms to music and sing them with us every day. So with Japanese gunboats in the harbor in front of our house and with guerrillas limping along Mule Road behind us, bloodied from their nighttime skirmishes with the invaders, we sang Mother's music from Psalm 91 at our family worship each morning:

> I will say of the Lord, He is my Refuge and my Fortress; my God, in Him will I trust. . . .
>
> Thou shalt not be afraid for the terror by night. . . . A thousand shall fall at thy side and ten thousand at thy right hand, but . . . He shall give his angels charge over thee to keep thee in all thy ways. . . .

Our family choir soared with the music, *to keep thee in all thy ways . . . Thou shalt not be afraid. . . .* We children had also sat in Sunday school, listening wide-eyed to spine-tingling stories of such pioneer missionaries—David Livingston in Africa, John G. Paton in the New Hebrides, and J. Hudson Taylor in China. Hudson Taylor, my great-grandfather, decided at twenty-one to give up his medical studies in England to pursue a dream—to take the Christian faith to every province in China. He sailed to China in 1853, and it was he who founded the Chefoo School in 1881.

He did not believe in public pleas for money or elaborate recruiting drives. He believed in God—and miraculous results. "We do not expect God to send three million missionaries to China," Hudson Taylor had said, "but if He did, He would have ample means to sustain them all." Hudson Taylor founded the China Inland Mission, and God sent a thousand missionaries—and money to support them. We Taylor children grew up on that kind of faith.

Our father was the third generation of Taylors preaching in China. It seemed only natural to us when, in 1940, Mother and Dad left us at the Chefoo School and returned into China to continue their work. After all, it was China's war, Japan's war. England and America were neutral. I was seven years old at the time. My brother Johnny was six.

On the morning of December 8, 1941, we awoke to find Japanese soldiers stationed at every gate of our school. They had posted notices on the entrances: UNDER THE CONTROL OF THE NAVAL FORCES OF GREAT JAPAN. Their Shinto priests took over our ball field and performed some kind of rite and—just like that—the whole school belonged to the Emperor! There was reason enough for panic. The breakfast-time shortwave radio reported the American fleet in flames at Pearl Harbor and two British battleships sunk off the coast of Malaya. When we opened the school doors, Japanese soldiers with fixed bayonets blocked the entrance. Our headmaster was locked in solitary confinement. Throughout the month, Mr. Martin, the Latin master, had been preparing a puppet show for the school's Christmas program, and as far as he was concerned, the war was not going to stop Christmas. Mr. Martin was like that. With his puppet dancing from its strings, he walked about the compound among the children and the Japanese sentries.

And the Japanese guards laughed. They were human!

But with the anarchy of war, the Chinese beyond our gates were starving. Thieves often invaded the school compound at night, and one morning we came downstairs to find, to our teachers' horror, that all the girls' best overcoats had been stolen. After that, the schoolmasters took turns patrolling the grounds after dark, and our Prep School principal, Miss Alisa Carr, and another teacher, Miss Beatrice Stark, started sleeping with hockey sticks next to their beds. Meanwhile in Fenghsiang, seven hundred miles away in northwest China, a Bible school student interrupted a faculty meeting and pushed a newspaper into my mother's hands. Giant Chinese characters screamed the headlines: PEARL HARBOR ATTACKED! U.S. ENTERS WAR!

Mother was stunned. America at war! She had visions of the Japanese war machine gobbling her children—of Kathleen, Jamie, Mary, and Johnny in the bloody clutches of advancing Japanese armies. She knew the stories of Japanese soldiers' ravishing the women and the girls during the Japanese march on Nanking. Numb with shock, she stumbled to the bedroom next door and fell across the bed. Wave after wave of her sobs shook the bed. Then—it might have been a dream—she heard the voice of Pa Ferguson, her minister back in Wilkes-Barre, Pennsylvania, speaking to her as he had when she was a teenager, saying: *"Alice, if you look after the things that are dear to God, He will look after the things that are dear to you."*

In later years she told the story a hundred times. "Peace settled around me," she said. "The terror was gone. We had an agreement, God and I: I would look after the things that were dear to God, and He would look after the things that were dear to me. I could rest on that promise." In the years to come, she said, as Japanese bombs fell around them, and armies marched, and mail trickled almost to nothing, "I knew that God had my children sheltered in His hand."

I remember so well when the Japanese came and marched us away from our school. By then the war had made us enemy aliens. Hong Kong, Singapore, and Malaya had fallen to Japan. Burma had collapsed, and U.S. Major General Joseph Stilwell put it bluntly: "We got a hell of a beating." The Philippines had toppled. It was November 1942.

Wearing olive uniforms, the Japanese soldiers led us off to our first concentration camp, three miles across town. A straggling line of perhaps two hundred children, proper Victorian teachers, and God-fearing missionaries, we went marching into the unknown, singing from the Psalms—*God is our Refuge and Strength . . . therefore we will not fear. . . .*

Local shopkeepers ran to their doors in astonishment. Chinese bystanders wept. We had become prisoners of war. We all had to wear armbands in those early days of the war: "A" for American, "B" for British. And when our teachers and the Japanese weren't looking, the American children turned the "A" upside down, chalked out the crossbar and proudly wore a "V."

We were crammed like sardines into the camp. There were four family-size houses, each bulging with sixty to seventy people. For ten months it was like this. We always sang to keep our spirits up:

> *We might have been shipped to Timbuktu.*
> *We might have been shipped to Kalamazoo.*
> *It's not repatriation,*
> *Nor is it yet stagnation.*
> *It's only con—cen—tration in Chefoo.*

We would hit the high note at the end and giggle. To supplement the dwindling food supply, one of the old Chefoo School's servants smuggled two piglets and some chicks over the wall for us to raise. For the first few nights, we hid the piglets under the veranda and fed them aspirin to keep them quiet. When the Japanese finally discovered them, they accepted them rather affectionately as our pets. In the daytime, propped up on our steamer trunks, we practiced our English lessons, writing iambic quatrains about life in concentration camp:

> *Augustus was a pig we had,*
> *Our garbage he did eat.*

At Christmastime we all felt sad;
He was our Christmas treat.

The beauty of it all! With soldiers patrolling the grounds with swaggering swords, with money supplies cut off, with rationed food and bone-chilling cold, children wrote poetry beneath The Rising Sun! After ten months the Japanese stacked us like cords of wood in the hold of a ship and brought us to Weihsien Civilian Assembly Center, a larger concentration camp across the Shandong peninsula. This camp held 1,400 prisoners, mostly British, Europeans, and Americans from Peking, Tientsin, and elsewhere.

In a prison camp, how do you arm yourself against fear? Our teachers' answer was to fashion a protective womb around the psyche, insulating and cushioning us with familiar routines, daily school, and work details.

Structure. Structure. Structure.

Our teachers taught us exactly what to expect. They marched us off to breakfast for a splash of steaming *gao liang* gruel (animal feed, even by Chinese standards). They trooped us back to our dormitory, mug and spoon in hand, to scrub the floor. We grouped for morning prayers—and sang:

> *God is still on the throne;*
> *And He will remember His own . . .*
> *His promise is true;*
> *He will not forget you.*
> *God is still on the throne.*

We lined up for inspection. Were we clean? Were we neat? Did we have our mending done? We settled down on our steamer-trunk beds for school: English, Latin, French, history, math, Bible. School must go on.

Structure. It was our security blanket. And years later, I would wrap it around my own frightened "prisoners" of another war.

The Weihsien concentration camp in northern China had once been a well-equipped Presbyterian mission compound, complete with a school of four or five large buildings, a hospital, a church, three kitchens, a bakery, and rows of endless rooms for resident students. The compound stretched only two hundred yards at its widest point and one hundred-fifty yards long. Though the buildings themselves were intact, everything else was in shambles, wrecked by how many garrisons of Chinese then Japanese soldiers. With 1,400 prisoners, it was hopelessly overpopulated. In the dormitories, only eighteen inches separated one bed from the next. Your snore, your belch, the nightly tinkle of your urine in the pot became your neighbor's music. For adults, this lack of privacy was the worst hell.

The grown-ups in the camp knew enough about war to be afraid. Indeed, a few came to Weihsien with the baggage of hate from earlier

Japanese prisons, but I saw the war through the eyes of a child: as an endless pajama party, an endless camp-out. I entrusted my anxieties to our teachers in the belief that they would take care of us. Our teachers could fix everything. Or if they couldn't, *God* would.

Our spirits could scamper to the heavens atop the hundreds and hundreds of God's promises like *All things work together for good to them that love God*. We could tell endless chains of Bible stories of God's rescuing His people: Moses leading God's children out of slavery into their Promised Land. The ravens feeding the hungry prophet Elijah in the wilderness. God's closing the mouths of the lions to protect Daniel in the lions' den. We could move mountains.

You could breathe the anticipation: God was going to add our very own story to the miracles of the ages. "I was not afraid of our Japanese guards or of being interned," our Prep School headmistress, Miss Alisa Carr, would write me years later. "There was no sense in taking thought for the future, for there was nothing we could do about it anyway. Occasionally I faced the end—whichever way it went—as being forced to dig a trench and then being lined up and machine-gunned into it, and I prayed that my turn might come near the beginning." I thought about it once when I was young, how curious it was that children watching enemy bayonet drills at dusk could know no fear.

Self-government at Weihsien ruled that every able-bodied person should work. The prisoners did everything—cooked, baked, swabbed latrines. My older sister Kathleen scrubbed clothes. Jamie pumped long shifts at the water tower and carried garbage. Johnny made coal balls. Before and after school, I mopped my square of floor, mended clothes, stoked the fire, and carried not coal but coal *dust*. The Japanese issued only coal dust.

Like every other Weihsien problem, coal dust had its dark side and its bright side. You could take your pick. You could grump yourself miserable about having only coal dust to burn; or, when you were breaking the ice in the water bucket in the morning to wash your face, you could count your blessings that you had anything at all to fuel the stove.

We younger girls made a game of carrying the coal buckets. In a long human chain—girl, bucket; girl, bucket; girl, bucket; girl—we hauled the coal dust from the Japanese quarters of the camp back to our dormitory, chanting all the way, "Many hands make light work." Then, in the biting cold, with frost-cracked fingers, we shaped coal balls out of coal dust and clay—two shovels of coal dust, one shovel of clay, and a few splashes of water. Grown-ups swapped coal-ball recipes. Winter sunshine baked the coal balls dry enough for burning.

One person in the camp who didn't work at a job was Grandpa Taylor. Almost eighty, and the only surviving son of J. Hudson Taylor, he had dwindled away to fewer than eighty pounds. His clothes bagged around his emaciated frame. "Grandpa Taylor," people begged him, "let us take in your clothes to make them fit." He always smiled, his face haloed with glory: "God is going to bring me out of Weihsien," he used to say, "and I'm going to fit in these clothes again."

He was right; he did survive the war and was flown back to England. The grown-ups said that Grandpa looked as though he had one foot on earth and the other in heaven. I snuggled up next to him on his bed and ran my little fingers through the crinkly silk of his snow-white beard to feel the cauterized scar on his cheek where a rabid dog had bitten him in his early days in China. Of all the children in the Chefoo School, we Taylors were the only ones to have a grandpa in the camp.

Why do I remember Weihsien with such tender memories?

Say "concentration camp" to any grown-up today, and you bring flashbacks of gas chambers, of death marches, of prisoners branded and tattooed like cattle. Auschwitz . . . Dachau . . . Bataan.

Weihsien was none of that.

Awash in a cesspool of every kind of misery, Weihsien was daily triumphs—earthy victories over bedbugs and rats and flies. If you had bedbugs, you launched the Battle of the Bedbugs each Saturday. With knife or thumbnail you attacked each seam of your blanket or pillow, killing the bugs and eggs in your path.

If you panicked at the summer's plague of flies, you organized the schoolchildren into competing teams of fly-killers. My younger brother, Johnny—with 3,500 neatly counted flies in his bottle—won the top prize: a can of *Rose Mille paté*, food sent by the Red Cross. If you shuddered at the rats scampering over you at night, you set up a rat-catching competition—with concentration-camp Pied Pipers clubbing rats, trapping rats, drowning them in basins, throwing them into the bakery fire. Our Chefoo School won that contest, too, with Norman Cliff and his team bringing in sixty-eight dead rats—thirty on the last day.

Oh, glorious victory! The nearest competitor had only fifty-six! Without dishes, you improvise. My own "dinner plate" was a can with its lid fashioned into a handle. Prisoners ate boiled cattle-feed from soap dishes, old saucepans, herring tins, enamel mugs, jam pots, or frying pans.

For one, two, three, four, five years I hadn't seen Daddy. I could hardly remember his face now, but I could still hear his voice: "Mary, Sweetheart,"—he always called me "Mary, Sweetheart"—"there's a saying in our family: A Taylor never says 'I can't.'" In the far reaches of my mind, like a needle stuck on a gramophone record, I heard the messages playing:

A Taylor never says "I can't."
Thou shalt not be afraid. . . .
For He shall give his angels charge over thee. . . .

Did he know I would need those angels again thirty years later? With four hundred school-age children in the camp, we shaped our world with childish innocence: We disarmed the Japanese guards with our curiosity about their swords. The soldiers let us take the gleaming steel out of the scabbard and sheath it gently back.

There were also sports. If the food supply is dwindling and starvation near, should you spend your energy on sports? In other Japanese prison camps in Shanghai and in Hong Kong, doctors advised against games and exercise because prisoners had no energy to spare.

But Weihsien was different. Nourishing the spirit was as important as feeding the body. So on any weekday after school, we children played basketball, or rounders, hockey, or soccer.

The man who organized these games was Olympic gold-medal winner, Eric Liddell—Uncle Eric, we called him. The Flying Scotsman. Almost everyone in camp had heard of Eric Liddell. The folklore about him seemed almost larger than life. In later years, the film *Chariots of Fire* would dramatize the accomplishments of this man who had refused to run in the Olympics on Sunday because of his religious convictions.

But Uncle Eric wasn't a big-deal type: He never sought the spotlight. Instead, he made his niche by doing little things that other people hardly noticed. You had to do a lot of imagining to think that Eric Liddell had grabbed world headlines almost twenty years earlier, an international star in track and rugby. When we had a hockey stick that needed mending, Uncle Eric would truss it almost good as new with strips ripped from his sheets. When the teenagers got bored with the deadening monotony of prison life and turned for relief to the temptations of clandestine sex, he and some missionary teachers organized an evening game room. When the Tientsin boys and girls were struggling with their schoolwork, Uncle Eric coached them in science. And when Kitchen Number One competed in races in the inter-kitchen rivalry, well, who could lose when Eric Liddell was on our team?

On a snowy February day in 1945, Liddell died of an inoperable brain tumor. The camp was stunned. Through an honor guard of solemn Chefoo and Weihsien schoolchildren, his friends carried his coffin to the tiny cemetery in the corner of the Japanese quarters. There, a little bit of Scotland was tucked sadly away in Chinese soil.

For a child who used to have to be bribed to take each bite of food as I was growing up, eating the concentration camp food was no problem. I was hungry! In the early days of the war, we lived on *gao liang*, the roughest broom corn, or *lu dou*, beans cooked into hot cereal for breakfast, and all the bread we wanted. Lunch was always stew, stew, stew. "S.O.S.," we called it: Same Old Stew.

Supper was more leftover stew—watered-down to soup. Only the stouthearted could work in the butchery with the maggot-ridden carcasses. Plagues of flies laid eggs on the meat faster than the team could wipe them off. When the most revolting-looking liver—horribly dark and cased with a hard, cream-colored edge—arrived with the day's food supplies, the cooks called in our school doctor for a second opinion. Was it fit to eat? Probably an old mule, he guessed. So we ate it.

If you wanted to see the worst in people, you stood and watched the food line, where griping and surliness were a way of life. Hungry prisoners were poised to pounce on food servers, who were constantly accused of dishing out more or less than the prescribed half dipper or full dipper of soup.

It was a no-win job. Having been taught self-control, we Chefoo children watched the cat-fights with righteous fascination. Shrieking women in the dishwashing queue hurled basins of greasy dishwater at each other. Fights were common but not among the Chefoo contingent.

Our teachers insisted on good manners: There is no such thing, they said, as one set of manners for the outside world and another set for the concentration camp. You could be eating the most awful-looking glop out of a tin can or a soap dish, but you were to be as refined as the two princesses in Buckingham Palace. Sit up straight. Don't stuff food in your mouth. Don't talk with your mouth full. Don't drink when you have food in your mouth. Don't lick your knife. Spoon your soup toward the back of the bowl, not toward the front. Keep your voice down. And don't complain.

We were God's representatives in this concentration camp, our teachers said, and God was not represented well by rudeness or grumbling. Food supplies dwindled as the war dragged on. If you wanted to be optimistic, you could guess that the Allies were winning and that you were going hungry because the Japanese weren't about to share their army's dwindling food with Allied prisoners.

Grown men shrank to 110 pounds. Our teachers shielded us from the debates among the camp cynics over which would come first—starvation or liberation. By 1944, American B-29 Superfortresses from bases in Calcutta, China, and the Marianas were bombing Japan. There were many meatless days. Even the *gao liang* and *lu dou* beans ran out and the cooks invented bread porridge. They soaked stale bread overnight, squeezed out the water, and mixed up the mush with several pounds of flour seasoned with cinnamon and saccharin. Only our hunger made it edible.

An average man needs about 4,800 calories a day to fuel heavy labor, about 3,600 calories for ordinary work. Camp doctors guessed that the daily food ration for men in our camp was down to 1,200 calories. Although no one said so out loud, the prisoners were slowly starving. The signs were obvious—emaciation, exhaustion, apathy.

Some prisoners had lost more than one hundred pounds. Children had teeth growing in without enamel. Adolescent girls were growing up without menstruating. That's when our teachers discovered egg shell as a calcium supplement to our dwindling diet. On the advice of camp doctors, they washed and baked and ground the shells into a gritty powder and spooned it into our spluttering mouths each day in the dormitory. We gagged and choked and exhaled, hoping the grit would blow away before we had to swallow. But it never did, so we gnashed our teeth on the powdered shells—pure calcium. Still, there was a gentleness about these steely teachers.

On my birthday, my teacher created a celebration—with an apple—just for me. The apple itself wasn't so important as the delicious feeling that I had a "mother" all to myself in a private celebration—just my teacher and I—behind the hospital. In cutting wondrously thin, translucent apple circles, she showed me that I could find the shape of an apple blossom. It was pure magic. On a tiny tin-can stove fueled by twigs, she fried the apple slices for me in a moment of wonder. After forty years I still look for the apple blossom hidden in apple circles. No birthday cake has ever inspired such joy!

It was a lasting gift these teachers gave us, preserving our childhood in the midst of a bloody war. But if we children filled our days with childish delights, our older brothers and sisters had typically adolescent worries: college, jobs, marriage.

Kathleen—quite head-over-heels in love by now—was sporting a lovely page-boy coif with a poof of hair piled modishly over her forehead. "God has forgotten all about us," one of her friends moaned one day. "We're never going to get out of here. And we're never going to get husbands." With malnutrition slowing down my hormones, no such foolishness entered my mind.

The Chefoo School had been called "the best English-speaking school east of the Suez," and our teachers had no intention of dropping the standards now. In times of peace, the Sixth Form (roughly equivalent to the senior year in an American high school) boys and girls crammed each year for their Oxford matriculation exams. From these, a passing grade would open the doors to universities in England. And jobs. Nothing will change, our teachers said.

You will go to school each day. You will study. You will take your Oxfords. You will pass. Sitting on mattresses in the dormitory, we conjugated Latin verbs with Mr. Martin while across the room Miss Stark fried bread in peanut oil. In summer heat under the trees we studied Virgil, and Bible history, and French. Between roll calls, scrubbing laundry, scouring latrines, hauling garbage, stoking kitchen fires, the Sixth Form boys and girls crammed for their Oxford exams. In the blistering August heat of 1943, eleven sweltered through the test—and eleven passed. The next year, Kathleen and her thirteen classmates took the exams. They all passed. The year after that, eleven more sat for the exam. Nine passed. And when the war was over, Oxford University confirmed the results.

The missionary and education community of north China in those days was a remarkable collection of talent. Besides teaching the young, the internees organized adult-education classes on topics that ranged from bookkeeping to woodworking to the study of such languages as Chinese, Japanese, Mongolian, and Russian. They could also hear lectures on art, or sailing, or history, and they could attend lively evening discussions on science and religion, in which agnostics debated Roman Catholics and Protestants about Creation, miracles, and the Resurrection. On Sundays there were early morning Catholic Masses, then Anglican services at 11:00 A.M., then holiness groups, Union Church, Sunday night singspiration. We also worshiped in glorious Easter-sunrise services.

Weihsien was a society of extraordinary complexity. It had a hospital, a lab, a diet kitchen. It had its own softball league with the Tientsin Tigers, the Peking Panthers, and the Priests' Padres playing almost every summer evening. Though we young ones never knew, it had its prostitutes, alcoholics, drug addicts, and roving bands of bored adolescents, and scroungers and thieves who filched extra food from the kitchens and stole coal balls left to bake in the sun.

Compressed into that 150-by-200-yard compound were all the shames and glories of a modern city, including music. Someone found a battered piano mouldering in the church basement and made it the centerpiece of a twenty-two-piece symphonette. It was a glorious combination—brass by the Salvation Army band, woodwinds by the Tientsin Dance Band, and violins and cellos by assorted private citizens. There was also a choral society that sang classical songs and madrigals—Handel's *Messiah*, Mendelssohn's *Elijah*, and Stainer's *The Crucifixion*. And yet another group of prisoners organized a sophisticated drama society whose ultimate triumph was its production of George Bernard Shaw's *Androcles and the Lion*.

To costume ten Roman guards with armor and helmets, stagehands soldered together tin cans from the Red Cross food parcels. The church was always jammed for these performances. It was our escape from police dogs, barbed wire barriers, stinking latrines, and gnawing hunger.

Some of us children had grown more than a foot taller since our parents had sent us off to Chefoo School. Providing clothes for a school full of growing children was going to take a giant miracle, but hadn't God promised: "If God so clothe the grass of the field, shall He not much more clothe you, O ye of little faith"? Clothes and shoes for us little ones were easy: We grew into hand-me-downs. We patched and then patched the patches. But clothing the older boys posed a serious problem: They were facing the third winter of the war—with no winter trousers—until Mrs. Lack had her dream. In her dream she was going from mattress to mattress looking for dark blankets that could be made into winter slacks. Blanket for trousers. Of course! Why hadn't they thought of that before?

In the dinner queue—where hunger heightened contentiousness— the skeptics started on Mrs. Lack. "Trousers out of blankets?" "Blankets, my dear, aren't made of woven fabric. The seats will be out the first time the boys sit down." How could they understand that if God had told her to make trousers out of blankets, He would make it His business to keep the seats in? But just then a kindly old stranger interrupted. "I used to be a tailor in Tientsin," he told Mrs. Lack. "I'm old and not much good these days, but maybe I could help you cut them out."

By early December when the thermometer dipped to seventeen degrees, the trousers—hand-tailored—were ready. Temperatures dipped to three below zero that winter. At the end of April when the last snows were melting, the first boy came to Mrs. Lack. "May I wear my khaki shorts now?" he asked.

"It's still a bit cold now, isn't it?" she asked.

"But the seat is splitting in my trousers." He blushed. After five winter months, the first seat had given way!

We would win the war, of course, and when we did, we would need a victory march. So on Tuesday evenings—all so clandestinely, in a small room next to the shoe-repair shop—the Salvation Army band practiced a newly created victory medley. It was a joyful mix of all the Allied national anthems. Because the Japanese were suspicious of this "army" with its officers, its uniforms, and military regalia, the Salvation Army in China had changed its Chinese name from "Save the World Army" to "Save the World Church."

The Salvation Army had guts: Right under the nose of the Japanese—omitting the melodies so the authorities wouldn't recognize the tunes—Brigadier Stranks and his fifteen brass instruments practiced their parts of the victory medley each week, sandwiching it between triumphant hymns of the church—"Onward, Christian Soldiers," "Rise Up, O Men of God," and "Battle Hymn of the Republic." We would be ready for any victor—America, England, China, Russia—or God. And victory would surely come.

In May 1945 the war was escalating to some kind of climax.

In the darkness, I sat bolt upright in my bed. Off in the distance the bell in the bell tower atop Block 23 was ringing. Within moments the camp was in pandemonium. On the roll-call field, angry Japanese voices shouted a staccato of commands. It was clear that they hadn't rung the bell. A bell tolling at midnight—what could it mean? An escape signal? A victory signal?

Numb with sleep and dressed in pajamas, we stumbled outside to the roll-call field where an angry soldier, pistol drawn, barked line-up orders at us in the darkness. They counted us and counted us again.

The Japanese demanded explanations. They were particularly angry, we found out later, since the bell was their prearranged alarm to call in the Japanese army that night if we prisoners reacted with a disturbance. It was one o'clock before they finished the head counts and sent us back to bed, but by then the rumor of what had happened filtered through the ranks. The Germans had surrendered! Chinese coolies (either repairmen or "honey-pot men") who carried out the nightsoil from our latrines and cesspools and smuggled coded messages in and out of the camp—our "bamboo radio"—had brought the news: The war in Europe was over!

Months before, on a dare, two prisoners had made a pact that when the Allies trounced the Germans, they would ring the tower bell at midnight. The camp was delirious with hope. We had licked the Germans, and we were going to lick the Japanese. One month? Two months? Three months more? We dreamed and conjured up visions of The End.

It was Friday, August 17, 1945. A scorching August heat wave had forced the teachers to cancel classes, and I was withering with diarrhea, confined to my mattress atop three steamer trunks in the second-floor hospital dormitory.

Rumors were sweeping through the camp like wildfire. The prisoners were breathless with excitement—and some with terror. Although we knew nothing of the atomic bomb, the "bamboo radio" had brought the news two days before: *Japan Has Surrendered!*

Was it true?

Mr. Izu, the Japanese commandant, was tight-lipped, flatly refusing to answer questions.

Lying on my mattress in mid-morning, I heard the drone of an airplane far above the camp. Racing to the window, I watched it sweeping lower, slowly lower, then circling again. It was a giant plane, and it was emblazoned with an American flag. Americans were waving at us from the windows of the plane! Beyond the treetops, its olive belly opened, and I gaped in wonder as giant parachutes drifted slowly to the ground.

Weihsien went mad.

Oh, glorious cure for diarrhea! I raced for the entry gates and was swept off my feet by the pandemonium. Prisoners ran in circles and pounded the skies with their fists. They wept, cursed, hugged, danced. They cheered themselves hoarse. Wave after wave of prisoners swept me past the guards into the fields beyond the camp.

A mile away we found them—seven young American paratroopers—standing with their weapons ready, surrounded by fields of ripening broom corn. Advancing toward them, intoxicated with joy, came a tidal wave of prisoners. Free in the open fields. Rag-taggle, barefoot, hollow with hunger. They hoisted the paratroopers' leader onto their shoulders and carried him back to the camp in triumph.

In the distance, from a mound near the camp gate, the music of "Happy Days Are Here Again" drifted out into the fields. It was the Salvation Army band blasting its joyful Victory Medley. When they got to the "Star-Spangled Banner," the crowd hushed.

> Oh, say, does that star-spangled banner still wave
> O'er the land of the free and the home of the brave?

From up on his throne of shoulders, the young, sun-bronzed, American major struggled down to a standing salute. And up on the mound by the gate, one of the musicians in the band, a young American trombonist, crumpled to the ground and wept. Overnight, our world changed. Giant B-29s filled the skies each week, magnificent olive bombers opening their bellies and spilling out tons of supplies.

While the B-29s supplied us with desperately needed food, they were also a menace. From giant parachutes, monstrous pairs of oil drums crammed with canned food then hastily welded together, bombarded the fields around the camp. On one such drop, a crate of Del Monte peaches crashed through the kitchen roof. Outside the walls a falling container fractured the skull of a small Chinese boy. Our teachers issued orders for us to run for the dormitories whenever we sighted bombers. They were not about to have us survive the war and then be killed by a shower of Spam.

One Saturday in September as I was running for cover from the bombers, my dorm mate ran toward me, shouting, "Mary! Mary! You may be leaving on the next plane." The following Monday, on the tiny landing strip beyond the camp, Kathleen, Jamie, Johnny, and I boarded an Army transport plane.

After being separated from Daddy and Mother for five-and-one-half years, we were headed home. We flew six hundred miles into the interior, traveled one hundred miles on a Chinese train, and found ourselves at last on an old-fashioned, springless mule cart for the final ten miles of the trip, escorted now by a Chinese Christian friend.

It was a rainy September day, and as the squealing, wooden cartwheels sloshed a foot deep into the mud, it seemed to us that the journey would never end. We finally decided to brave the world on our own, running ahead on foot while our escort, Mr. Soong, brought the baggage along after us in the mule cart. Chinese peasants in the fields along the road blinked in amazement at the four "foreign devil" children struggling through the mud. We were a soggy mess!

Along the lonely, mud-clogged road the *gao liang* corn stood tall in the fields—the frequent hiding place for brigands and bandits to pounce on unwary travelers. Evening was coming, and off in the walled town of Fenghsiang the giant city gates would close at dark— shut for the night to protect the populace from bandits. Kathleen and Jamie, who knew about these things, worried about the city gate.

Would we reach Fenghsiang before it closed for the night? If not, would the gatekeeper break the rule and open it to strangers? But on that night of miracles—September 11—at eight o'clock, the city gate stood wide open as we approached.

On we walked, through the gate and along the main street lined with packed-mud walls. Without electricity, the town was black, the streets largely deserted. Kathleen walked slowly to a man who passed us in the darkness. "Would you take us to the Reverend Taylor of the Christian Mission?" she asked in her politest Chinese. The man muttered something and moved quickly away. In China, no nice girl approaches a man. Neither does she walk in the street after dark. Kathleen approached a second man. "Would you take us to the Reverend Taylor of the Christian Mission?" she asked. His eyes adjusted to the darkness as he looked at us. Four white children. "Yes! Oh, yes!" he said. The man was a Bible School student of our parents, and he recognized at once that these were the Taylor children for whom the Bible School had prayed so long. He was gripped with the drama of the situation.

Down the block, through the round moon gate into the Bible School compound he lead us, stumbling as we went. There, through a back window, I could see them—Daddy and Mother—sitting in a faculty meeting. I began to scream. I saw Father look up. At the front door the student pushed ahead of us through the bamboo screen. "Mrs. Taylor," he said, "the children have arrived." Caked with mud, we burst through the door into their arms—shouting, laughing, hugging—hysterical with joy. And the faculty meeting quietly melted away.

3

GEORGE DUNBAR'S ESCAPE

The Camden County Children's Shelter was a mixture of foundling home and teenage lockup. From 1925 when it was built, this sprawling three-story building reflected America's split personality—a sorry mix of pity and punishment for handling throwaway children. Children slept on metal prison beds lined up in rows in fourteen-bed dormitories upstairs. To prevent escapes, they were forbidden outdoor recreation but on some lucky nights were sent to bed with pitchers of hot cocoa at bedtime. The Shelter struggled with contradictions.

Wayward girls slept on the second floor. An odd assortment of misfit boys slept on the third. They were children who had skipped school or run away from home. Boys who stole hubcaps and snatched pocketbooks. Youngsters who broke into parking meters.

Occasionally the Shelter became a drop-off point for unwanted children, usually when a parent was heading for vacation. The Shelter staff had no way to screen admissions. In those days parents could file papers saying a boy was incorrigible—lock him up—safe—while they vacationed faraway. If a parent produced the official complaint, the Shelter could not refuse. These were children—seven to fifteen years of age. Sometimes seventy-five youngsters crowded the place.

Located in Pennsauken, just a stone's throw away across the border from Camden, it was a stately, three-story brick trash bin for Camden County's unwanted children. Marble stairs, fifteen-foot ceilings, and green linoleum polished to a spit shine. It had teenagers, children, and babies locked behind steel doors and bars.

In the juvenile courtroom facing the street downstairs, black-robed judges sentenced the county's bad boys to locked cottages at the Training School for Boys in Jamesburg, to be rehabilitated among cows and corn on the rolling farmlands there. Girls who couldn't act nice at home—so-called incorrigibles—were sentenced to the sprawling campus of the State Training School for Girls in Trenton.

In 1963 the county renovated a building that had once housed nurses and the county morgue, and moved the Children's Shelter and the Juvenile Court down-county to the county's sprawling, 684-acre

Lakeland campus. It was a move of convenience. The Children's Shelter was now connected to a crumbling hospital for the elderly. Up an enclosed ramp, orderlies pushed giant metal food carts—creamed chipped beef on toast, creamed eggs—food for old folks who had no teeth—now also served to teenagers—carts pushed from the hospital kitchen through padlocked steel doors that opened into the Shelter. For medical care, officers escorted handcuffed teenagers down the ramp to the doctor's office in the hospital basement. A blast of a buzzer summoned someone to unlock the metal doors. Trucks carted linens to and from the hospital laundry.

Steel beds brought from the old Children's Shelter were bolted to floors in bare, high-ceilinged cells. A steel bed. Bare walls. A radiator. Exposed pipes. Nothing else. Angry boys, locked in for days, urinated on the pipes until the place often smelled like an unflushed toilet in a hothouse. The place had no thermostats to control the heat in the cells.

There were no foundling babies anymore—the Shelter was designed as a temporary holding center for youths seven to fifteen years of age. Sixteen- and seventeen-year-olds began arriving when judges rebelled against subjecting older teens to horror stories in the county jail's notorious "J-block" for juveniles. It was the kind of tough love that the nation believed in: locks, metal, brute force, making nobodies feel even more like nobodies—then maybe they would change. A folder in the office file listed boys admitted *wearing long hair*. The definition of long hair, it said, is "any hair that covers the top of the shirt collar or longer."

By the 1970s, Steven Termy's hair had grown from collar to shoulder length. So had almost everyone else's on the list, which stretched down the page. Most residents at the Shelter were teenagers in trouble.

No one asked many questions about the Shelter—until George Dunbar hanged himself in 1973.

><+>-O-<+><

George Dunbar's foster mother was in the hospital with pneumonia, and his father was working the night shift in a factory in Camden the night that George started arguing with his little sister. George's job was to keep an eye on his little sister.

Next-door neighbors in Berlin Township had agreed to look in on the children from time to time. A latchkey watch. The neighbors broke up the argument that cold March night.

They told George's foster father about the fight. A payback thing—throwing rocks through several windows of the neighbor's house. George didn't like people ratting on him.

Despite the foster parents' making restitution, the neighbors signed a complaint against the boy, and George Dunbar, who had never before been arrested, was taken by the Berlin Township police to be locked up at the Camden County Children's Shelter. He was fourteen years old—charged in front of a black-robed judge with the crime of mischievous behavior.

At the Children's Shelter, no psychiatrist called. No counselor came. The foster parents, Mr. and Mrs. Harris, said that Mrs. Harris's illness and her husband's job kept them from visiting. George had lived with the Harris family since he was eighteen months old.

At breakfast time ten days later on a Thursday morning in Room 205, George Dunbar hanged himself. An eighth grader who played the saxophone and loved basketball, George took a sheet, made a noose of it, and hanged himself from a pipe in the ceiling. Nobody knew why.

Daisy Harris, his foster mother, said the boy had never been into crime or violence, though "maybe George did need some help," she said. Since January he had been hassling his teachers.

The Berlin Township police chief said that he didn't think that the boy deserved to be locked up in the Shelter with muggers and purse snatchers, but they had to put him somewhere because the foster parents couldn't handle him.

The police complaint that put George Dunbar into the lockup was signed by a policeman named Jay Clancy. The complaint said: "The child is a ward of the state, and the parents do not want him back."

Samuel and Daisy Harris said they *did* want George Dunbar back; they loved him very much, they said, but they couldn't handle his problems during Daisy's illness.

There were only nineteen boys and girls in the Shelter that March morning when George Dunbar hanged himself. While the medical examiner took the body out, Ed Deitrick, who had found the boy hanging, and Bob Beaver, the recreation man, took the North Side boys across the street to a meadow to play tag football. No one wanted to sleep in Room 205 after that. Forever after that, Greg Lyons, who had tried without luck to cut the boy down from the pipes with a butter knife, always came to work with a pocket knife tucked ready in his trousers.

What was happening at the Camden County Children's Shelter was not so different from what was happening to troubled children all across America.

From one coast to the other, juvenile and family court judges were locked in debate: Should judges and police be locking up children who run away from home or refuse to go to school? Should they lock up disobedient children? Judges called it the debate over "deinstitutionalization."

Some voices said judges *should* control children—even lock them up—to save them from themselves—save them from pimps and drugs and sex and dangerous streets.

But there were other voices, too. In Tucson, Arizona's juvenile court, presiding Judge John P. Collins took off his gloves: "We send a kid to juvenile court to teach him a lesson," he said. "If only *we* realized what lessons we are teaching. . . . The learning in our institutions is phenomenal. Any eleven-year-old can, within forty-eight hours, learn to pick locks, hot-wire cars, shoplift without getting caught.

"We are an equal-opportunity institution. We will jail anyone—especially the least qualified to otherwise survive. We take the poor, the helpless, the downtrodden—we pretty well exclude the rich, the powerful, the influential. We will take any child that society doesn't want to put up with."

Children were beginning to get rights that adults had long taken for granted. In Globe, Arizona, in the 1960s, when fifteen-year-old Gerald Gault was convicted of making lewd and obscene phone calls, the court sentenced him to the state industrial school until he was twenty-one. For making obscene phone calls, a fifteen-year-old got a six-year sentence—longer than some grown-ups were sentenced for murder!

No one notified Gerald's parents that he was in custody. No one required the complaining witness to be present at the hearing. No one told Gerald or his parents that he could have a lawyer, that the boy could remain silent. No one made a transcript of the hearing. He was refused a chance to appeal. The United States Supreme Court said the boy's rights were violated. With that decision, the Supreme Court gave a list of rights to children that every adult already had: a right to remain silent, a right to have a lawyer, a right to confront accusers, a right to be told specific charges, and enough time to prepare a defense.

In Camden County, New Jersey, George Dunbar's death turned on the floodlight.

In much of America, elected officials who run county governments are called county commissioners. New Jersey calls them freeholders. When the prosecutor and county officials went to the Children's Shelter to investigate the hanging, freeholder Lewis Katz was appalled at what he found. One eleven-year-old boy had been locked in isolation for five days, allowed out only to use the bathroom. A nine-year-old who had been sodomized by his mother's boyfriend had been brought sobbing to the Shelter and locked alone in a cell until the state could find him another home. First-time runaways were locked up with young criminals. Katz saw rainwater flooding the soggy basement Ping-Pong room, the Shelter's only indoor place to play. The Ping-Pong table was warped from the rain. The Shelter had no social workers. No counselors. The only full-time staff were guards.

To Lewis Katz, who had two children of his own, the Children's Shelter was a pit. He spoke his mind. This place was a page out of *Oliver Twist*, he said. And the newspapers printed every word.

Lewis Katz's outrage brought a trail of investigators. The Prosecutor came to see. Elected officials. A blue-ribbon panel. Horrified ladies came. They were observers from the National Council of Jewish Women who were studying juvenile justice that year.

If children had known torment in the Shelter for how many decades, now the staff would know it, too. Staff limped home from their eight-hour shifts under a barrage of newspaper stories and reports that labeled them as dogs. Some were interrogated.

"We've been in hell down here ever since that boy was killed," Monahan, a Shelter janitor, told anyone who would listen. "We're not even allowed to say boo to the kids now, and that kid, Dunbar, was vicious, he was a mean little . . .

"The other week, we shot a little Mace on this kid's stomach and they were screaming about it. . . . We can't lay a hand on the kids anymore. Now if we have trouble we call the cops in. They can get away with it—we can't."

Chemical Mace was locked in a big green cabinet in a closet on the South-Side wing. The rulebook didn't put any limits on who could use the Mace. For ang boys, locked into cells and banging on their doors, a blast or two of Mace from the black aerosol cans was crisis intervention made easy: You quieted down the whole floor by shooting a stream of Mace into a locked room. One boys' supervisor made a discovery: He could drape a blanket over the see-through grill on the cell door and spray Mace onto a blanket draped over the hot radiator along the cell wall. For a whole shift it could keep a boy crying and choking. The Mace would never dissipate.

From the day that I arrived, I heard stories of Mace at wake-up calls: "This one dude come walkin' down the hall—'Good morning, Henry, *pshtt! pshtt!*'"—the boy raised his hand and squirted an imaginary Mace container at me.

From late afternoon until breakfast, when the superintendent was absent, no one was supervising employees.

A North-Side boy said a janitor was fondling him when he was assigned alone to help the man sweep the downstairs office hallway. He couldn't get anyone to believe him.

Boys said that staff assigned to the midnight shift slept throughout the night. Boys urinated on floors and security screens when no one awakened to unlock their doors for toilet calls.

Sixteen-year-old Mark Henson recalled the way Harry Wilkins was treated: Harry got his food on the floor—in a dog dish. Harry was a deaf mute who was sent to the Shelter because he wouldn't cooperate at his special school. He had been running away from foster homes for years. Harry was a legend at the Shelter even after I came—a very sloppy eater, Mark recalled. Boys' supervisors had made Harry crawl like a dog for his food and lap it up from his bowl.

The *Philadelphia Inquirer* trumpeted the news that a lot of the employees "aren't fit to care for animals, let alone children." A

Shelter volunteer had dared to tell it like it was. She was barred forever from the place.

Fifty-nine-year-old John Milton Slim had been Shelter director for almost twenty-five years. Before that he had been a probation officer. Almost every boy's supervisor could remember Mr. Slim's recounting his day in the "killing room" at Trenton State Prison. By invitation— to an execution, in every detail . . . the guards . . . the death switch . . . the lights dimming in the prison when they threw the switch . . . the jerking body . . . how he had watched this "poor b____d die." It was a story that Mr. Slim told over coffee in the South Side, where the younger boys were housed.

Mr. Slim came from a different generation of child care. He couldn't understand the questions that kept coming after George Dunbar died. "These kids are out on Friday and back on Monday—they like it so much," he said.

"They grow up here. They like it here. It's clean and they get three meals. They have companionship. . . ."

But not George Dunbar.

4

FOOTPRINTS
THAT LAST FOREVER

The boys were endlessly curious about how I came to such a place. The story of how I got to the Youth Center became my trademark. I called it "Footprints That Last Forever."

Sometimes I told it to a boy while we perched within touching distance in his room. Or in my office. Whenever anyone asked the question about how I came there, they got the story.

Table by table, the officers are leading the older boys from the cafeteria at lunchtime on a sullen day in winter.

David sits next to me near the salad bar, finishing his pepperoni pizza. "How come the judge don't let me go home?" he asks me. "I ain't messed up."

"Maybe your record?"

"The way I see it, I finished three years at training school, maxed out on parole. . . ."

"And now you're back in trouble."

The clatter of trays being washed in the kitchen makes it hard to hear. I signal the other boys to tune in.

"David wants to know how come the judge won't let him out of here."

A chorus of "yehs."

"Do you know the word *reputation*? Good record?

"Bad record? Leaving an impression?" Sneakers kick the table leg. "Everything you do leaves a record."

"Like a footprint." Chris joins in.

"People always remember. Like police. Ever know a policeman to forget your record?" Heads shake from side to side.

"And judges. You want to go home, Daniel? Judge gets a secretary to pull out your record." Long pause. "Good record. Bad record. Leaving footprints. Footprints that last forever."

Forever. I can practically see that idea penetrating like ink onto a blotter. *Forever.*

"Can I tell you a story?" I wait. "Any of you go to Camden High?"

Chris nods. And Daniel.

Everyone in Camden knew the stately landmark of Camden High, like turrets of a giant castle alongside the park. "The Castle on the Hill." We were a handful of novice teachers, fresh with new ideas from college—walking in awe in the footsteps of teachers whom the boys called the "blue-haired set."

"Not too long out of college . . . teaching five years at Camden High School. You didn't know that, David?"

He shakes his head.

"I was about this tall, this big" (I measure with my hand). Teaching English and journalism, I was so young that everyone thought I was one of the kids.

"A long time ago. Would I figure any of the guys were measuring me, sizing me up as to what kind of person I was? You never know. I was a young teacher who looked like a kid." I let them adjust their mental picture of me.

"Well, this one student was sizing me up. Checking me out. This one boy in my home-room, Lewis Katz, who was always into mischief—smart but always playing. Like he was the one who went around the Castle, put the muscle on the twelfth graders—the strong-arm guys. He and his boys threatened everyone, making them vote to dedicate their yearbook to me. Vote for Mrs. Previte—or else."

The boys sniff as though they know that game.

"My second year, with seventy teachers in the school, they dedicate the yearbook to me—you know, *The Purple and Gold.*

"A teacher gets a pretty good idea in her head. This boy is going to be someone important, that girl is going to make it big. Gut feeling. Right?"

By this time, except for our table, the cafeteria is empty. I can see the wheels turning in their heads. Nobody moves.

"Well, I could tell that Lewis Katz was a boy who would make it big. He was in national speech competition, had good grades, that kind of thing.

"Sure enough, this boy went to Temple University. He was a classmate of Bill Cosby. Buddies. Bill Cosby was in charge of inviting famous entertainers to the campus, and Lewis Katz was in charge of inviting famous politicians. They were friends.

"After he got out of law school, I used to see Lewis Katz's name in the newspaper. I had quit teaching to be at home with a new baby daughter while she was growing up. Ten or twelve years went by.

"You paying attention, David?" I watch the boys around the table, finishing their pizza and trying to imagine me as a young teacher.

"Ten or twelve years after he left Camden High, Lewis Katz decided that he wanted to run for freeholder—freeholders are the people who run our county government," I tell the boys, "—run for election. The funny thing was, no one thought the political machine could be toppled.

"This guy remembered me from ten or twelve years before at Camden High. He sat in my living room and asked me to be his campaign manager. Help get him elected. Send letters. Shake hands. Pass letters door to door. I remember sitting on the red couch in my living room when he asked me. From all those years before, he remembered what kind of person I was, what kind of work I did.

"All those times when kids from the journalism class piled all over the floor in my living room, putting the student newspaper together. Going for the state basketball championship—in the bleachers, I'd line up all the twelfth graders and make them quote Macbeth: *Tomorrow and tomorrow and tomorrow....* I always made them memorize from *Macbeth* in my English class. Can you believe it!" I always got carried away, remembering, every time I told the story— "Shakespeare, *Macbeth*, at the Camden High basketball tournaments! That was the year Camden High started winning state basketball championships. Empowered by Shakespeare, no doubt.

"Well, this man Lewis Katz remembered."

"'Membered your reputation," says Chris.

"Right. Well, we won the election. A fluke. I had never run an election campaign—not in my whole life."

Sitting at the lunch table, I can feel that long-ago wonder again— now, how many years later. "I could not believe we won. An upset. Elected freeholder, my former home-room student Lewis Katz put in charge of the Youth Center—except it was called the Children's Shelter in those days."

"Messed up!" David looks out the window, points across the ball field. "That building?"

"The two-story one." I nod my head. "The place was a snake pit. You can't even imagine how bad it was. A boy had hanged himself upstairs on the North Side. George Dunbar. My assistant, Mr. Lyons? He cut the kid down, a boy just turned fourteen. From that day on, Greg Lyons has carried a pocket knife to work just in case, ever since that day, in case he would ever again have to save a kid from hanging. There were riots and sheriff's officers called in almost every week . . . rainwater and backup from the toilets all across the basement. Kids had to go down in the basement and sweep up the stuff.

"Lewis Katz began looking for a new person to run the place, remembered from Camden High what kind of teacher I was—liking kids, knowing every kid's name, staying after school. After all that time, he remembered.

"People never forget. He hired me."

The boys sit thinking in silence. "One thing," says Chris, wiping pizza from his fingers. "People never forget what you do."

David takes longer to answer. "The way I see it, something you do when you young—it can affect you later on—for a long, long time."

In the election-night fever on a November night I could not believe that we had won. With strained, anxious faces through election evening, hour by hour, watching vote tallies changing on the wall. I was crushed inside this tiny room, sweaty and crowded with anxious bodies wearing giant blue-and-white buttons, *Lewis Katz for freeholder*. All of us who had put up signs, passed out flyers door to door, handed out literature at shopping centers, organized coffee klatches. A shoestring operation of political beginners with makeshift blackboards for vote tallies tacked up on the walls and win-against-anything hope. Red, white, and blue streamers and campaign signs were everywhere: *Simon and Katz*. It was a staggering election upset: two young political upstarts toppling a powerful machine and BANGO! We had done it. Won. We had beat the machine.

Within a year of Lewis Katz's election, the victory propelled me into the halls of power. I had become his administrative assistant. In the mornings I now drove to Camden, walked up marble steps into the vaulted marble rotunda of the courthouse, and sat behind a freeholder's polished wooden desk in an office on the second floor. Inside these massive halls, black-robed judges married and divorced people. Juries found people guilty or innocent. Homeowners registered the deeds to their homes. Freeholders spent millions to build roads and college buildings.

In Lewis Katz's office on the second floor, I handled his county business and wrote his letters. He had never known failure. The trappings of success were everywhere. On the walls of his hideaway hung framed black-and-white pictures of Lewis Katz with Walter Mondale. Another with Lyndon Johnson. A steady stream of people wanting political favors hovered around freeholder offices and cozied up to secretaries.

Even in these halls of power George Dunbar's death was intersecting with my life on a path that was leading me to the Shelter. In the file cabinet in Lewis Katz's office, a folder bulged with testimony about the suicide of the boy.

Starting in 1974, a young reporter from the *Philadelphia Inquirer* scorched Camden County political leaders with almost daily investigations of the Children's Shelter: SHELTER UNFIT FOR ANIMALS— ABUSE CHARGED AT SHELTER—STATE TAKEOVER URGED.

Rod Nordland was a firebrand reporter fresh out of Penn State's journalism school. In later years, he would risk death to expose the filthy soul of a local motorcycle gang known as the Warlocks. He would give horrified Americans an inside look at death camps in Southeast Asia. A motorcycle-riding, ponytailed rebel bred in America's 1960s, he put nothing off-limits in his search for justice. He wrote about runaways being locked up with murderers. He quoted Shelter staff who said judges treated black children differently from

white. He wrote when riots disrupted the Shelter school. Nordland's
stories soon attracted cameras from Philadelphia's television news
teams.

George Dunbar's death and the daily spotlight of stories in the
Philadelphia Inquirer forced the issue of who was going to run the
Children's Shelter. Nordland's stories hit readers who were sick of
injustice. John F. Kennedy was dead. Martin Luther King, Jr., was
dead. Vietnam had divided the nation. In Camden County, Nordland's
stories were a daily embarrassment to political leaders. They stirred
up do-gooders and activists.

In a generation past, John Milton Slim had been picked to run the
Children's Shelter because he had the no-nonsense background of a
probation officer. Times had changed. A fourteen-year-old boy had
hanged himself. Runaways were being locked up like criminals.
Children were being Maced. If change was to come, it would start at
the top . . . someone with a sunnier view of children. Lewis Katz
would make the choice because the stinking Children's Shelter was in
his department.

Lewis Katz was a lawyer, born and reared in Camden's inner city.
He was a father of two and a Jew with a profound sense of social
justice. I was the contradiction of everything that had come before.
Choosing his high school home-room teacher—the sprout who could
stand by the chalkboard and capture the room by quoting the Bible
today and Tennyson tomorrow. It was like deserting the predictable,
giving the future of a buildingful of hell-raisers to a novice, an
unknown. Lewis Katz was hit with a barrage of questions with his
choice . . . "Where did she come from?" . . . "Why does she need
curtains for the windows?" The *Philadelphia Inquirer* trumpeted its
judgment: "political appointee."

I was asking for a small miracle. But I believed in miracles. I had
walked with angels and miracles all my life—wonders and mysteries
beyond what I touched and saw and smelled: What angel guarded my
bed in China when I was seven years old and my appendix ruptured?
Who made the miracle when our baby Alice was born, when I had
almost given up dreaming that I could have a child? Who sent the
anonymous check when my daddy—a young man—first came to
America from Shanghai on a miracle—no money and his pockets
empty? My world was full of mystery and surprise. You sailed into
this giant ocean, moving away from the safety of the shore, not
knowing the destination—but knowing One was there. The world
isn't flat—the way folks said. It is round, with distant shores to find.

This new step was a leap of faith. I had been locked up for three
years myself as a child and knew what helps a child survive. I stepped
into hell, brandishing an almost girlish brand of triumph. We had to
reinvent the place—reimagine everything. Reimagining was indis-
pensable. It was not inevitable.

I didn't think about it as a child, but Taylors were never ordinary people. We Taylors believed that we could beat the world. My mother did. My father did. I thought that everybody felt that way. It came from a feeling that God has His kindly hand on us all.

>‑+‑<>‑O‑<>‑+‑<

For a Taylor, being rich has nothing to do with money. James Taylor, my father, said that the fruit of the Spirit is love, joy, peace, gentleness, goodness, meekness. Just as the Bible says. My father and mother always taught us who we are. In our family, our value was never measured by what we wore or what we had. My father wanted character—not show.

If someone wanted to know who the Children's Shelter's new administrator was, they might have looked to my parents, James and Alice Taylor. They had spent a lifetime telling their children: You can be anything.

Alice Taylor said that God called her to go to China when she was a teenager growing up near Wilkes-Barre, Pennsylvania. She was one of seven children. Their family, the Valentines, had pioneered and settled in the Endless Mountains of northeastern Pennsylvania. When I thought of my grandmother and of my mother after her, I could picture pioneers challenging the continent in wagons. They were from that kind of stock. For two generations, if there was a church to be planted in the mountains of China or Taiwan, Mother was the pioneer who went out first, with steamed bread for food and turnips tucked in her pouch to quench her thirst.

If her Bible School student was struggling in childbirth, Mother was the midwife summoned to deliver the baby. "I made the young fathers stand beside me to watch," she would say, "so that next time they'd know what to do in case I might not be there to help." Mother used to boast that she had delivered more babies than most American doctors ever had.

Mother was appalled that girl babies disappeared—hundreds, thousands, millions over the years—because Chinese society preferred boys. There were missing baby girls—killed at birth, or starved because they were given less food than boys. In Chinese villages, she gathered girls and women around her. Her *Lai, lai, lai* (Come, come, come) along dusty paths assembled women with bound feet, women who had never learned to read. She taught them to break loose from the centuries of China's social bondage that had held women back. She unwrapped tiny feet crushed by footbinding. She taught women how to read. My mother took seriously the words of Jesus: "Inasmuch as you have done it unto the least of these, my brethren, you have done it unto me."

Pioneering and church-planting in Taiwan in the 1950s, she taught in a Bible college throughout the day then took to the streets to preach in the evenings. Into the night she collaborated on a Chinese translation of a textbook on New Testament Greek. She helped start twenty new churches, most in remote mountain villages. She walked. She biked. She rode a motor scooter. She was a superwoman before anyone ever used the term. Her Chinese scholar-partner who accompanied Mother at the street meetings said that she worked harder than any person he had ever known.

The setting or audience made no difference. Mother could be crowded in a train compartment hurtling through the frozen Chinese countryside with a Chinese Army chief-of-staff—or sharing a mud bed with an old peasant living in a mountain cave in northwest China—or playing her accordion in Taiwan on the rocky paths of mountain villages, trailed by curious children and tribesfolk. Her message was always simple and direct: God loves you. Let Him guide your life. She went into places where women were not wanted, championed the rights of the downtrodden, spoke loathingly of communism in every form—the Communists had killed her friends, she said. She pricked the conscience of sleepy American churches—did largely as she pleased despite the myriad conventions of a more restrictive time.

In conventional terms, my mother lived an outrageous life. It never crossed her mind to ask whether the order from the apostle Paul, *Do the work of an evangelist*, was only for men. She knew that people needed help, and she was going to do something about it.

She approached hesitant young people with encouraging words: "You have a gift. Use it for God's glory."

When Father became pastor of the Free Methodist Church in Spring Arbor, Michigan, Mother—more than any social worker—knew every needy family in the area. She knew which children needed clothes or shoes, or a ride to Sunday school, or money to go to camp meeting. She dispatched the Sunday school buses into the countryside to bring the children in. My mother saw six fires burning at once and converged on them all.

Mother approached her adventures just as Moses did. "I want you to show me your way," Moses had said to God when he was about to lead the multitudes of Israel in a lifetime journey across the sea and deserts and mountains to the Promised Land. God always had an answer for Mother as He did for Moses: "I know you by name. My presence will go with you" (Exodus 33:13–14, 17).

That was my mother's secret. I always thought that God knew my mother by name. She felt that God walked beside her.

Alice married James Hudson Taylor II in 1924. They had met at Greenville College. And so she joined the Taylor family—missionaries to the Chinese since the 1850s. James was the grandson of the famous pioneer missionary, J. Hudson Taylor. James and Alice complemented each other. He was the gentle scholar; she was the dynamo. They held tent meetings on their honeymoon.

My mother was never a typical, nurturing, always-attendant mother. It isn't a milk-and-cookies-at-the-table-after-school picture that comes to my mind when I think of her now. Teaching values came first. My memory picture of her has Japanese gunboats in the harbor at Chefoo. If you put most mothers in a scene like that, you'd see them wrapping their children in their arms. Mother was not like that. With gunboats in the harbor, lobbing artillery into the hills overhead, Mother gathered us around her knees at the pump organ in our living room and poured faith into our hearts with her music and her singing:

He shall give His angels charge over thee to keep thee in all thy ways . . . Thou shalt not be afraid. . . .

As Henry Ward Beecher said, "What the mother sings to the cradle goes all the way down to the coffin." I never forgot.

My picture of her is that of a world-class storyteller dressed in a Chinese gown on platforms from coast to coast. She could spellbind an audience. She made her listeners hear the bombings. She made them itch with bedbug bites. She made them weep.

Mother didn't hug and kiss, nor did her mother. Mother expressed her tenderness in action. When Kathleen was dying of lupus—at the age of twenty-three—to be near her, Mother slept night after night on a mattress on the floor at the foot of Kathleen's bed.

Mother inspired wonder in people. She was tough as nails.

I often saw her in myself—a vision I alternately accepted and rejected. My girlfriends envied my Alice Taylor mother. Sometimes I envied their milk-and-cookies moms.

Mother left no doubt that she would leave an imprint on her children and her world. She was always prodding, instructing, encouraging, fine-tuning us. When we turned the tables on her, with a twinkle in her eye, she would boast to audiences across the land that "I'm the best brought-up mother in America."

In our family, doing well was achieving in academics, being polite, talking honest and clean. These were not a choice. I often saw myself as a connecting link for that wisdom, one hand touching the past, the other holding the future. I was a link in a chain—from Mother and Father and Chefoo School teachers to generations they would never know.

How many times would I sit with the boys in the cafeteria, nudging a wayward arm or elbow off the table—with Chefoo School teachers at my side, real in my memory, doing the very same thing to me.

My father taught me pride and the importance of a pat on the back. Those lessons turned up as daily Clean-and-Tidy contest stickers on Youth Center bedroom doors, pictures of student winners posted in our Hall of Fame. They showed up with Youth Center's highest achievers marching in Guard-of-Honor glory for the whole Youth Center world to see.

My father preached kindness. He taught me what a woman should be. Among her attributes, he said, kindness ranks near the top. In the Youth Center cafeteria, I find my hand gently resting on the shoulder of a twelve-year-old, whispering to him to eat the carrots and green beans he has buried beneath his napkin—and remembering my father's doing the same to me. He used to quote from the Proverbs: *What is a virtuous woman?* He always picked this verse: . . . *and in her mouth is the law of kindness.*

A generation later these words still leave my father's mark on what I touch. On a bright winter day, a visiting judge from Japan is finishing a tour of the Youth Center as part of his study of juvenile justice in America. He has seen bedrooms papered with certificates of merit. Classroom doors posted with photo collages of happy Youth Center students and their teachers. Snapshots of mock trials, spelling bees, Halloween masks. He has watched an angry boy in the schoolroom hallway on a time-out, an officer's hand resting gently on his shoulder as he talks the boy down.

The Japanese judge reaches for American words tinged with a Japanese accent. "I am surprised," he says. "Very surprised. How clean is your building. And how kind."

James Taylor would have liked that.

>─◆>─○─<◆─<

I inherited a building of wounded spirits.

When AT&T cut back its staff—Greg Lyons among them—a follow-up to an employee's being laid off was an aptitude test—a step to finding another job. The test said that Lyons should work with kids, maybe as a phys-ed instructor. Lyons had just turned twenty-one . . . didn't have a college degree to be a teacher so he got a reference from a local politician to be an officer at the Shelter. "A job," he said. "What the hell—I had a car payment to make."

Nothing prepared Greg Lyons—or any other officer—to be psychologist, priest, teacher, and child guru at $2.50 an hour. Officers making $5,600 a year—parents coming to them—"I don't know what to do with this kid." All the man had was a ringful of keys. There was no training. He walked up onto the second floor. Someone pointed to a couple of men standing there. "This is Joe and Tom"—strangers who were to be his partners—and "This is the logbook. See you tomorrow." That was it.

The headlines had worn them down. The health of John Slim, the superintendent, was failing, and staff was left wondering who was in charge.

Some officers looked at their group and saw children and boys: Fun. Kids. Playing around. Lyons himself got into big trouble for having a snowball fight with the younger boys in the hallway of the south corridor one afternoon. Children playing hookey from school were held routinely overnight, locked in with car thieves, purse snatchers, and burglars.

Other officers looked at the group and saw animals. It was a self-fulfilling prophecy. The boys always seemed to riot when these officers were on shift.

Greg Lyons was with the North Side boys when the word was announced that a woman from Lew Katz's office had been named administrator.

"I'm not going to work for a g_d d__n woman," he said to one of the boys.

Some, as reported from the Italian contingent, were more succinct: Women were good for making babies and spaghetti. That was it. Never to my face, of course. They were polite—but always it was politeness touched with I'll-wait-and-see.

I found a strange mixture of hope and we'll-wait-and-see. Most of the officers were desperate for the riots to end. Physical danger and the Shelter's notoriety had worn them down. But could one trust a politically appointed suburban housewife who said she doesn't like uniforms? Maybe yes. Maybe no.

Abandoning the uniforms was the emotional watershed. For some, giving up the uniforms meant giving up authority and power. For others, it was a step into a new approach with youngsters. Giving up the word *inmates*—that was another watershed. I called them *residents* and *students*. Names create attitudes, I told the staff. Call me a *student*, and you'll treat me one way. Call me an *inmate*, and you'll treat me another. Call me an *officer*, and you'll treat me one way. Call me a *guard*, and you'll treat me another.

Greg Lyons felt a glimmer of something new, a feeling of hope. I promised a very tired group that the Children's Shelter was going to become a model. I also promised to do something about the pay. That talked the loudest.

I don't know why they believed me. Perhaps it was seeing instant results. I took boys swimming the first week. Within a month, we added staff. The riots stopped. Out of a twelve-year maternity leave, I was stepping into a war and preaching to the walking wounded a new battle plan. New weapons: We would program the youngsters with success, I told them. For delinquents in a pretrial juvenile detention center—teach them "success skills." *Make* them succeed. *Make* them grow.

Loyalties change slowly. It was no surprise that more than half the staff were waiting to see how long—or *if*—I'd last. I could see the message in their eyes: They would politely wait me out. Officers who had gotten their jobs from political godfathers felt that they held the trump card of political power in their pockets. I got a weekend call at home one day from a well-placed official asking me to set aside the union seniority rules to give a politically favored officer a different shift. I was suddenly walking a tightrope. Say no to a politician and watch him say no to you. I was polite. And firm. I couldn't bend rules.

I held a trump card called success. For one thing, I had the unwavering support of freeholder Lewis Katz. I also had another: Embarrassing newspaper stories about the Shelter had changed. The newspapers now showed Shelter teenagers jumping in sack races like any boy-next-door. And when Lewis Katz and I chipped in together to buy a Saint Bernard puppy for the place, a roly-poly ball of fur with giant paws—PUPPY AT THE SHELTER—made newspaper and the nightly television news.

The day I became the administrator, John-John and John were locked in together. They were roommates on the South Side. John-John was twelve, from affluent Cherry Hill, a boy who kept running away from home because his mother beat him with a shoe. John was fifteen, from Camden, and was charged with murder.

A new law changed all that. Children who run away, skip school, or act unmanageable at home would no longer to be treated as criminals, not be locked up with children who were accused of committing crimes. In a one-hundred-year-old building across the street, on the third floor, we opened an unlocked shelter for children with family problems. I called it *Cloud Nine*. The Children's Shelter now became two programs—one locked and one unlocked. Twelve-year-old John-John was with the first group to move in to Cloud Nine.

The old Shelter building—the lockup—was a mouldering mess. Water flowed through basement storage rooms, so Viola Slim, the stock clerk, worked her shift in rubber boots. When the bases of her metal storage cabinets crumbled in rust, she propped them up on wooden slats to keep supplies of T-shirts and sheets and toothpaste from mildewing in water. When the sewer backed up and human waste flowed through the basements and flooded the elevator shaft, officers recruited boys to scoop up and sweep away the fetid mess. Flood marks from rising water marked the walls. Moisture seeped from the basement throughout the building. I was seated at my desk one morning when plaster above the door erupted onto the floor in a shower of humid powder and yellow paint. County painters could not keep up with the rust. Broken windows in the attic left ceiling floorboards heaped with pigeon droppings from decades of roosting birds.

Then I saw a small item in the newspaper about the federal government's boosting the nation's economy with community projects. Construction money. I sat down and wrote my congressman.

We launched a thousand helium-filled balloons when we broke ground for the new building. The Camden High School band played under a perfect sky. Bricks and mortar rose in an asparagus patch beyond the softball field. New walls. New colors that looked like children. New skylights to let the sunshine in. New name—the Children's Shelter became the Camden County Youth Center.

>⊶⊷⊙⊶⊶⊰

I inherited one demoralized teacher and a budget that gave me fifty cents per child that year to operate the school. *Fifty cents per child!* Hardly enough to buy crayons and colored paper for busywork—one group in the morning, the other in the afternoon. A one-room school in a classroom with steel-meshed wrap-around windows that had once been the juvenile court. The curriculum had two majors: buffing floors and watching television. I saw before my eyes the formula for riots: Lock up a teenager with bursting teenage energy—dress him in baggy clothes and her in a shapeless housedress, then give the youngster absolutely nothing to do.

A warden friend of mine who runs a prison had it right: "You can run the Big House with cops for a little while—but without the programs, without the teachers, the place is going to blow."

I battled for school books, but when I asked the courthouse to buy books, an administrator asked me: Can't you go begging for used textbooks from schools in the area?

I wouldn't.

These youngsters were tough cookies. Some had been spanked too much. Others had never been spanked. Or loved. But more than that. Any teacher who has ever staffed a detention room at school would recognize them. They were the mouth-offs, the angry teenage bullies, the see-if-I-care kids, see-if-you-can-make-me. The boy on the edge whose parents never show up at Back-to-School night. They were teenage failures who wind up on the streets—dropped out or expelled from school. A few were from gangs who carried knives and brass knuckles. Gangs called The Kakalaks or The Wrecking Crew.

School could make us. Or break us—youngsters spending half their waking hours in school. I wanted life. I wanted color. I wanted action. School had to grab them—more than buffing floors and watching television.

I would have to take on the top brass who throttled the budgets for troubled children. Take on the staff who believed that "nothing works." Take on these kids who dreamed no dreams for themselves. No pinching pennies on school books.

When I was driving to work in the morning, fresh from a good night's sleep and sparked by a cup of coffee, I was always ready to win. Youth and vigor and gaudy self-confidence. By the end of the day, bloodied from eight hours of challenges, I whispered to myself that I wasn't sure I could ever—ever—make it all happen.

I discovered immediately that it doesn't cost money to raise morale. I did need a typewriter. On Day One, I had started a Memo to Staff. Town crier. Morning headline. Hand-typed by me. It celebrated our successes. It wept with our sorrows. It was full of breezy news tidbits, love notes, announcements, rules, and thank-yous. Bulging files of Memos to Staff turned into the Shelter history—where you were as likely to see a snapshot of clerk Sylvia Shuster's honeymoon picture in Atlantic City fifty years ago as an announcement of a meeting. People always grabbed them to get the latest news.

I felt like a parent being watched for playing favorites: Staff or residents—whom does she love the best? If I added recreation for residents, did I love the residents more than the staff? I was forever being weighed on that balance.

I went over and over it in my mind. What could I give my staff? Feeling safe—survival training for staff came first. If our officers weren't free to walk the halls in safety, no other perks mattered. I was after their hearts. Their loyalty.

MEMO TO STAFF April 1, 1974: *DISARMING NEWS: A 210-pound, 5' 11½", 28-year-old police patrolman will launch a week-long staff training program in unarmed defense techniques today. Wear sneakers, sweat suits. No blouses with buttons.*

We pushed back the furniture in the girls' lounge and spent hours learning self-defense, how to hold and not to hurt. That class struck a landmark: It was the last use of chemical Mace in the Shelter—I myself volunteered to get the last blast of the stuff on my shirt below my chin to show its effect. I wept through the class.

Then there were the afternoons I invited freeholder Lewis Katz to chat with the staff in the classroom at the end of the school day . . . a rolled-up shirtsleeves, town-meeting-kind of government with a freeholder talking freely to county employees in the trenches. Employees talking back. No one had ever heard of such a thing.

"I want to give you the feeling," an officer told Lewis Katz one afternoon. "Two o'clock in the morning. Mice. Roaches. Two, three hell-raisers banging on the doors at once to use the bathroom. You don't know what they want—you or the 'can.' No back-up standing by." I heard a murmur of agreement from all the line staff on the 11-to-7 shift. "You *know* you can get hurt." . . . raw truth it was. Before the week was over, Katz had another officer on the midnight shift.

If safety was an issue, so was violence. From my first day, I investigated every incident when a boy was buffeted by the staff or staff by residents. The riots stopped in one week. There were incidents, but they were rare. Inch by inch, officers were coming to work in a Shelter that was behaving more predictably. Residents were waking up to a world that was feeling safer. Safety had to be number one.

How do you turn a dangerous lockup around? I relied on little more than decency and fairness. What more did I have? I loitered everywhere in the building and in the play yard. Listening. Seeing. Noticing—all signals to grown-ups and children that I was open for business. Officers called it "the open door." I hadn't even heard of "dressing for success." A lady in slacks or something casual, sitting by a girl on her bed, poking at a rusting door, noticing pats of butter stuck to the ceiling. Even a small problem—it might be the biggest problem they had—a roommate who wouldn't wash, a hair in the food, an officer complaining that his relief was always late. I couldn't blow it away. If we were going to turn this place around, we had to deal with the cause of everyone's discontent, summed up in one word: hopelessness. People—grown-ups and children, too—had to start feeling like people.

Children needed concrete rewards: increased visits and telephone privileges—contact with home.

This was not the sort of thinking that won friends in a world that pushed for tougher sentencing. I was neither indifferent nor apologetic. I had known every rage and revulsion when my own home had been broken into. I understood how victims felt. But I couldn't run the Shelter with a mind clogged with hate. All that had failed. Who wanted to come to work in a place where hell-raisers threw food, and spat, and hid excrement behind a heated radiator?

We would create a world of predictable consequences for teenage felons: Good consequences. Bad consequences. The boys and girls would have to choose. The assaults dropped dramatically. The riots stopped.

Then I discovered money in federal grants. That fall, the Memo to Staff trumpeted a federal windfall: *October 10: SHELTER GETS $28,000 FROM FEDS: for mini-bus, staff training, Director of Volunteers, art therapy consultant, arts, crafts, hobby supplies, recreational equipment. We're applying for another $30,000 grant— to arrive, we hope, by the end of the year.*

Now when the school day ended, boys and girls went to arts and crafts . . . art and dance therapy. Muslim lecturers and the Reverend and Mrs. Winsor Cooper came to preach the Word. Volunteers joined the girls to decorate the girls' wing. Blue curtains fluttered on the windows. Girls posted a wish list that included a gerbil cage. The Public Defender brought one of the girls a guitar. I love the Bible story of Noah and the Ark. Noah looks across the flood for a sign that the devastation is ending . . . and sees a dove with an olive leaf in its beak, flying back to the ark. I walked into A-wing one day and heard guitar music and gentle singing coming from "D.J.'s" room. It was *my* sign.

Officers on the 3-to-11 shift teamed up with the teachers to plan a Parents' Night. We would hook the students' dads and moms. A committee of the youngsters joined in mailing invitations. One team spruced up the classroom. Another set out cookies and juice. Another coached student hosts and hostesses on how to be the welcoming committee. When Parents' Night arrived, at 7:00 P.M. the boys kept watching for headlights in the parking lot. And again at 7:30.

By eight o'clock we knew. No one was coming. We could change our world inside the Youth Center. But not the outside world.

We ate the cookies and drank the juice. And the children pretended that they didn't really mind. Pat looked up over her orange juice. "All the more for us," she said, but her brown eyes didn't smile.

These were not ordinary teenagers. *Battered spirits.* I stood before Civil Service commissioners and said: Don't give me officers who only can pass a written test. Make Civil Service tests that give me "soul." I discovered that the net that catches idealists also catches "moonbeams." My freshly hired recreation leader closed his recreation periods with the girls by setting them one by one on his knees, kissing them good-bye on the mouth. He was the first of many good-byes.

Another, the officer newly hired, awakening me one night with a telephone call that she was seeing snakes in a resident's hair and a ghost in the hall upstairs. Another, fresh from the college, dragging to work late almost every day because of her drug habit. Another, who couldn't remember rules—like keeping closets locked. From that mistake—youngsters raiding medicine shelves—three girls overdosed on pills, rushed to the hospital to have their stomachs pumped.

It would be years before police background checks became routine across the land for child-care workers. It would be even longer before we required preemployment psychological, medical, and drug screening of applicants.

What do you give to a staff in a place like this, I wondered, after you give them safety? I went for pride. I went for the pocketbook. Most of the men held second jobs to support their families. Like many officers, Greg Lyons was earning $7,290—$3.50 an hour—when I arrived. Lyons had been hired in 1971 for $2.50 an hour.

I could attract promising young college students to the Youth Center for their first job, but at $3.50 an hour I would never hold them there. Kiddie court, kiddie prosecutors, kiddie officers—anyone who wanted respect in the judicial system across the land headed for respect—and better pay—in ivory towers that served adults.

Staff training now became a serious effort. Teams of officers went to be trained in Trenton at the Correctional Officers Training Academy. After the center launched a major course in Parent Effectiveness Training, one of the clerks announced that the course had actually improved her marriage. We added training in effective listening skills.

People who worked with children were used to tiptoeing with polite requests. I wouldn't tiptoe. And I wouldn't give up. "We are training the staff as professionals," I wrote to the courthouse. "They should be paid as professionals."

My advantage was that I had had no experience. No reason to think that anyone would tell me no.

By late 1974, I chose a new approach. I would compare wages. Sheriff's Officers earned $8,900 a year. Officers at the Youth Center earned $7,500. We stepped up the pressure with a staff lobbying committee. Where was it written that guarding adult felons should be valued more than counseling and watching over prodigal sons and daughters?

On December 14, 1974, just in time for Christmas, freeholders voted officers' salaries from $7,290 to $10,395. In ten months, a $3,105 raise.

WHAT'S HAPPENING

If this was a student newspaper, it was unlike any that Lamont had ever seen before.

He was gangly and teenage-awkward, sitting beside me in my office, so close that we almost touched. He couldn't take his eyes off the newspaper's handlettered headlines: A GUY NEEDS A FATHER—MY STEPFATHER RAPED ME!—PARENT TROUBLES—TEENAGE HOOKER—MY BABY'S DEAD.

Lamont's fingers zigzagged slowly down the page, his lips forming the words as he read. He was mesmerized—so much so that he temporarily forgot to be embarrassed over his struggles to read.

"These stories be for real?" he asked.

"For real," I said, trying not to break the spell. "Make-believe stories don't talk to you the same as true stories."

I could see him pause, wondering if he could trust me with a family secret. "My stories be like these," he said softly, ". . . just like these." As he began to tell me a story from his own life, I typed the words out for him on the page: ·

LIFE AND DEATH IN THE GHETTO

Living in the projects when I was a little kid, I seen my grandfather smack my grandmom—POW!—in the face.

I went to call my uncle to help because I was only 6 years old. And my uncle came and tried to get him to stop. I remember still.

Then my grandfather went under the bed and got a machete and swung it and sliced my uncle's arm, and the meat was hanging. Blood running all over the floor.

My uncle knocked him down so he hit his head on the ground. My grandfather died in the hospital.

When that story was done, he told me another.

>─┼◄►─○─◄┼◄

TAKING CARE OF MY MOM

I seen my stepfather hit my mother in her face. My mom started cryin'. She told me not to get involved. But I told my mom I was gonna get him. I was gonna get one of my friends and get his gun and shoot him. He be doing this since he first knew her. I be helpin' her to find another place to stay.

I got one of my mom's boyfriends real good—I was 12 at the time—bust him in the back of the head with a two-by-four 'cause he threw an ashtray and busted my mom's forehead.

At the age of sixteen, Lamont is locked up at the Youth Center because he assaults people.

>⊶⊷⊶O⊷⊶⊷⊰

Sometimes when my ears grow tired of meetings and my mind wearies of paperwork, I push all that aside and just listen to the stories the children tell. If I listen gently as they talk, they unlatch the barrier gates and admit me into their shadowy world—a world where children barter their bodies with grown men, where giant fists smash into fragile faces. Where fathers disappear and moms run off with motorcycle gangs. It is a world where pushers own the streets. And children sometimes want to die.

For the last twenty years at the Youth Center, these children and I have published a student newspaper—*WHAT'S HAPPENING*. In it, no real subject is off-limits because in this place you can write a story like "The World's a Jungle," and a chorus of kindred voices will echo its agreement. *WHAT'S HAPPENING* has become a collection of personal stories—whispered to me in the safety of my office. I write down exactly what the children tell me. Sometimes the stories violate my peace of mind. Sometimes they give me moments of pure and undiluted wonder.

Here is a sampling of what they have told me over the years.

THE WORLD'S A JUNGLE
by BERNADETTE, age 15

I started selling reefer and "girl-boy" (cocaine) in Atlantic City. I couldn't go home—didn't want to.

I don't stay nowhere. I been in 13 foster homes. I don't stay in them.

This guy goes to the bus stations looking for runaway girls. He go all over getting the girls. He put 15 of us in his house. He like to have sex with some of the girls.

But mostly guys come and pay him to watch us girls having sex with each other.

The world's a jungle and full of creeps.

LITTLE KID WALKIN IN MY FOOTSTEPS
by DUECE, age 16

Little 8-year-old boy on the corner. Comes to me, says, What's up? Asks for some money. Plays little games.

I give him a dollar. His eyes light up. Like he never seen so much. First question he ask, Is all that yours?

I've suddenly become his idol—a real man that he can count on. He hangs around a lot.

I go to school. He goes to school.

I make jokes. He makes jokes.

If I get new sneaks, he want new sneaks.

I walk to the next corner. He walks with me. Little kid . . . he's always in my footsteps. To him I am the good life.

It'll be a couple years—an he'll be sellin drugs.

IT MESSED UP HIS PRIDE
by KEVIN, age 15

This guy Joey that I know. He's 13. He got raped by some older guy. He was embarrassed to go out after that. Everyone knew about it. It messed up his pride.

My love affair with student newspapers was an accident. My father and mother both loved to write. And I was a high school English teacher. But journalism and sponsoring a student newspaper—that was a different story. I knew nothing about that. I had never taken even one journalism course. Teaching journalism and sponsoring the student newspaper were thrust upon me without warning, part of a last-minute teaching package when I went to Camden High. I was a substitute for a veteran journalism teacher recuperating from an operation. I was to sponsor *The Castle Crier*. The newspaper's deadline days invariably meant a tumble of student reporters and editors in our home, sprawled on our carpets and kitchen table, fortifying themselves with pizza amidst paste-ups and galley proofs.

I loved fat, red editing pencils—marking papers and editing copy. With red markers, I swooped down with red happy-faces and exclamation marks, spiraling red stars to cheer my students' successful writing. I snarled and pounced with giant red circles and splashes of "For Shame!"—always "For Shame!"—around misspelled words, trite thoughts, and dangling modifiers.

The fat, red markers and "For Shame!" became my trademarks. No Christmas ever passed without student editors' rewarding me with bundles of new, red editing pencils wrapped up as gifts. With my fat, red pencils—I swooped. I splashed. I pounced.

But not with *WHAT'S HAPPENING.* Here, we tiptoe. We whisper. We cotton fragile feelings onto the page. Here in my office, where we write together, the mood is different. I try to create an atmosphere that's quiet and safe for feelings. Safe for misspelled words and stumbling English. A world safe from fat, red correcting pencils. Safe from failure.

There's a ritual to it all. By the office door, the youngsters explore a robin's nest with a blue egg and bits of broken shell. Under the skylight, they inspect my airborne kite to see what holds it so mysteriously in midair. They stroke the shell of a box turtle that my daughter, Alice, and I found one evening along the fence at home. The shell is chipped from curious handling now. Their fingers find the little dents that once made room for tail and legs and head. They reach for the tassels of handmade Chinese lanterns swaying like Spanish moss high above my bookcase and chair.

"Every person has hundreds of stories inside," I tell them as we settle close beside my typewriter. "Your own true stories. Happy stories. Sad stories. Maybe a proud story."

I show them an issue of *WHAT'S HAPPENING.* Seeing what others like themselves have dictated to me over the years always seems to prime the pump.

I talk softly, "You know what the very best stories are? Big feelings. Heart-thumping feelings most often on your mind. Maybe you want to tell the happiest thing that ever happened to you. Or maybe the saddest."

In all my years of listening, only one or two boys have kept the stoppers in. For most, it's like uncorking the Mississippi. Elbow to elbow we nestle as their whispers become black letters on the page. And when it's done, we go next-door to the copy machine and push the button marked: TWO-SIDED COPIES. On side one we print a copy of their story. "Now, put your hand on the glass right here inside the machine," I tell them. It's like a game. "Now close your eyes from the light." I watch a flutter of eyelashes as I push the green button marked PRINT. Out prints their handprint on side two. It never fails. Wide-eyed, childlike wonder. "The hand of the author," I tell them. They see it all with such a glow of bashful pride, sometimes they ask if they can have an extra copy—or 4 or 5 or 6—for Mom.

GADGET IS DEAD
by ABRAHAM, age 17

It was a day everybody wanted to get drunk. They wouldn't believe it. That's how it is when a kid gets shot.

Gadget was a month away from his 17th birthday. We was so best friend that we used to fight together. One day we be playin together on the street. The next day he be all dressed nice in a suit, lyin dead in a casket at Mayer's Funeral Home with a photograph next to him and a lot—a LOT of flowers.

All these people coming in—as soon as they walk in the door they just be cryin a lot. You see his mom, his girlfriend, tears be fallin out.

I was just so cryin and cryin, I couldn't hold it—to see him lyin there. I stood and prayed and kissed him in the front head. My friend Bird and I just huggin together and cried.

I went to the bar and got drunk.

"It's a shame about their grammar, isn't it?"

Some businessmen at Rotary breakfast meetings in fashionable places like suburban Cherry Hill where I often go to speak may never, ever understand.

>─◄─>─O─◄─►─◄

The colors on the Youth Center doors sing of childhood—yellow, blue, orange, red—but the locks say "Prison Hardware." The sky outside is full of puffy clouds, but the sunlight sparkles on windows of triple-layered, bulletproof glass.

Their numbers often overflow the thirty-seven beds, and we have to put down mattresses on the floor. Between 7:00 o'clock wake-up and 8:30 bedtime we cram their day with school, recreation periods, visiting hours. They take courses in Success Skills and Parenting for Teens. They are watched over round-the-clock by juvenile detention officers.

My assignment as the new administrator of the Youth Center was to clean it up. I began to think that if we could connect with the child inside those grown-up bodies, we wouldn't have to tangle so often with their savage physical strength.

I wondered how we might do this. I thought about the triumphs of my own daughter's growing-up years—the ways I had tried to make her feel treasured. The tender "I love you" note in her schoolbook on the first day of school. The report card with the proud A's mounted on the refrigerator alongside a string of first-place ribbons for mother-daughter, three-legged races on the Fourth of July. Our uproarious celebration when she installed the sparkling yellow toilet in the upstairs bathroom all by herself. All the praises heaped on her joyful successes—*these are the nourishment that feeds a child's soul*, I thought.

Changes came slowly at the center. None of it seemed like very high-powered stuff. We got a Saint Bernard puppy that the boys named Mr. Tim. We started the student newspaper that published stories they had never dared tell before. We awarded blue wristbands for progress and gold wristbands for honors. We had photos of honor residents mounted proudly on giant stars and spotlighted in the "Hall of Fame." Eugene DeLarge, one of our officers, videotaped the kids' most successful moments. Mark Williams, a shift commander, helped them start a vegetable garden.

We had the Student of the Week lead opening exercises each day on the intercom. We gave Athlete of the Week citations. We conducted Clean-and-Tidy competitions, with happy-face stickers on the bedroom doors of the winners. We held a ceremony in the gym, where the highest achievers were congratulated by an honor guard of all the staff. We sent letters of honor to the judges who had placed these kids here and proudly forwarded copies to Mom and Dad.

This may seem an odd, even naive, way to deal with hard-core young thieves and drug traffickers, but it worked. For seven straight months after we started teaching them Success Skills, we didn't have to use locked isolation even once. Initially reluctant staff members soon became true believers.

But the parents were the most astonished. I answered the phone one morning to a gravelly, unfamiliar voice. "You the one who wrote this letter 'bout my daughter?"

I felt myself gearing for defense.

"Sir?"

"This is Molly's father." I knew he meant Molly who had killed her baby. "This letter you sent . . ." His voice broke. I could hear him start to cry. I knew then that he was holding my letter announcing his daughter's latest honors. It would happen again and again through the years, parents weeping over letters like that—in all their lives, their child's first official recognition of success.

>-•-◦-•-<

Some of the younger boys were hovering at my elbow, begging me to score their lunchtime manners on the daily Good Manners Checklist. José nudged me.

"You see that?" Loretta, on the girls' team, had her arm resting on the table, which meant a point deducted in the manners competition. The younger boys, who struggle with such niceties as talking only when their mouths are empty or keeping arms and elbows off the table, are always joyful when they catch a competing team member in a mistake.

José whispered seriously in my ear. His tone was that of a brother watching out for his little sister, protectively instructing about the streets. "Y'know, in the streets it's okay to eat with your elbows on the table."

I beckoned some of the boys around for the kind of super-secret conversation they love most, up close and private, with the girls excluded.

"José just told me that arms-on-the-table is okay on the streets."

They nodded seriously.

"Rules for being successful on the streets—we don't teach you about that. You already know about that," I said. "Shall I tell you my dream for each of you?" They pressed in closer. "I have a dream—that every one of you will someday have a chance to make it someplace better than the streets. When you get there, you'll remember the right manners. You'll feel comfortable because you'll already know exactly how to act. You know the rules." I paused. "That's why we teach you Success Skills and good manners here every day."

No one spoke. For one hushed moment, a dozen wide-eyed, tousled boys considered a different picture of what life could be.

Most days, though, it is I who look through the keyhole into their world, and it makes me shudder at the endless ways people find to torture their children. I wonder who is going to anoint America's children with hope.

MOMS ARE A PROBLEM
by GERRI and CINDY, both age 13

Moms are a problem!
They hit you with things like extension cords, knives, wine bottles, and sticks.
They tell you you're a problem and call you names like Bitch, Whore, Slut, and No Good.
They don't let you have no boyfriends and won't let you go outside.
I wonder what kind of mom I'm gonna be?

Gerri never found the answer to that question. Both she and Cindy were child prostitutes, and not long after they wrote this story, the police found Gerri's body alongside Farnham Park near Camden High School. Word filtered back to us that she had been executed by her pimp.

It was mid-December, and the streets of South Camden blew cold enough that even the hookers, "geezed out" on cocaine pipes, were out of sight. Out at the Youth Center, though, the Christmas tree was loaded down with tinsel in the visitors' lobby, and white snowflakes floated from the ceiling in the dining room. Santa Claus was already wrapping socks and stocking hats for Christmas. So if Tina was planning to be locked up, this was definitely the night for it. Tina is a street urchin, a lovable nubbin who was first hauled in to the Youth Center when she was nine years old. Her mother is a junkie and a prostitute; her father is in prison.

"I went up to this cop on the corner," she told me, "and ax him, 'You be lookin' for me to lock me up, I s'pose?'

"He say he ain't. So I ax him if he sure. He say he sure."

She skipped away. In no time she was swaggering back in front of the cop, flaunting a new pair of jeans—twice her size—freshly stolen from the nearest store. For a repeat delinquent, it was just enough to get picked up.

People ask me what topsy-turvy world makes a child choose lockup over being safe at home. Tina told us when she wrote her stories for WHAT'S HAPPENING. I called her whole page "Tina's World."

BEATINGS AND BRUISES THAT POP OUT
by TINA, age 12

I ran away when I be living with my dad's mom because she was beating me with thick sticks real hard that I get bruises that pop out. So I ran away to my mom for three months. Beating makes you worser.

RAPED

Do you know what it feels like to be raped? TERRIBLE!

You be doin somethin that you don't want to do. He be forcin you, makin you while you be fightin to get free. DIRTY!

You don't feel human. Like you ain't nobody. No one listenin to your screamin and hollerin.

I been raped twice this year.

I get tired of the righteous and the comfortable in this land who send arms-length sermons to children like Tina: "Stand tall," "Just say no," reach for "higher motivation"—without giving them any authentic opportunity. Hope is not a slogan that can be marketed like blue jeans. Hope is a legacy that comes best from parent to child. This is a twelve-year-old child of America, cheated since the day she was born.

Parents need to listen to their children. "Research shows that the average amount of time kids and parents have two-way conversation is fifteen minutes a week," says Robert Bowman, Ph.D., of the faculty in the department of psychology at the University of South Carolina. "Contrast that with the fact that kids watch thirty hours of TV a week." Bowman thinks that teenage suicide and drug abuse go hand in hand with the fact that families aren't listening to their kids anymore. I agree.

In the stories young people tell me, the most common message is, "Listen! Won't you please *listen*?"

I FOUND SOMEONE TO LISTEN
by LIZA, age 17

My father grabbed me by the back of my head and threw me up against the dining room wall. I blacked out. I woke up laying on the floor.

He walked away and went back in the living room, propped his feet up, puffed his cigarette, and watched TV. I was 8. And I was scared that he would hit me again. So I told my mom. But she didn't believe me.

No one would ever listen to me at home, so I started hanging around with older people who would listen. They were bikers and street people, too. But when I cried, they gave me tissues. They were good to me. I thought they could do no wrong. They took drugs, so I did, too. At 8 years old.

No one at the Youth Center was surprised that after nine years Liza was still running away and taking drugs. Medical experts who deal with child abuse and neglect have a clear message for the country's juvenile and family courts: If you see children running away, skipping school, or abusing drugs, look for the signs of neglect or physical or sexual abuse at home. "The correlation between abuse and adolescents' acting-out behavior is high enough that it should be considered in every case that comes before the family court," says Robert ten Bensel, M.D., a professor at the University of Minnesota School of Public Health.

"In the 1960s," says Cynthia Myers of the National Runaway Switchboard, "it was more common for kids to run to something. Now they are running away from something."

"It's much more a survival issue," says Roy Jones, director of the Detroit Transit Alternative, a shelter that provides housing and counseling for thirteen- to seventeen-year-olds whose families are in crisis. What children are trying to survive and run away from, he says, is often physical abuse, neglect, and incest.

LOVE (SEX) IN THE FAMILY
by POLLY, age 15

My mom and her boyfriend together tried to force me.
I was 14.

She said it was better if you do it with your mom or any member of your family first.

I told her I never heard of anyone going about that.

They both wanted me the same night. They were both naked and he grabbed me in their bedroom. I punched him in the stomach so I could get away from him. I tried to push her away. But she kept pulling at me.

She had been drinking.

In the middle of the night I got away by running to my boyfriend's house.

Alcohol is a factor in 83 percent of all reported cases of physical abuse of children, says ten Bensel, who often speaks to gatherings of family court judges around the country. Drugs and alcohol, he says, accompany almost every kind of sexual abuse.

I have never seen one good thing that comes from teenagers' using alcohol or drugs. I see messed up, burned out, wasted kids—and parents too frightened to say, "Don't do it."

Teenagers get alcohol in their homes. They get it from their parents, who often feel, or say they feel, that they are teaching their children to drink responsibly.

I DON'T DO DRUGS—I DRINK
by GEORGE, age 16

I first started drinking when I was 12 or 13. It would be in the house a lot and I just pick it up and start drinking. My parents rather see me drinking than using drugs, then it got to the point that I couldn't really talk to anyone without having a drink in my hand. I got kicked out of school because of it and my grades and everything started falling. Then I started getting in trouble out of school.

When I drink, I just can't control myself. If I wasn't drinking, none of this trouble would have happened.

George (me) without a drink is a nice guy—never been in trouble. But when I'm drinking, look at the trouble I'm in.

Our social worker wanted me to meet Ann. She was a ringleader of a band of girls hell-bent on vandalizing her stepfather's house with rocks. I had seen that kind of rage against men before.

MY STEPFATHER RAPED ME
by ANN, age 16

When my mom was in the hospital, my stepfather used to come toward me and tell me to take off my clothes. I was only 12 at the time and I didn't know how to react.

My mom called me a liar when I told her what happened. One night when I was sleeping, I felt him getting in my bed and I was shocked to see him. He put his hand over my mouth and said, "Don't move or say a word. Just lay there and let me do it."

He did it. My little sister seen it. I felt creepy about my body because he was the first one. And I felt that no other guy would want me if they found out about my stepfather being the first.

I told my mom and nobody believed me, except my grandmother and my aunt. I pressed charges, but no one believed me.

But I was taken out of my home and lived with my grandmom. I dropped the charges because he would of gone to jail and my mom wouldn't have any way to pay the bills.

Ann is white. I mention this because, out there in our havens of decency—the PTAs or Lions or Rotary—the white folk listen to my story of Ann and ask if her family is black. The black folk listen and ask if she's white. The truth is, incest victims at the Youth Center come in white and black and olive.

Melinda is black. Her two front teeth are missing. Her father kicked them out, down in a shadowy basement when she couldn't swallow his semen. As they took Melinda's father off to prison, she heard him calling her a little bitch. "Melinda's to blame," he told her mom. "She tried to turn me on."

The father who rapes his child kills a spirit. Sometimes forever. The child couldn't even tell me what she felt. She wrote her feelings in a crumpled little note. "I'm all confused," Melinda wrote. "Most people I know tell me I'm bad. Some people say I'm good. And I don't know who to believe."

Experts who staff crisis hotlines estimate that one in every twenty women in America is a victim of sex in the family. Among girls under eighteen, the estimates are about one in four. At the Youth Center our statistics are much higher. It's most of them.

What a way for Daddy or Uncle or Pop-Pop to teach a child what girls are for. "He made me feel like trash," one girl from suburban Cherry Hill told me. "So that's what I would be."

➤━◆➤━◯━◆━◄

"I hated gym the most," Cynthia told our social worker, "undressing in the Camden High locker room. That high-fashion school and all them girls with pretty underwear. We ain't even have no money for toothpaste in our house.

"And me with only one pair of panties . . . I quit going to school.

"I knew the way to get them pretty threads. . . ."

Cynthia's mother didn't ask her where the new clothes came from or why.

Sex with children turns America on these days. Look at the pitiful trade of children along Camden's seamy Admiral Wilson Boulevard. And across America, look at the "chicken hawks" with boys and girls for sale. *Pretty Baby* runs in America's movie houses, and Rent-a-Kiddie-Porn passes for home entertainment in proper living rooms.

Dawn, fifteen, is a wide-eyed elf. Her belly stretches with the baby she'll deliver in a few weeks. Down in the darkness, prowling men pay for sex with this pregnant child. She was arrested a few blocks from the peep shows and porno shops along the Boulevard and brought to the Youth Center still sucking her thumb like a toddler.

It's America trashing its children. We charge them with prostitution and bring them in in handcuffs—the Cynthias, Dawns, Angels. Their stories sound so much alike.

HOOKING IS HARD WORK
by ANGEL, age 16

A lot of kids are prostitutes at 16. I meet a lot of them. And it's easy to get started. You need money because you're running away and there are a lot of pimps out there.

I've been propositioned by five pimps in one day. They're nice to you the first time. You have to go to bed with them. But if you don't give them the money they beat you up.

It's tiring when you have to work all night, especially when you have to stand out in the rain. I go out at 9 p.m. and come in at 4 a.m. And then I want to sleep all day.

I make about $350 a night, but I have to give it all to the pimp. Most girls my age don't work this hard.

Teenage pregnancy is so common in this nation that if trends continue, 40 percent of today's fourteen-year-olds will conceive before their twentieth birthday.

In Camden, one out of every three babies has a teenage mother. In fact, Camden's fertility rate is so high now that about half the population is under twenty years of age. Twenty of every 1000 Camden babies died before they could celebrate a birthday. It was an infant death rate double that of the rest of the country.

TEENAGE MOTHER
by KENYA, age 15

I didn't want to have no baby. A 13-year-old shouldn't be having no baby—no money, nowhere to stay.

Retha was born when I was 14. I knew I wasn't finished growing up, that I still be going out, partying, doing what I wanted to do.

My body was grown up enough to be a mother, but I wasn't ready.

TEENAGE FATHER
by PABLO, age 15

My girlfriend isn't a very good mom to our baby. She's 16 ½ and she still wants to be a teenager instead of a mother. She likes to have more fun and pay attention to the people outside instead of to our daughter—like dating and partying.

She don't come back until late at night. Her sister take care of the baby—and she's 14 and not very responsible.

It worries me what's going to happen to that baby.

In the telling of America's stories, whose is the authentic American voice? WHAT'S HAPPENING takes a chain saw, chops up the American myth of childhood, and reassembles it in strange shapes.

On a hot summer day in North Camden, boys play Stuntman or Suicide, jumping back flips from the fourth floor of abandoned houses onto a wobbly platform of mattresses and old tires on the ground below. On an overpass by the river, children dive off moving trains into the lazy current. For two hours, in a squad car, Detective Lenny Hall and I have been patrolling the city's hottest drug spots. Hall is a Camden-High-School-basketball-hero-turned-inner-city-cop in the city's Youth Task Force. After twenty years on the force, Lenny Hall is known to every kid in the city.

"I stopped a kid the other day," he says "and told him to go to school, get an education.

" 'How much you make a week?' he asked me. I told him. He said, 'I make four times that much.' Said he was hustling two grand a week."

We pass a new gray Corvette nestled in a garage near Wildwood and Empire Streets. "The big guys have big cars. The little guys have big cars—even got guys chauffeuring for them. It's a multimillion dollar business up here," Hall tells me.

LOVE ME—WITH MONEY—PLEASE
by RASHEED, age 17

The drug dealers are starting off young these days because money talks. Most of the teenage girls go for the guy that can give her gold and furs and diamonds.

I had a girl like that.

I was a drug dealer for a while—bought her gold, clothes, leather coats. And every night when I came home with a pocketful of money, she seemed happy. Told me she loved me. And I believed it. Until I decided to quit dealing and got a job in the laundry-mat, making $160 a week.

I thought that was good money for a 17-year-old. One day I came home and seen a guy there with a fancy car and a lot of gold. She told me, "That's my new boyfriend."

I told her, "I thought you loved me."

She told me, "I don't love nobody. I don't want to be tied down."

Rasheed, who wrote that story, was mowed down on his doorstep at 5:00 A.M. just three years later. In a one-page edition of *WHAT'S HAPPENING*, Rasheed's memorial, I typed them out—the two stories he had written with me, knee-to-knee: "LOVE ME—WITH MONEY—PLEASE," and "THEY LEARN FROM THEIR DADS AND MOMS." On the back of the page I printed the newspaper account of his murder and put a copy on every bed. Everyone knew Rasheed. At twenty, they told me, he had become one of the biggest dealers in Camden. A "big boy." Flashy clothes. Flashy cars. They nodded knowingly. He had crossed someone.

>−+◆>−O−<◆+−<

A group of grubby drug pushers scurry like roaches as our patrol car approaches. "It's a drive-up drug business," says Hall. "Just stop your car, blow the horn. Someone'll come right to you. Little kids are the warning system." I watch two little girls, seven-year-olds, maybe—all ribboned and innocent strolling their Cabbage Patch dolls to the corner. "They don't stand a chance when they get older," Hall says.

Along the Morgan Village section, we drive by a young prostitute. Red spikes tapping on the cement. Leopard sash nipping in her waist. Wet tongue licking her lips slowly at the men who pass. "The girls come early in the morning along here," Hall says, "to serve the truckers."

"How does a kid survive in a place like this?" I ask Hall, who grew up in Camden and brought up his six children there.

"A drive to do something else," he says. "Each generation tells their kids, 'You got to be a little bit better than me.' I always told my sons, 'Two things we ask of you. One is respect. One is education. The respect is for me and Mom. The education is for you.' A kid that survives here can survive anywhere else in the country. But we've got to get parents involved in what's going on with their kids."

I keep wondering what happens to kids who keep crashing into the same brick walls of frustration. What do you dream about, spending your day at curbside with friends?

"There are three things I want to be real bad, " Lamont told me one afternoon. "A police officer, a basketball player, a football player. But for me and my friends—our dreams don't come true. Did you ever have a dream come true?" he asked.

My voice felt clogged.

He leaned forward and spoke softly: "I just want to have *one* dream come true."

The experts who know about such things say that by the turn of the century, roughly one out of five teenagers entering the labor force will be from a minority: young blacks—many of them like Lamont, struggling to read, many brought up without fathers, amid crime and squalor—and young Hispanics, many resisting assimilation into an alien language and culture. Lamont's mother is thirty-one. She has borne eight children. One mother. Eight children whose baby-sitter and teacher is the TV set. Three different fathers, not one of them currently at home.

Lamont and his friends are not just someone else's problem. In many inner-city black neighborhoods, more than half of the teenagers fail to graduate from high school. While Lamont and thousands like him waste away on the streets—lacking the skills increasingly demanded in the marketplace—America's banks, hospitals, hotels, and insurance companies say they will have only half the qualified workers they need in the next generation. Chemical Bank interviews forty applicants to find one who can be trained as a successful teller.

Children like these will be the workforce and the parents in the year 2000. Unable to earn a living. Unable to support a family. They will watch their families fall apart, their children lost to drugs and grimy streets. And when we condemn them for failing—for not even wanting to try—as we always do—will we remember how we failed them in the first years of their lives? So *whose problem are these kids?*

>—•◆•·O·◆•—<

A boy named John sat talking with me in my office one afternoon. Fifteen years old. Sparkling bright. Top dog in the residence wing.

"You know what I see when I look at you?" I said.

He looked curious.

"Two perfect hands. Two perfect feet. Sharp mind. And when you talk, all the guys want to follow. A whole life full of big possibilities"—I paused—"Except you're wasting your talent on crime."

I watched the tug-of-war I'd seen so many times before. Part of him was saying, "I want to believe this lady, that she sees good inside me." Another part was saying, "She ain't know nothin'. She must be pullin' a con."

So he was listening for the catch.

"Did you ever think what a good job you're giving me?" I said. I had caught him off-guard. "Not a bad living, watching over boys like you."

He was very quiet.

"Did you ever think you could be doing something good for *yourself* instead?"

He didn't answer.

I gave him some homework. Write me your dream—of John five

years from now. Make it a picture with very clear details: What will you be wearing? What will your house be like? What will you want your job to be? Will you have a wife, some children? What will it take to get there? "Make me a real picture," I said. "Start making it come true."

He asked me for a pencil and paper to take back to his room. An hour or so later, John was back to see me, stuffing his word picture, "John's Dream" into my hand.

It could have been the dream of any American boy, anywhere. Nice house. Nice car. Pretty wife. A good job as an electrician, making about $100 a day. Working on cars at night. Two kids.

As I tucked "John's Dream" into my desk drawer, I saw an awkward P.S. scrawled along the bottom of the page.

"P.S.," it said. "I'm gonna make it."

6

TWO HUNDRED MILLION GUNS

The dead body of the baby sparrow lay skewed on the concrete landing for a week. Naked, crushed from its fall out of the straw and string of its nest behind the concrete facing along the roof above the Youth Center door. It lay there among the telltale bird droppings on the concrete ramp. Flies buzzed around.

Mies van der Rohe, a twentieth-century architect, said: "God hides in the details."

I needed to blank out the details that spring. There were just too many. I couldn't see the nests. Only the broken fledglings.

>──+─◄►─○─◄►─+─◄

The tire suspended from a tree in Junior's fenced backyard was for me the symbol of the city's violence. It was Rambo's teething ring. Rambo was Junior's dog—an old-time fighter, scarred head-to-toe from battle wounds but undefeated in fights in Camden and Philadelphia. Out in Franklin Township, in Camden's rural suburbs, you could buy pit bulls trained for fighting or for baiting.

For hours the man swung the tire. He hammered it into the muzzle of his pit bull until the dog's teeth locked onto rubber. Along the fence, children in the neighborhood watched with fascination—a man who kept his killer-dog mean. On the 32nd Street posse, everyone said that no dog on either side of the Delaware River was Rambo's match—even when it meant a fight-to-the-death.

Junior trained the dog on Goodyear rubber and raw meat.

Tyree was awakened by the shouting underneath his aunt's second-floor bedroom window. Baying dogs. Bellowing boys and men. It was the shouts of "Kill 'em" that dragged the boy to the window, still rubbing the sleep from his eyes. Tyree was ten years old that summer.

Pit-bull fights in East Camden were set in the summer either on the giant softball field of Dudley Grange or on the parking lot right around the corner from Bob's Market. No one really wanted the little kids to see the fights. There were standards of decency mixed in with the blood, which was why they were staged in early summer mornings at

a time less likely to attract the police—or children, who were
supposed to be still in bed.

Tyree looked down to the fury in the parking lot below. He had lost
track of how many pit-bull fights he had watched. Fifty? A hundred?
Men in Raiders caps, jeans, sweatpants. Boys. Ripped and bloody dogs.
One time his own pit bull, Uzi, had ripped the bite-proof mask off
Rambo's mouth. Uzi was one of Rambo's pups. That's when Junior
had had to beat Rambo with a pipe to pull him away.

"Uzi is dade now."

In my office, a kite with one red, one yellow, one green tassle sways
gently over the boy's head. Tyree repeats it to me as he talks. "Uzi is
dade now." Quietly.

I am listening to the voice of a child talking softly about fights to
the death, an every-week part of his summertime. Jumping rope with
neighborhood girls, long bike rides to Tippins Pond, splashing in the
open hydrant in Dudley Grange park—and pit-bull fights. Children
watching dogs kill each other.

It is this odd combination of fun and violence that chokes in my
throat. I feel both horrified and baffled as I listen to the boy. A small
boy talking softly of a Saturday morning on Beideman Street where a
crowd of men and boys entertain themselves with violence. Boys are
gleeful.

On the peppered brown carpet in my office, Tyree plays with a
memory toy from my own childhood, a wooden thread spool notched
into tractor wheels. Tyree is thirteen years old now. As he winds up
the rubber band, the tractor climbs over a pencil on the floor.

Now in the sixth grade, the child missed one hundred days of
school last year. His caseworker from the street says he can't walk
from one corner to the next without getting in trouble. He told an
officer today that he'd like to stay at the Youth Center forever.

Rules were a comforting road map when I was growing up: *Thou
shalt not* . . . at home and school and church. Miss Stark told me to sit
up straight. Daddy banned *gosh* or *gee* or anything else that defiled my
mouth. Kathleen and Jamie kept my elbows from resting on the
dinner table when I ate. I'm not sure when America set aside the rules
and stopped saying *NO*. Tyree has never heard *Thou shalt not* . . .
Maybe it was gradual. Someone said it was undemocratic to have
rules—threw out the agreed-upon values. Grown-ups among the rich
and famous began preaching that "Greed is good." Winning by
intimidation made best-seller list and TV talk shows. "Attitude" and
"in your face" became fashionable.

Who shaped the values of this thirteen-year-old boy playing on my
carpet who entertains himself on summer days with pit bulls fighting

to the death?—Stuck forever in a ghetto listening to Oprah Winfrey on TV and gunshots at night. Every day I look out at children addicted to risk and violence—bonded with their own initiation rites, their own set of rules. Anything goes. The ancient morality of an eye for an eye—paybacks—is not enough. Violence is now an initiation rite: Grab guns and bricks and bottles and bats. Fight and beat. Stomp a rival. *Yo, man, you're down. You're in.* With no benchmarks for the young, we are haunted by their violence. *Not one thread tethers the boy to the rules in my world.* A child with no feeling that he belongs. If Tyree doesn't think he'll be alive tomorrow, what value does he put on my life or anyone else's?

In my office, Kevin sits clicking the much-used Viewmaster stored in my desk drawer from my daughter's childhood. He turns the frames with the viewer pressed to his face as I read the story aloud to him—Walt Disney's *The Aristocats.* One minute a lovely child with the most beautiful eyelashes framing his brown eyes lost in a cartoon fantasy of adventuring cats. The next minute—jerking to the next subject that jump to his mind—

GUNS IN MY TREEHOUSE
by KEVIN, age 12

Most kids I know want to be in a gang.
There's a test to join. All these guns and stuff in our treehouse on 33rd Street—my friends take these guns and do stuff.
Bad stuff. Then they in.
They gotta wear FILA sneakers. Gotta wear the red-and-white scarf. Or black and white.
Then they in.

One out of four of our boys and girls these days is fourteen years of age or younger. Babies. When I was fourteen, I was still wearing little-girl pigtails down my back. Reading Nancy Drew stories.

Hundreds of golden trumpets of daffodils sway today in the sunshine by the Youth Center door. I think of John McCrae's war poem I studied as a teen: "In Flanders fields the poppies blow"—a poet's mournful look at blossoms blooming silently over the graves of England's sons. I don't know why the flowers remind me of death—perhaps the violence that everyone is talking about inside.

Three weeks ago, Pain was shot to death—Pain was Tyree's friend. Jermaine "The Pain" Purcell.

"Pain"—he used to walk me to school through a back way, roundabout, to keep people from botherin me. Pain got killt. He my friend. Three people shot dead. . . .

Tyree can name them all—these ghosts of violence that haunt their lives.

And now, on a Monday morning bathed in spring sunshine, there is nothing but talk of the latest weekend killings in Camden. Four people blown out—murdered—within five hours in a twenty-square block area of the city. Police say it's all drug-related—the Sons of Malcolm X trying to take over the drug trade in town. Killers killing killers. Or maybe it's initiation rites—who knows? You wanna prove yourself, you gotta kill.

War between the Sons of Malcolm X and Three-Two. North Camden against East Camden.

Terror fills the streets, the *Courier-Post* reports. No one will talk. "You talk, you die."

"All the killer got to do is start putting together the pieces, and they start blowing people out."

The voice on the Youth Center telephone at 3:52 in the dark hours on a Saturday morning is our first warning—war between the posses is reaching down county to us. The voice is a trusted friend, Camden police detective Leroy Palmer. Expect admission of one of the Sons of Malcolm X, he says. The word from the street says—and now his voice gets urgent—the Sons are planting one of their posse as a hit man to rub out a rival already at the Youth Center. Gerard against Nickee. Police say the "X" in the gang name stands for execution.

One hour later, police bring Gerard to the Youth Center to be held on drug charges.

The shift commander posts Gerard's and Nickee's names on the Youth Center's KEEP-APART list until Gerard leaves for the state training school.

People ask me if I'm ever afraid of being locked in with killers. The answer is no. Maybe my childhood stories of Daniel in the lions' den have never left my mind—the hand of God across the mouths of the lions. Maybe it's a talented staff.

The Youth Center is safer and more orderly than most high schools in America. In A-wing, twelve-year-old Maury follows me from door to bedroom door like a shadow, whispering just the right word for me to write on each Clean-and-Tidy inspection sticker for the day. One

for every door: "Super-star," or "Fat," or "I love to inspect this room."
Like any boy.

In B-wing, sixteen-year-old Rick, drags me into his bedroom to show
me his latest drawing for WHAT'S HAPPENING, penned with felt-tip
black, a drawing of a raggedy boy digging for food in a wintry trash
can. Like any boy. In C-wing, thirteen-year-old Shakeem challenges
me to a game of Ping-Pong, letting me win a few unanswered serves.
Like any boy.

There is a difference. Maury is here for hitting a teacher in his
school. Rick is here for trying to kill his father with a knife. And
Shakeem—I don't even know why Shakeem is here. The daily list of
names and charges sits on my desk, but I rarely look at the charges.
Shakeem plays Ping-Pong with me. Maury opens my milk carton for
me at lunch. Rick brings me his drawings. Why would I be afraid?

＞―◆＞―◯―◁◆―◁

The May evening that the city's twenty-fourth victim is gunned
down this year, I drive down Thirty-second Street. The crumbling
neighborhood of Thirty-second and Beideman streets, home of the
East Camden's Three-Two posse. A teenage boy in a black, hooded
sweatshirt breaks away from the posse of boys on the corner, hoping
to flag me down to sell. He sees me as another white, suburban
stranger—there to buy cocaine.

When it comes to purchasing drugs there—nearby the brick walls
and stately courtyards of Woodrow Wilson High School—drug buyers
throw caution to the wind. Buyers wearing guns walk by undercover
detectives, walk by a police van with eight-inch-high letters painted
on the side: CAMDEN COUNTY NARCOTICS TASK FORCE.
Buyers are bold. Sellers are bold—even with detectives fanning out in
the area, imitating drug dealers. In one week this May, drug sweeps
catch seventy-four buyers in mass arrests—buyers from as far away as
Texas and Pennsylvania. The boys will tell you that the best
customers come from the Camden suburbs—Cherry Hill, Atco,
Pennsauken.

Six million Americans used cocaine in 1990, according to government figures, but that number told only a small part of the story: The
child of a parent who abuses substances is four times as likely to
become an addict as the child of a parent who doesn't. Substance
abuse is a family problem that almost predicts that a child will get in
trouble.

＞―◆＞―◯―◁◆―◁

In New Jersey's cops-and-robbers world, most people had once
thought of "organized crime" as being the Italians, La Cosa Nostra,
and the Mafia. The greatest source of revenue for the Sicilian Mafia in

America is narcotics trafficking. Not until it was too late did law enforcement and the popular media acknowledge that organized crime was always much more than La Cosa Nostra and the Mafia. It included gangs of almost every ethnic origin. Colombians first burst into organized crime in the early 1970s, serving mainly as suppliers to other groups.

Cocaine was grown for four dollars a pound in Peru or Bolivia, processed at $6000 in Colombia, and sold at well over $100,000 on the streets of New York. It didn't take the Colombians long to recognize the tremendous profit to be made by expanding into every phase of the business—from processing to smuggling and money laundering. When a Colombian terrorist group in South America kidnapped the sisters of one of the leaders of an independent trafficking group, drug groups there joined hands to free the victims and to wreak vengeance against the terrorists. The coalition—at first a temporary alliance—became the Medellin cartel. By the 1980s, the Colombian Medellin cartel had become the largest and most powerful drug-trafficking organization known to exist. In New Jersey, Colombian crime groups became the primary suppliers for cocaine.

No one in New Jersey had thought much about black crime syndicates—that is, not until their drug posses had already terrorized neighborhoods, corrupted urban teenagers with the bait of fast money, inflamed city streets with violence. Jamaicans, Dominicans, Haitians, Nigerians, and Americans of African descent—their posses had already damned the cities by the time New Jersey's State Commission of Investigation sat down in the early 1990s to discuss what they called Afro-Lineal organized crime. By that time, urban street corners had become open-air drug markets. Some—like Camden—had become war zones.

Jamaican dealers considered New Jersey a safe place to hide from New York police. The syndicates flourished, using New Jersey hotels and motels as "stash houses" to store marijuana and later to distribute it back across the border into New York. By then, five syndicates had blanketed a drug-operation network across the state.

There was nothing mysterious about the rise in violence. It was the onslaught of crack. With crack came soaring crime rates and violence. Police began picking up teenagers with Uzi submachine guns, .357 magnums, Tech-9s. By 1987, when New Jersey said it would get tough on drugs, it was much too late. The first vials of crack cocaine had shown up in Camden in 1985. Drug posses already had a chokehold on the cities.

Born in the poverty and political turmoil of Kingston, Jamaica, posses had been trafficking the high-grade sinsemilla strain of marijuana called "Jamaican Gold" since the mid-1970s. Jamaica had once been the world's chief supplier of bauxite, the principal source of aluminum. When the demand for bauxite declined, the collapsing

Jamaican economy pushed thousands of desperate workers into the cities looking for jobs—especially into Kingston. Many of the city's black residents had already embraced Rastafarianism, a religion that includes in its teaching a belief that marijuana—"wisdom weed"—is an aid to meditation. The island's poverty, widespread use of marijuana, and political corruption gave birth to violent street gangs. Violence was an initiation rite for a posse member to demonstrate his manhood and to develop a reputation in the neighborhood for being aggressive.[1]

Posse was a word the Jamaican underworld chose to create the right images of violence—just like the Wild West—shoot-outs and terror in taking over neighborhoods. By 1984, posses had become active in transporting and distributing cocaine and crack, also called rock cocaine.

In Camden, Jamaicans dealt primarily in marijuana, cocaine, and weapons, using suppliers from New York and the Junior Black Mafia in Philadelphia. Everyone in Camden could identify the Jamaicans: Their island accent identified them as different from the Dominicans and the Latinos. At first the Jamaicans moved quietly into Camden neighborhoods, connecting themselves as suppliers to freelance drug sellers until they controlled the area. Police called the process "quiet takeovers." No shoot-outs or beatings to muscle into power. In Camden, some of the takeovers took ten years. Young street dealers had no idea who the ultimate boss of the operation was. The ordinary street soldiers, usually between thirteen and twenty-four years of age, got their supplies of drugs from trusted middlemen called "big boys."

In places where the takeover was obvious, violence was bound to erupt in a bloody defense of the turf. In a park in Oakland, New Jersey, on August 4, 1985, a gun battle between the Shower posse and members of the Spangler and the Dog posses left three people dead and nineteen wounded. Police seized thirty-three weapons at the scene and more than 1000 spent bullet casings.

In Camden, drive-by shootings terrorized neighborhoods: one set trying to force another out. The other retaliating with hooded soldiers—some in ski masks—fighting back. Conflicts turned into armed confrontation and murder.

Rage and sorrow take different forms. Raman, from the Three-Two posse, was breathless with rage over his lost friend: Pain was dead.

Nickee was almost curled over with depression. He lifted his sleeve to show me the *SOMX* tattooed on his left shoulder—Sons of Malcolm X. In the corner over his Youth Center bed, the boy had taped the newspaper clipping, neat letters in black and white telling

---

[1] 21st Annual Report, State of New Jersey Commission of Investigation, 1989, 28 West State Street, Trenton, NJ 08625, 36.

the bloody details of the death of Lenwood Thomas. Lenwood was his friend.

When police found Lenwood Thomas's smouldering body near the goal of a North Camden football field, all of Camden shuddered. Every citizen in town felt suddenly within range of flying bullets from gang wars. Games played in the nighttime youth basketball league dwindled. Some residents refused to brave the streets.

"You get used to hearin' 'bout people getting shot and killed . . . robbed . . . beaten up," Jamar told me. "So when you walkin' home at night, you be hearin' leaves fallin' thinkin' it be someone comin' up behind you. Cars followin' you. At night I really never feel safe."

Eric came banging on Nickee's door in Parkside while Nickee was still asleep.

"You hear what happen to Lenwood? They found him dead."

"WHAT!"

"They found him killt. . . ."

"Stop lyin'."

"For real." Lenwood was only eighteen.

Nickee was still half asleep and couldn't believe it. Eric said it was on the news. Nickee shook his head and began to weep.

"Shot six times . . . head and back . . . set on fire." They had found the body ablaze under the goalposts of a football field in North Camden.

Nickee went back to his room and pulled out snapshots of him and Lenwood dressed in jeans and black, hooded, Raiders jackets on the corner. Sons of Malcolm X wear black. Pictures of Lenwood and Nickee going to parties.

Nickee had chewed every fingernail back to the quick as he talked to me by my desk. Between snatches of sentences, I had the feeling that his consciousness ebbed in and out of our conversation. The boy slumped beside me like a crumpled rag.

". . . started looking at the pictures that me an him took . . . just couldn't believe it . . . murdered.

". . . used to drink together. Go to parties. Talk about girls together. Listen to Ice Cube rappin'. Smoke Bland-and-Milds cigars together on the corner. Go to Ruthie's together for cheese steaks. There was a lot of us that was close to him."

The boy had drifted away from me again to some other world.

"You hear it . . . you be thinkin' a lot . . . lotta stuff run through your mind . . . 'f it could be Lenwood . . . it could be me next . . . 'cause you ain't know who killed him. . . ."

Prosecutor's investigator told me that Nickee was as good as dead, marked on the hit list by his brothers in the Sons of Malcolm X. At the Youth Center he was safe. Once he left our doors, I did not know.

"My aunt wants me to move someplace else—outa Camden," he said.

I have read of people dying under the power of a voodoo curse. Nickee walked like a boy under the curse of death. Like a boy from the grave.

". . . know Lenwood for a long time. He ain't done anything to be killed over. It wasn't right . . . murdered . . ."

A mural memorial to Lenwood's death appeared within days of his murder, a brightly painted monument at Ninth and Vine Streets. Under the banner, *Died a soldier*, Lenwood stood—firing his MAC-10.

Nickee didn't know who his friends were anymore.

"You don't know. The cops are pickin' up the Sons of Malcolm X . . . people rattin'. . . ."

Nickee's world had crumbled. A boy who had been bonded to his posse brothers for as long as he could remember now believed that a posse brother could kill a friend. The anger, the despair, the naked fear—they were gone. Death looked out of his eyes.

He had started selling drugs when he was thirteen—the days of playing basketball and football and Monkey in the Middle. "Jason ask me . . . did I wanta sell drugs." Nickee turned to me to ask me if I knew Jason.

I knew Jason. I posted his picture on my wall—Scotch-taped it to the wall near my desk maybe two weeks before he was shot to death on the streets. I couldn't bring myself to take the picture down.

"Jason ask me . . . did I wanta sell drugs? . . . 'cause a lotta kids have nice clothes, shelltop Adidas . . . everybody want shelltops. I was mad that I didn't have what they had. My mom never gave me that much money. Jason ask me did I want to start sellin' drugs. I say, 'Na . . . because my mom . . . if she find out, she gonna hit me an' all that.' But same day he ask me, we began. Northside posse.

"The streets are dangerous. You get hurt over somethin' dumb . . . someone wants you sneaks. Sneaks cost a lotta money—sneaks like these costs $120—Michael Jordan sneaks. Or gold, special gold round your neck. People gonna stick you up . . . they kill you for stuff like that. Happens a lot in Camden . . . you could be in front of your house . . . car drive by . . . buncha guys shootin' at you . . . automatic weapons . . . if they do it right, you don't know who . . . ski masks on . . . dangerous . . . so it's common for kids to carry guns. Almost all of them in my posse carry guns."

In a country of two hundred million guns, it was hard to convince a boy that guns lead to more guns, more violence, more hate, more huddling behind locks—an endless cycle of fear and fury.

"Don't any of them say, ''s not worth it'?" I asked Nickee.

"Nah."

"They all keep doing it because it's going to happen to somebody else and not to them?"

"See, it's the money you make . . . $800 to $1000 a day . . . kids see

the money comin' in . . . get more money than their mom would . . .
mom and dad's paycheck. Once they know they get a lotta money . . .
more than parents, they gonna keep do it . . . want to show off to their
girl, buy fancy clothes, give girls whatever they want . . . like a big,
expensive car, stuff like that. . . . Save your money . . . like buy a
corner store . . . you have people workin' there for you . . . an' all that
. . . like the young boys, they see that . . . they gonna wanna do that."

"How many people do you know that have saved their money until
they own a corner store?" I asked.

"None."

I found it hard to imagine—for money, for things—a youngster
willing to risk his life or being locked up.

>-+-+>-+-O-+-<+-+-<

The snow melts and the grass turns green before I hold in my hand
the court transcript of Nickee before the judge: Test Night in a Killer
Gang.

Nickee: "A couple of days before that—before the night of March
13—a fight had broken out on the corner between two other guys.

"The head of the gang got mad, because when the rest of the guys
jumped in, we didn't. So on the 13th, he said I had to prove myself.
They seemed to think we were scared."

On a clear night in March six young men toting a Mac-11, semi-
automatic pistol, pile into two fast cars and drive up and down the
streets of Camden looking for victims . . . it will be random killings
. . . "to prove ourselves. To shoot people."

After a debate about killing girls, they bypass two women walking
on the street. Then the order, "Shoot this guy comin' off the bridge."
Lamont Jones, thirty-four, is shot twice in the head at Eighth and
Tulip Streets near his home.

"Did you shoot him?" the judge asks Nickee.

"I had three shots, and then I passed the gun to somebody else, and
that person had shot him."

"And that was for the purpose of proving yourself?" the judge asks.
"Yes."

"Was he involved in the fight?"

"No."

"Just happened to be somebody who happened to be on the street?"
"Yes."

Three people shot to death that night: Damon Rhodes, eighteen;
Lamont Jones; Earl "Yock" Wilson, forty-one.

"Did all of you discuss the fact that you were going to go out and
ride around and find somebody to shoot? And kill them?"
"Yes."

>━┣━━◇━━┫━<

In East Camden at the cathedral, just a short walk from the drug corners on Thirty-second Street, the snaking line of silent people marches by the cross—a thousand strong. A cross of two charred beams pulled from the city's 4000 burned and abandoned houses. An empty cross but for three red-tipped hypodermic needles impaled in the crumbling wood and a single sign in English and Spanish: CAMDEN CRUCIFIED—CAMDEN CRUCIFICADO. As the line files past the cross, haunting voices read the names of Camden's murder victims for this year:

Richard Biles, 29, black male, killed with a gun.

Robert Gore, 20, black male, killed with a gun.

Trevin Lamont Oglesby, 18, black male, killed with a gun.

Tiffany Leeper, 19, black female, killed with a knife.

Alberto Santiago, 17, Hispanic male, killed with a knife.

Steven Green, 21, black male, killed with a gun.

Charles Williams, 34, black male, killed with a gun.

Jermaine Purcell, 20, black male, killed with a gun.

William Pratt, 30, black male, killed with a gun.

Lamont Davis, 27, black male, killed with hands.

Joseph Trolio, 65, black male, killed with hands.

Lamont Jones, 34, black male, killed with a gun.

Earl Wilson, 41, black male, killed with a gun.

Daymond Rhodes, 18, black male, killed with a gun.

Jessie Pinkney, black male, killed with a gun.

Lenwood Thomas, 19, black male, killed with a gun.

Paul Glover, 21, black male, killed with a gun.

Leonard Bonilla, 14, Hispanic male, killed with a gun.

Parmit Singh, 32, Asian male, killed with a gun.

Ada Lara, 26, Hispanic female, killed with a gun.

Gregory Tyree Roundtree, 20, black male, killed with a gun.

Tyrone Simon, 24, black male, killed with a gun.

Nicole Evans, 3, black female, beaten to death.

Tyrone Damon Harris, 18, black male, killed with a gun.

James Nock, 39, black male, beaten to death.

Anna Mulero, 29, Hispanic female, stabbed to death.

Luz Castro, 19, Hispanic male, killed with a gun.

One year only halfway spent, and already twenty-seven.

I suppose I've been dragging the war inside me all my life, reading with fascination stories of World War II. In the oral history, *Japan At War*, Shozo Tominaga recalls the summer of 1941, when a half-million Japanese and uncounted Chinese had already died, and he had to pass his final test as a platoon leader. It required beheading an emaciated, blindfolded prisoner. A lieutenant demonstrated, shouting "Yo!" as he stretched out his sword in a long arc. Almost unable to breathe, Tominaga recovered his composure, unsheathed his own sword, and swung at the next kneeling victim.

"At the moment," he confessed a half century later, "I felt something change inside me. I don't know how to put it, but I gained strength somewhere in my gut." Butchering had become easy.

It has in America.

7

FATHERS

NOT ONE HOUSE HAS A FATHER
by CORY, age 17

On the street that I live, not one house has a father livin there. My dad left when I was 4. I knew my father's name but not his face. I didn't see him again until I was 13.

When I finally saw him again, we never got that father and son feelin. He was like just another guy.

If a kid don't meet their father till they grown, it's too late for a dad to start acting like a father then.

These days, friends is more family to a kid than a boy's father.

IF A DAD CARRIES GUNS, HIS KID WILL CARRY GUNS TOO
by DESTRY, age 17

A boy's gonna copy what his father does. If his father's out there selling drugs, the boy's gonna try doing the same thing.

If his father is hitting on his mother, the boy's gonna grow up hitting on his girlfriend or wife.

If a father's carrying guns around, the kid's gonna carry guns around too.

If a father's out there getting a job and losing a job and getting a job and losing a job, always depending on his wife, the boy's gonna always depend on his mother—never on himself.

If his father gets an education, the kid will more likely get his education to make his mother and dad proud of him too.

He gonna follow his dad.

Spring Arbor, Michigan, was a postage stamp along the two lanes of highway that connected Chicago with Detroit. It was a tiny village that grew up around a small Free Methodist college and its big, stone church beside a ribbon of highway called M-60. That's where our family settled after World War II—a town with no stoplight. Along one side of Spring Arbor's single business block were Del's, the

Delamarters' restaurant; Archie Woodhurst's Grocery Store; Orville's Barber shop; and the post office. You could mail a letter in those days with a three-cent stamp. Spring Arbor College and the church were across M-60 from Orville's Barber shop. Orville Fitzgerald was among the men who joined my father at six o'clock every morning to pray at the church. Archie and Del attended the church on Sunday mornings. Modest houses on Cottage and College streets hemmed in the cluster of brick buildings that made up the college. The war was over, and soldier boys trooped to the village to attend Spring Arbor College on the G.I. Bill. They settled in Vetville, a rim of prefab houses assembled around the college playing field.

Spring Arbor had a *Good Housekeeping* feel about it. The village was full of saints. When we settled in the old farmhouse across from the college in 1946, the townsfolk welcomed us with an old-fashioned "pounding." Neighbors opened up their pantries and brought us a pound of this, a pound of that. Sugar. Flour. Rice. Staples to help us through the Michigan winter. It was an old tradition in the town.

Townsfolk rallied that winter, opening their homes to offer beds to icebound travelers. These were complete strangers, stranded on a Greyhound bus by a nighttime sleet storm on the highway that cut through town. Winters in Michigan could sneak up with frost in September and stay eight months. In the cocoon of ice that night, the college opened its dormitories to the strangers. And when they still needed beds, in our upstairs bedroom, heated only by the chimney from the potbellied coal stove downstairs, we sheltered two women from Washington, D.C. They slept between flannel sheets in the double bed where Kathleen and I usually slept. The next morning, they washed from a china pitcher and basin on the dresser. Our house had no running water, just a pump at the kitchen sink. The Greyhound Bus Company responded with tangible thanks to the college the following spring, loaning—lease free—a luxury bus for the college's annual Easter-week concert tour for its *a cappella* choir.

The farmhouse across from the college was as primitive as anything we had known in China. The bathroom was an outhouse on a path behind the kitchen. The kitchen soon became the hub of our world. Taylor teenagers came and went through the kitchen door to the high school and college across the street. In a house with no heat but a potbellied stove in the living room, the kitchen was big and warm. In the corner, Mother cooked meals, baked bread, and heated water on a cast-iron stove fueled with coal. To save money, she bought fresh milk from Max Videto's farm along M-60, where cows grazed along the highway. My brother John peddled it home on his bike, and Mother pasteurized it by simmering it on the kitchen stove. We did our homework at a white enamel table in the middle of the room. And on Saturday nights, baths were a family ritual performed in a metal washtub behind a screen next to the kitchen stove. We took turns for who got first bath, when the water was warmest and cleanest.

John, one year younger than I, was getting his first touch of adolescent independence. He wanted to be *modern*. Even bread got into John's dispute with Mother about being *modern*. It was a way to pinch pennies, I think. But Mother baked homemade bread every week. For John, homemade bread was too old-fashioned. He wanted store-bought Wonderbread—modern and soft and wrapped in paper. Mother finally gave up baking bread when John would return from school in the afternoons and devour a whole loaf at one sitting. She just couldn't keep up. Mother nicknamed him from the Scriptures: John was her "bottomless pit."

Spring Arbor was never trendy. Mother was outraged when John sneaked off to Orville's Barber shop and paid sixty cents for his first crew cut. Taylor menfolk usually got their haircuts from Mother in our kitchen, in the corner over by the ironing board. It wasn't just the lost sixty cents. Crew cuts were just too modern. To Mother, *modern* meant *worldly*—and *worldly* bordered on *sinful*. Crew cuts might be stylish in Jackson, nine miles up M-60. Compared to the rest of the world, Spring Arbor would always measure itself with a different yardstick. For a week, Mother made John cover his shame, doing his penance at family mealtime with a hat hiding the offending "butch."

>─◄►─○─◄►─◄

The summer had been full of picking wild huckleberries and strawberries for homemade jam, baking bread, family singing around the pump organ in the corner of the living room, scrubbing clothes on a washboard on the porch. Corn growing fast enough on the farm to be first on the market at Sault St. Marie, Ontario. The sawmill screaming against blunt-edged saplings up by the woods, leaving big heaps of fresh sawdust. Our first summer out of China. I was a child of fourteen, with playful pigtails touching my shoulders on a sunny August evening in Canada. With Father and Mother crossing America in meetings, John and I were summering with friends on St. Joseph's Island. John and I were close enough in age to be taken for twins. Two peas from the same pod.

Alone by the woods, I felt the screaming jolt—the split-second whine of the buzz saw. I took two steps forward in the heaping sawdust beneath my feet before looking down. One minute the hand was tanned brown from the Canadian summer, with slender fingers stained from wild strawberries. Teenage-nibbled fingernails. One bump and one scream of a buzz saw later, it was a bloody, mangled mess. Two steps and one glance down.

Oh, please God, no!

A bloody, butchered left hand, mangled lengthwise. A palm neatly split open, top to bottom, flopped in half. I screamed to the farmhouse, busy with evening chores, not like the scream of a silly girl surprised by a grasshopper on her dress. This was a different scream.

Like a scream for the end of the world. The revolving buzz saw—I never knew just how I bumped it—out there all alone near the woods where they cut the logs for fish crates.

I awoke in an all-white room, my eyes blurry with ether and morphine. A pigtailed child, facing the wall, measuring a left arm against the right. The left arm was swaddled in bandages. It stretched short.

I fell asleep and awoke, measuring again. Two hands. Comforting. Two hands. I felt two hands. I could feel them there beneath the bandages in this narrow, all-white room. Four comforting fingers and a thumb. I could feel them all. Under white bandages, I played "This Little Piggy" and commanded them to move. Four fingers and a thumb. "This little piggy went to market. This little piggy . . ." The fingers would not move. I measured arms again. "This little piggy . . ." The left arm measured a whole hand short. In the daylight I could screw up my courage. I could feel the fingers. In the darkness my courage softened.

White world . . . white room with whispering people . . . whispering people with no tongues . . . One day, two days, three days . . . White bandaged arm measures one whole hand short . . . Measure again, Mary, again . . . again . . . again. This little piggy went to market . . . four comforting fingers . . . one . . . two . . . three . . . four . . . and a thumb. And this little piggy had roast beef . . . A whole hand short . . . And this little piggy had . . . some . . . yes, some . . . Move little piggy . . . Please, move little piggy . . . Please . . . Big, wrapped-up arm . . . fills the whole room . . . chokes it . . . pushes everybody's tongues back into their heads. You people coming and going, whispering . . . smiling pretend-smiles . . . afraid of the one question you don't want to answer . . . pretend-talk . . . pretend-smiles . . . Please, little piggy . . . wee, wee, wee, wee, all the way home . . . Please little piggy . . . mo-o-o-ve . . . mo-o-o-ove . . . I will not cry . . . They'll see . . . brave.

Maybe it's wrapped bent backward to make it short . . . A Taylor does not cry . . . Proud of me . . . Give them back their tongues . . . give them back their smiles . . . a brave girl. Brave. A Taylor.

I was frightened by truth. Not knowing gave my terror someplace to hide. I measured arms and dreaded. Dreaded to ask. *Dreaded.* Until morphine and sleep wrapped me in peace.

Kindly old Doctor Trefry bolstered himself with a roomful of people when he told me. The hand was gone.

I looked out at all of them with big, unblinking eyes. My throat felt lumpy. The child inside harnessed every muscle to drag back the ocean that wanted to spill out. I wanted them all to go away, GO AWAY! *Stop the pretend-talk of modern miracles.*

I didn't want to hear about artificial hands. Fourteen years old and artificial hands? My teeth clenched.

No miracles! No artificial hand. NO ARTIFICIAL HAND! GO AWAY! Give me back my hand. GO AWAY! Leave me—just me and Johnny, my brother—Johnny stay with me.

I would test out new thoughts, one by one, as they peeked around secret corners of my brain.

Do you think boys will like a fourteen-year-old girl with just one hand? Braiding pigtails, tying shoes, playing the piano—can I do it— with just one hand?

Home again in Spring Arbor, Father tiptoed through his grief. He gave me time to hate my handless arm. I loathed it. For weeks I couldn't even look at it. The monster arm that made me different.

Dad's best presents were always Taylor stories, told in his gentle Scottish accent. He agonized. A child of his was looking out at a world defined by what she could *not* do. He was braiding my pigtails for me, wrapping the ends in rubber bands one day.

"Shall I tell you a secret, Sweetheart?" I loved his just-for-me secrets.

"When Bertie first heard you had lost your hand, do you know what he said to me?"

I waited.

"He told me, 'Now Mary won't be able to ride her bicycle.' " Bertie was my little brother, not yet seven. I suspected he was eyeing my new British Raleigh with its hand-grip brakes. "And do you know what I said to him?" Daddy paused.

"I told him, 'Well, I don't know why *not*.' "

"**Well, I don't know why not.**" I tacked them up like a banner hanging forever on the wall of my heart—not just the words.

Well, I *don't* know why not.

The believing. My daddy believed in me. My father's voice was the rhythm of my childhood. I looked down at wondrous fingers on my right hand, fingers that could tie shoelaces with one hand. I braided my hair, trading the three strands between my mouth, my armpit, and my hand. Mother, who never let any Taylor hide behind the nonsense of "I can't," enrolled me at the college for Hammond organ lessons. I would play the keyboards with one hand and two feet. She would not rest until she had tracked down piano music and typing instruction books written for just one hand. And excuses about not doing dishes? A Taylor *never* says "I can't," she would remind me as she lined me up with the rest. *Absolutely, yes! You will take your nightly turn at dishes with everybody else. You will do everything*, my mother said. Everything! Then she sat me down and taught me to crochet.

When my year rolled around to the eleventh-grade English term paper, it was Dad who settled with me on my research topic— *HANDICAPS?* It was a father-daughter project. We set off looking for the triumphs of Helen Keller and President Franklin Roosevelt. Helen Keller, a child with no hearing, no sight, and no speech could learn to read and write and speak. Franklin Roosevelt, a paralyzed president, who could inspire America from his wheelchair.

My father taught me *cans* and *coulds*. My father taught me that handicaps come only from the inside.

James Taylor believed that knowing God changes the way you look at the world. For how many generations of Taylors, a kindly heavenly Father had held us in His hands. God's words, God's laws were the comforting, unshifting bedrock for our family.

The Bible was his guide. The Ten Commandments. The Sermon on the Mount. The Psalms. God's Word. He believed that a father is God's representative in the home. The teacher of Truth by word and by example. He told us that the ancient Hebrews used to carry the Truth of the Almighty wrapped around their heads and attached to the door frames of their homes. Dad knew that he would just as deliberately write God's values on the tables of our hearts. That was a father's job.

He did it with stories. Next to my mother, he was the best storyteller I ever knew. Dad didn't tell family legends just to tell a story. There was always a lesson to be learned. Stories with a moral, about character. My childhood favorite was *Chips and the Smelling Salts, and God Answers Prayer*. This story had everything: Dad's pet monkey freezing—lifeless—in his cage on the window ledge in Shanghai, China. Dad, a teenager praying with newfound faith in God to save his precious Chips. The frozen monkey sneezing at the smelling salts when the prayer was done. Chips was alive! A miracle! Dad always attached a word from God to the happy ending to this story: *If you have faith so much as a grain of mustard seed, you can command this mountain to be moved, and it will be moved.* The verse became Taylor family bedrock. You can move mountains.

Then there was the *Why-I-fell-in-love-then-broke-up-with-May Twigg* story. May Twigg was Dad's first love in Shanghai in the early 1900s before he came to America to college. This story had the handsome suitor (James Taylor), the beautiful maiden (May Twigg)— and her unwilling father, who viewed James Taylor as a young lad quite without promise. That, of course, was the problem. If May Twigg married James Taylor, she would be breaking one of God's Ten Commandments.

"Well, how come you didn't marry her anyway?" This was the part I hated. I wanted happily-ever-after endings to my stories. And anyway, what kind of evil man could think James Taylor lacked promise? The man who would someday be my father lacked promise?

"But, Dad . . ."

"Well," he would ask, "what does *Honor thy father and thy mother* mean? Mr. Twigg didn't want his daughter to marry me." As far as

Dad was concerned, heartbreak or not, there was only one acceptable ending to this story. God's. You could break up a romance, but you couldn't break God's law. I always secretly felt that it served Mr. Twigg right. James Taylor came to America and married Alice Hayes.

Even the walls at our house preached my father's values. Did we need to improve our understanding of the world? He tacked a giant *National Geographic* map of the world to the dining room wall. With cities of the world, we played Who-can-find-it-first? Durban. Vladivostok. Quito. Qingdao.

Did I need a reminder that God watches over me? He hung artwork with a message on my bedroom wall, a framed picture of the guardian angel hovering over two endangered waifs crossing a yawning chasm. And always—always—he posted the Taylor family motto around the house, a motto passed on for at least five generations: *As for me and my house, we will serve the Lord.* That's how it was with Dad—just like the ancient Hebrews: *Bind God's Word around your head. Write it on the tables of your heart.*

Even a stranger would have been excused for believing that God lived with us. Our family certainly believed that He did. My father talked to God every day. And God talked to him. So Dad became my pipeline to the Almighty—I always felt connected to a safe, recessed Place for gathering strength. He could almost always find a bedrock word from God there in the Secret Place. We sang Psalm 91: *He that dwelleth in the secret place of the Most High shall abide under the shadow of the Almighty* (KJV). The Secret Place had nurtured miracles for at least four or five generations of Taylors.

We grew up at family worship every day, listening wide-eyed to stories of God's miracles: Moses' leading God's people out of Egypt into the Promised Land. God's closing the mouths of lions to save Daniel in the lions' den. God's sending the ravens to feed his prophet Elijah in the drought-dried wilderness. Opening the doors of the jail to set free his apostle Peter. There were modern-day miracles, too. When the young James Taylor, who would one day be my father—who couldn't sing—prayed for a wife with a gift for music, God sent him Alice Hayes, who would charm the children of China with her accordion and her singing.

If Mother took us by the hand in search of johnny-jump-ups and jack-in-the-pulpits in Michigan woodlots that she loved so much, Dad took us exploring through the well-worn pages of his Bible. He took me through its groves and streams and much-walked paths in search of God. I was a teenager curious about God. "How will I know when I've found God?" I asked my dad one day.

You will seek me and find me when you search for me with all your heart. He leafed to Jeremiah. In these father-daughter walks, I could hold his hand to touch the face of God.

Dad showed me God's Word. I watched him live it every day. I saw it work.

Baby Alice died in Washington, D.C.—he told me about it so many years later—his firstborn child. He trusted God. Then little Jeannie died of pneumonia in his arms in far-off China—his second child. In faraway Henan there was no doctor. He trusted still. Then Kathleen— a girl who survived a bloody war and Japanese concentration camp— returned to America and died of lupus at twenty-three—his third child. I was a teenager in college then, watching my father—my idol—torn between being head-of-the-family strong and opening his broken heart. I wanted to hold him in his grief. How many years later, when we buried Father in the little cemetery along M-60, we laid him next to Kathleen. From four treasured daughters—every one a gift from God, he said—he was left with me. He called me his "Mary, Sweetheart." I watched him find his strength and comfort in his Secret Place—on his knees, his Bible open. He trusted God's goodness and God's kindly purpose. When I looked at my father, I saw God. I thought that God must be like my father.

Even today I find myself studying the hair above my forehead to see if I have the one curl over my temple that my daddy had. Maybe even God has a curl like that. A child should want to be like her father or her mother. I did.

Dad expected absolute honesty, clean speech, good manners. To Dad, bad manners were very close to sin. Any offending elbow that lingered on the table at mealtimes would be cracked sharply on the table by the nearest brother or sister. After all, Dad preached chivalry that blended the tenets of King Arthur, Sir Galahad, and Emily Post. If our English teachers didn't make us memorize great thoughts, my father did:

> My strength is as the strength of ten
> Because my heart is pure.

Abraham, Moses, and King Arthur costarred in his sermons from the platform of the old stone church in Spring Arbor. In the 1950s he had become the pastor of the college church in town.

If you want to find who shapes America, dig for the childhood memories, those snapshots of past. The real history makers of America are its fathers and its mothers. What they talk about. What their attitudes are. What they do for a living.

Dad was always our cheering section in filling our minds with great poetry. He loved the ripple effect—Jamie practiced his memory work on me in the living room near the potbellied stove. I practiced on John. As each successive Taylor reached Miss Celestine Carr's English literature class, one child poured lofty thoughts from Tennyson and Shakespeare and Alexander Pope into the ear of the next. Lofty thoughts, high ideals—they stuck forever. Forty years later I still remember:

Vice is a monster of so frightful mien
  As to be hated, needs but to be seen.
Yet, seen too oft, familiar with her face,
  We first endure, then pity, then embrace.

* * *

The quality of mercy is not strained.
  It droppeth as a gentle rain from heaven. . . .

* * *

We think our fathers fools so wise we grow.
  Our wiser sons, no doubt, will think us so.

When the family budget could afford it, the prize for our successes was a joyful trip to Loud and Jackson's Dairy Bar in Jackson to buy a five-scoops-of-ice-cream milk shake for a quarter. The biggest prize was having a father and mother being there to see our triumphs. My father was proud of me. That was what fueled much of my drive to achieve.

Family talk is the indelible message from our childhood. It marks us like a fingerprint—unique. I remember standing in the doorway of the old stone parsonage on a February day, still cold from Kathleen's funeral. My big sister was dead at twenty-three. Kathleen, who had sent me off to college with her favorite blue satin dress. Of four Taylor girls, I was the only one left. "Remember, Mary," Jamie, my oldest brother, stood beside me. "It's your responsibility now for the girls in the family." When I need to remember, I go to his words in the yellow pages of my scrapbook.

I was the inheritor.

>─<>─O─<>─<

Many children in America inherit something less wholesome. At the Center, we knew what set the stage for youthful killings. Boys learned violence by watching it; feeling it at home. Someone taught them.

By the time he was eight, Ricardo had seen more violence than most of us have seen in our lifetimes. Street fights were a boy's curiosity. Something to watch like a carnival or dogfight. They were nothing like the throat-grabbing terror that always choked him when his father's fists crashed into his mother's head. Boys learn by watching. In the streets of Humacao in Puerto Rico where he grew up, he learned the sound of *machetes* hitting flesh. In his home, he cowered from his father's drunken fists and tongue.

Ricardo did not know exactly what caused something inside his mother to break. Maybe it was the strain of trying to stretch the foodstamps and $984 a year in welfare checks for her five children. Or the shame of not being able to find the fifteen cents for each child's lunch money every day, knowing that they would preserve their honor among friends by saying that they weren't hungry. Maybe it was the repeated beatings from a drunken husband. But one day she just snapped. Even when he tried to hug and comfort her, she pushed him away.

They took her away to the mental hospital, and for the next two years, Ricardo bounced between two sisters. No dad. No mom. No anchor. When she returned, she packed the children, and with disaster relief money from Hurricane David, headed for the better life she was sure awaited her in Camden, New Jersey, where her uncle ran a carpet business.

Ricardo was nine years old when he arrived in Camden, wearing a new zippered sweater. He felt proud inside, wearing the jackets that other Americans were wearing. If his mother's dreams saw Camden as rows of lovely houses and neat lawns, Ricardo already knew better. For more than two years in Humacao, Uncle Juan's son had been telling him legends of the fights in Camden.

The night had pulled a dark mask over Camden's gutted houses and boarded-up shops when they arrived. In his van, Uncle Juan drove the family from the Philadelphia airport across the darkened river to Camden. Ricardo's mom awoke to daylight that told her that Camden was not the beautiful city that she had imagined in her dreams. She found burned-out houses and trash.

None of Ricardo's family spoke English. On the street, he tried hand signals that promptly got him labeled as "a faggot." In return, his foot landed a karate kick that blackened a playmate's eye. Ricardo found himself a scrawny, tempting target. The new boy on the block. With hair cropped almost cue-ball bald, he had no hair to pull. So they pulled his ears. They called him "lizard."

That was his first day in Camden.

Ricardo had learned his first lesson in the street rules of respect. The playmate with the swelling black eye didn't mess with Ricardo— not ever again. *Macho* was the standard for survival, and Ricardo had learned the rules. Only a punk would not fight back.

When it came to fighting, Ricardo was one of the boys. When it came to personal habits, he wasn't. He didn't drink. He didn't do drugs. "I never even hold a cigarette between my two fingers," he liked to boast. He despised people who took drugs. "Drugs . . ." he used to preach to his little brother Jorge, "if you do drugs—you get even be worse. Cocaine make them feel big and *bad*. You know . . . when they smoke a joint or whatever . . . they got a big *S* on the middle of their chest because they Superman—got a beer in their hand . . ." He didn't want Jorge to have anything to do with drugs.

Ricardo wanted to be a *real* American—with a lamp in the house, a sofa, a refrigerator for his mother. It wasn't just furniture that the family needed. It was winter clothes. Through the biting winds of winter that whipped down Federal Street, he watched his mother walk coatless to the welfare office to pick up the family check. At ten years of age, Ricardo blamed himself that he was too young to work.

The things that Ricardo wanted—how could he ask his mom? She was struggling to pay the rent, the electric and the phone bills. She hardly had clothes for herself. How could he ask for the seventy-dollar sneaks he wanted for school when his mom couldn't find the money to pay the electric bill?

Ricardo sold his first joint of marijuana when he was twelve years old. In school.

Then he sold to all his uncles. Uncle Juan from time to time would hand the boy five dollars for seed money—a boost for his new enterprise on the street corner.

"Do it the smart way, if you gonna do it," his uncle told him. "Stand alone." The boy had found no heroes. Except an uncle who taught him, "I only stand by myself."

With drug money, he bought a .22 for eighty dollars from a desperate drug addict—a geezer with a bagful of guns at the top of the hill at Thirty-second Street was the home of the Three-Two posse, the largest gang in East Camden. Ricardo was now a twelve-year-old with a gun.

Guns and gold and clothes meant respect out on the street. People knew his name. People greeted him with "What's happenin', man?" "What's happenin'" was the street code—he was *in*.

The neighborhood was an open drug market. "Dime" bags of cocaine for ten dollars. "Twenties" for $20. "Sixties"—two or three "twenties" put in a little bag—sold for $50. "Eight-ball"—six or seven "twenties" put in a bag for quick sale—went for $100. Quarter-ounce cost at least $300. Half an ounce for $550-$600. A whole ounce cost $1000 or $1050. The "big boys" could buy half a kilo for $15,000 or a kilo for $30,000. Ricardo had arrived at adolescence just as the cocaine epidemic hit the streets. It was 1987.

Selling drugs and going to church didn't mix. Pastor Angel Luis Guzman preached to the faithful each week against the scourge of drugs. Selling was a sin, the pastor said. Buying was a sin. Drugs would destroy the city. They would destroy your soul.

Ricardo knelt by his bed each night. Apologizing to God became a nightly ritual. "Forgive me for all the bad things . . . God, you can see inside my heart . . . what my family needs." There was a single thread that wove through the ribbon of all his prayers: *Please, God, PLEASE don't let there be any damage from what I sell*. He didn't want to awaken with blood on his hands.

At East Camden Middle School and at Woodrow Wilson High School, Ricardo estimated that seventy-five percent of the students smoked marijuana. A kid could sell five bags while changing classes. Easy. Teenagers who cut class to sell the drugs could earn as much as one hundred dollars an hour. Trapping—selling on the corner drug sets—youngsters could make three hundred an hour. Friday and Saturday nights on the corner were a feeding frenzy. So was the first of the month when welfare checks arrived: A boy could pocket fifteen hundred dollars in one night.

The drug trade was the fastest route to respect. That's what everyone on the street lived for. Respect. *RESPECT* was a street word all in capitals. You lived—or died—for RESPECT. One-hundred-dollar Nike and Air Jordan sneakers bought respect—and status. So did Toyotas, Mazdas, and Raiders' jackets numbered with 32 on the back. Headbands of red and black. Or red and white.

In the projects where Ricardo lived, there was an unspoken agreement between some of the police patrols and the boys: The cops would sweep the corners and let the boys sell in the middle of the blocks. It was the corners, after all, that were giving Camden a bad name—boys scurrying round like cockroaches on corner sets, accosting cars, hawking their favorite brand of drugs.

By the time he got to East Camden Middle School, classmates were using guns to settle fights over girls, over boys. Life without meaning and the gaping poverty of the city came together at the barrel of a gun. Death was worth only twenty-five cents—that's what a bullet cost. Sometime—amidst all the violence—the boys on the corners stopped talking about fighting. Now they talked about killing. Next thing you knew, it was *bang, bang, bang*.

At fifteen, Ricardo Fontanez was on the run.

Nothing about the murder on the night of September 9 made sense. Nor did his immediate impulse, dragging him back like a homing pigeon to Humacao and his father.

He hated the man.

He loved the man—or at least he kept building an imaginary father that he could love.

Violence and drunken stupors tangled in almost every memory of his father. Yet even at fifteen, Ricardo kept making up visions so clear that he could see them. Father-love was easy as a wish: He could close his eyes and dream. Father-and-son picnics. Ricardo, Sr., and his little Riquito. Man-to-man talks along the beach at Seven Seas. Fantasy.

With police in Camden looking for witnesses to the killing of Julio Matos, Ricardo had fled to Puerto Rico. Someone had told him that he could find his father at the carnival, a stone's throw beyond the housing project at Humacao.

The winking lights on the merry-go-round splashed yellow on the men drinking at the beer and hot-dog stand on the midway. Ricardo recognized his father right away in the crowd of men, the same curly hair—like his. In his mind Ricardo knew exactly what would happen. He had talked it all out to himself: *First I open my arms to hug him. Then my dad reaches to do what a lot of dads would do when they ain't seen their son for six, seven years. "Ricardo, how you doin'!" He hugs me. "Oh, my God! You grown so much. Oh, so tall! All that gold. You lookin' good. That's your girl!"* That's how it would be.

Ricardo was pulling his lovely Marielle, his girlfriend, toward the man with the mustache, the curly hair, the mirror image of himself. It would be a proud six-feet-one-inch hugging a joyful five-feet-nine-inch and 123 pounds.

Ricardo touched his father's shoulder. He was stepping into the story he had told himself a hundred times.

"Ricardo," he said.

The man ignored the touch, concentrating on his drink. Ricardo tried again.

"Ricardo."

"What?" The man growled at the interruption.

"I'm your son."

"What you mean you my son?"

"Remember me?"

"No, I don't remember you."

Ricardo opened his arms. "I'm your son."

Word had reached Puerto Rico almost as fast as it had reached the Camden police. Someone got shot. Someone died. Ricardo would be coming to Puerto Rico. Now a father was jabbing a finger at his son's collarbone, pointing to the gold chains.

"What kinda life you think you livin'?" In the blur of beer and the mugginess of the tropical night, the elder Ricardo moved his hand from the gold chains around the boy's neck and started tapping on the boy's forehead. "I bet you sellin' drugs." Beer slopped from the can clutched in the man's hand.

Ricardo felt a rush of anger and disappointment. His dream was melting in front of his eyes. "And this is the type of life you been living since I was three . . ." The boy tapped the beer can in his father's hand. ". . . prob'ly the type of life you been livin' since before I was born."

The clownish hurdy-gurdy music grinding on the midway mocked them. Veins began throbbing on his father's throat. "Look. You want to talk to me, you talk to me tomorrow." He started walking away.

Ricardo put his hand on his father's shoulder to hold him back. "Na. I wanta talk to you right now." He had been so sure of his this-is-how-it's-supposed-to-be meeting that he was unprepared for rejection. "You don't even care about your *son.*"

Like lightning, his father struck the boy hard across the face. Ricardo reeled. Marielle gasped. The man's six-feet-one-inch frame was towering over the boy. This scrawny, loose-lipped twirp challenging him in front of his friends. "I should punch you."

Ricardo started taking off his gold, handing it to Marielle.

"Whacha gonna do, boy?" His father was poking his finger now in Ricardo's face, looking down at all 123 pounds of the fifteen-year-old boy who was challenging him. "You gonna hit me?" he laughed. "You gonna hit me?"

"You disrespect me," Ricardo said. Respect was the badge of manhood on the street. Disrespect was the one act a man could never forgive. Ricardo had been "dissed."

"I see—what kinda dad you are. I don't ever want to see you again. I'm never gonna forget—you disrespect me."

Even two years later, he remembered it like a video playback. "I went off," Ricardo told me. "I mean, after six or seven years, he's gonna give me that! I had this dream, like he was gonna be my father. I thought my dad was gonna be like: *I'm glad you're back. I'm gonna get you a job.* He has his own business—a carpenter—big connections—that he was gonna help me instead of puttin' me down. But he never gave me that. That night I jumped all quick from sad to angry."

Ricardo would not let go. The boy kept reaching, clutching for the dream: In that six-feet-one-inch carbon copy of himself he kept inventing a father that believed in him, that hoped for him, that was proud of his son. He wanted advice. Man talk. A man in Camden was dead.

The carnival had been Friday night. By Sunday, Ricardo's fantasy was tugging him again. *Maybe my father was drunk on Friday. Six years later you surely gonna be glad to see your son.* He and Marielle went over to Maricutana Street, his father's house.

"I couldn't see you real good, Friday night," his father said. It sounded like the beginnings of an apology. "I guess I was a little bit drunk." The man turned away—slowly—toward Marielle. Across the room, he started blowing her kisses.

The man's nostrils quivered. "What you see in Ricardo?" His voice was husky. "What you need—" he paused as his eyes caressed her body—"is a real man."

On the day he decided to return to Camden to turn himself in, the boy went looking for his father one more time. "I opened the door like if it was my house," he confided in me two years later when he finally dared to face the failure of his dream. "I hugged my grandmom. 'Look, I'm goin' back to Camden tomorrow.'"

"'Yeh, that's good,'" my father said.

"I had this picture I wanted to give him—give him a picture of me—'Look, it's for you.' "

Neither Ricardo knew what to say. Neither knew what to do.

"He was suspecting for me to go like this." (Ricardo motioned to me across my desk, reaching out both arms as if to embrace his imaginary dad.) "I gotta go now. A'right?"

Ricardo paused again in telling me the story, still stunned with disbelief. "He—only—shake—my—hand. I walked down the steps. I closed the door on him in my heart." It was almost a whisper—flat, empty of feeling. I was watching a boy who didn't dare unlock his anger as he told me the story.

"Incredible! Incredible! I didn't believe it was happening.

"Love. That's all I needed. Love. But you don't go—you ain't seen me six years that you don't see me—go smack at me. If my father would of give me the type of love I deserve—even if he would smack me around—long as he teach me good from bad . . . from time to time talk to me. . . ." Ricardo's voice trailed off. The chair he was sitting in squeaked as he swiveled angrily left to right and back. I heard it every day—the simple, endless hunger of a child for a father who had disappeared.

"Please . . . if he only talk to me from time to time. . . . If I go back to Puerto Rico and he know how to be a dad—or a close friend. . . ." Ricardo's chair squeaked again. He struggled with his father's rejection. How could a father not want to be a father?

"Even if he don't want to be a dad, I just want him to be my close friend."

Ricardo killed the pain with fantasies. "My dad gonna look back— 'After all, Ricardo didn't kill anyone. He prob'ly just there at the wrong time.' All this smackin'. He gonna realize it was a mistake. So I prepare for him to be a good friend with me, you know, to do things with me, go out places, go to the beach, have picnics. . . ."

Something important had collapsed. Here came the twenty-first century, a nation wringing its hands: Why were more than a million Ricardos behind bars?

Every time a boy pulled a gun on the streets, parents searched for some reason why it was an unusual case, why it couldn't happen in their community, but the exception to the rule had become exceptionally common. In ten years, there had been a 79 percent increase in the number of youngsters in America who commit murder with a gun.[1] Ricardo was one of the accused.

Murder was the leading cause of death for black males age 15–19. Eleven firearm deaths a day for youth in that age group. Child victims

---

[1]Crime in the United States 1991, Uniform Crime Report. U.S. Department of Justice, p. 297.

were getting younger. Firearms were the second leading cause of death for all children aged ten to fourteen, after motor-vehicle accidents. More male teenagers were being killed by gunfire than by all diseases combined.

Teachers' groups said 100,000 children carry guns to school every day. Children carried guns not only to commit crimes but to settle conflicts that once ended with fistfights.

What happened to teaching right and wrong? *Thou shalt* and *thou shalt not*? And when did we substitute the banner *It is forbidden to forbid*? If a father chose to leave his family, if a teenager in the slums chose to express herself by having a baby, it was neither good nor bad. It was just another option. Just another choice.

No law would cure the ultimate reason behind so many young murders—the tragic lack of stable, two-parent families and close communities that teach the value of all human life.

Absence of men in America's family life had become the trend that hit America harder than any other. Boys without fathers—the number-one predictor of juvenile crime. Seventy percent of youngsters serving time in long-term correctional facilities grew up without a father. Girls without a father—they were more than twice as likely to have children as teenagers and before they were married. Child abuse and domestic violence always showed up more frequently in homes where the man in the house is not the married husband and father.

Fatherlessness fueled the nation's most pressing social problems: crime, teen pregnancy, and domestic violence.[2]

Fathers are irreplaceable—shaping the character, giving kids skills. It was an undisputed fact from pediatricians to social scientists: Children who grow up with their fathers do far better—emotionally, educationally, physically—than children who do not. An intact family is the best crime-prevention program we know.

For Ricardo, any future meant keeping the past at bay. He returned to Camden. He turned himself in to the police two weeks after his sixteenth birthday. A skinny boy with big, brown eyes. Accused of murder.

IF MY FATHER WOULD OF BEEN NEXT TO ME . . .
by RICARDO, age 16

If a boy don't have a father, he ain't gonna beat the streets. The streets, the money, your friends control you.

You gotta have a strong man pullin you in the right direction, punishin you when you be doin wrong.

A boy's gonna listen to a father better than a mother. A mom like to

---

[2]David Blankenhorn, "The 'New Father' Is No 'Good Family Man,'" *Philadelphia Inquirer* (June 21, 1992), C9.

believe everything you tell her. A dad don't, because he was a teenager and know what the street is all about.

If my father would of been next to me. . . .

We lived in this world of *ifs* and *if onlys*.

At the Youth Center, visiting nights were a time for women. Mothers came. Grandmothers came. Girlfriends came. Fathers almost never came.

It shouted at me: Absent fathers—a mark of America's crumbling lives.

8

K–I–L–L

In the cafeteria, I reach my hand into the neck hole of a youngster's white T-shirt and put my finger in a bullet hole much, much too near the boy's heart. A bullet hole not three weeks old. Then I put my hand inside the back of his shirt and put my finger on the raw hole where the bullet came out.

Classroom 123 hushes when I write the letters on the board, big and round and black: **K–I–L–L.**

It is a lesson I have borrowed from the California Youth Authority in its work with gangs. In any ordinary high school, students would yawn about my playing such a game to get their attention . . . writing K–I–L–L across the board. But not this group.

"Ever hear of an endangered species?" I ask.

It is 9:15 on a summer morning. Outside the classroom window, tiny apples are beginning to form on the apple tree. Green pine cones grow fat among long-needle pines. Fifteen of the older boys bunch around the round classroom table, every one of them . . . yes . . . an owner of a gun . . . they have raised their hands . . . yes. And the officer in the room raises his hand too. Yes.

And why not? In America even the toy industry makes guns popular. In 1987 the U.S. toy industry spent more than $40 million on advertising new war toys that included water- and dye-pellet versions of the Uzi and AK-47.[1]

Toy guns are fun. So are real guns for risk-addicted boys. Semi-automatic weapons are the weapons of choice for the drug posses on the streets. With government restrictions removed for importing Chinese military surplus guns, a boy could get a real AK-47—$300—a cheap buy on the streets.

"An endangered species . . . is in danger of being wiped off the face of the earth," says Theaster, "because that's where most of the killings are happening. Wipe it off the face of the earth."

---

[1] J. Stewart and A. Alexander " 'Miami Vice' the trend-setter in assault weapons," *Atlanta Journal Constitution* (September 17, 1989), A13.

"That's what *you* are," I say softly. "An endangered species. Young men like you—killing each other off." With my boys and girls, potential and realities have never matched. The talent is here. But I also know the realities of this land: If you're a black or Hispanic family in America with a seventeen-year-old son, your son is more likely to end up dead or locked up than to become a doctor or a lawyer.

"We're going to write your answers on the board." I pick up a blue marker. "Good reasons to kill someone."

No one waits. Not one second's pause.

"Fightin'," says Troy. The answer does not surprise me as number one. Jeremy has just rolled up his right pant leg to show Troy next to him the scar of the bullet that went through his leg.

"Money." The answers come like popcorn.

"Females."

"Females?" A ripple of laughter crosses the room. "Yeh. Females." Coming faster than I can write.

"Drugs."

"Jealousy."

"Power."

"Hurt someone in your family."

"Kill to gain respect." Respect—I have known from the start that respect will be near the top of the list. The new values say, "Death before dishonor." Jostle your arm in the school hallway to make you spill your schoolbooks and someone will come back with a gun to retaliate for being *dissed*. You would *not* fight that very same day at his school, Jason says. Thursdays and Fridays were the days reserved for fights at Morgan Village School—you saved the fights for Thursday and Friday fights on the parking lot. Cars stopping . . . hundreds of people there to watch. Like gladiators. On schedule. It had a name: *Thursday and Friday Fights.*

I write "respect" on the board. People die for respect.

"Trash talk," says Kahlil. Laughter murmurs across the room.

"Wait," I say. "That's realistic." I point my blue marker at Kahlil. "Let's get clear exactly what you mean by trash talk—words that make you kill."

"Say something 'bout your mom or 'I'ma f__k you up.' Insulting your family."

"Threatenin' me." Jamie is seventeen years old. Accused of killing the owner of a candy store in a robbery attempt. Certain to be tried as an adult. I keep wondering in my head what the boy is thinking.

"Fight."

"Gang—posse fight."

"Fighting between posses?" I ask.

"Yeh."

"War."

"That's more like nation against nation." I take my marker away from the board. "Shall we leave that off? Not killing, like the United States against Iraq."

"No." Jamie insists. "I mean Three-Two against some other posse." Three-Two is *the* gang to reckon with in East Camden.

To me, war means Vietnam. Korea. World War II. To them . . . "Okay. Gang war. Like Three-Two against . . . "

" . . . anybody." I add "gang war" to the list on the board.

"Dead soldiers in gang wars," says Jack, who quotes from a recent story in *WHAT'S HAPPENING*, the youth student newspaper.

"Stealin' your stash."

"Someone talkin' to your girl."

"Someone sells you bad drugs."

"Someone steal your car."

"You are talking about . . . you would kill for someone stealing your car."

"Yeh."

"Territory."

"Explain what you mean—territory," I say.

"Trappin' where you' sellin' . . . Turf."

"Someone moving in on your territory."

"Yeh."

In the grown-up world, I think to myself, nations kill for economical survival. We call it war.

I write on the board "Moving in on your turf." "Keep talking. I know you've got a lot more reasons, because I've heard you tell me a lot more than this."

"Killing one of your friends."

"Revenge."

"Snitch."

"Someone ratted on you—like to the police? Snitched on you?"

"Any others?"

"Someone set you up."

"Someone kill you."

"Well . . . "

"Man, how you gonna kill someone if they already kill you?" Jeffery shouts across the room.

"Threaten you . . . so you kill them first."

With a lull in the answers, I start reading down the list. "Money. That realistic? Ever hear of someone being killed for money?"

The room is a chorus of "yehs."

"How about females?"

Shouts of "yeh."

"How 'bout drugs? We've got a lot on the list about drugs. Bad drugs. Someone said 'beat' but I didn't write it down . . . that's when a customer runs off without paying. Right? Shall I put 'beat' down?"

Howls. "Yeh. Yeh . . . " I have to wait till the laughter subsides.

The boys take proprietary pride when they succeed in teaching me the language of the streets.

"I'm doing okay. Right? You didn't think I knew about it, did you." They nudge one another. "Jealousy?"

"Yeh."

"Power."

"Power is like *juice*," Jack elaborates. " . . . earn more respect than others get."

"Respect."

"Yeh."

"Gain respect? Gonna hurt someone to gain respect."

No pause here. "Yeh."

"Like being the biggest, baddest, meanest person?" I ask.

"Yeh."

I move on down the list. "Hurt someone in your family? Ever heard of that?"

"Yeh."

"Trash talk? Insulting your family, your mom, your dad? Threatening you?"

"Someone hit your mom."

"Hit your mom? Okay. Let's put that down." I pause to think out loud. "You know what I didn't hear anyone say?—Someone looks at you weird."

"Grit."

"G-R-I-T—a look to kill."

"Yeh. If your eyes meet, the dude is looking for trouble."

If looks could kill . . . was a slang expression in my growing-up years. Today—looks do kill. Between street gangs—the "grit" look kills. A challenge with the eyes—it launches wars.

"Gang fight or war between posses? Wars in Camden just this year."

"True."

"Someone sets you up? Ever heard of killing for that?"

"Yeh."

"Sneakers." A shout from Jamar. "Sneakers can get you killed. Or in big trouble. Up on the telephone wire down on Thirty-second Street be more than hundred pairs of sneakers. Sneakers wars."

Perhaps we need the moment of diversion.

"Nike Patrol come out at night dressed all in black—and masks—they run up on people and take off their sneakers if they don't wear Nikes. Threaten. Tie the laces together. Throw the sneaks over the wire. Doin' it for the fun of it. Filas. Reeboks . . ."

Wearing the wrong sneakers—dressing for success has never been so hazardous. Lace-ups. Slip-ons. High-tops. The boys chime in as though they've every one of them been there.

"Champions."

"Spotbuilts. Adidas."

"Ponys."

"K-Swiss . . . they all could get you beat up—and your sneakers stolen."

Nike Patrol. About the time I was born, Sears Roebuck sold rubber-soled canvas sneakers for fifty-nine cents. Youngsters today wear Michael Jordans for $125. Shoes that get them killed. I shake my head and write "Steal your sneakers" on the board.

"Gold chain."

"Kill for stealing gold?" I ask.

"Put down jewelry." Someone by the window applauds.

"Someone set you up." I keep reading down the list.

"Hurting your little sister," says Kahlil.

"Gettin' you' sister pregnant . . ."

". . . and leave her."

I'm down to the end of the list. "Moving onto your turf . . ." I start counting. "How many do we have?"

"Twenty-seven . . . twenty-eight . . ."

In fifteen minutes the boys in Classroom 123 have filled the board with twenty-eight reasons to kill. Before my eyes on the board is the toxic residue of too much television, too many ghastly movies, too many violent video games. Life without a future. *It's like a game,* I think to myself. *Whoever gets the kids first, that's how they will turn out.* There is a very long pause. These boys know me well enough to know that this lesson is going somewhere else.

I feel an undercurrent in the room—something beyond my reach. Something no one wants to talk about.

"Another question for you." They are very, very quiet. "Which of these reasons . . ." I point to the board. ". . . would you die for? We're not talking about killing just for the fun of it." I look around the room. "If you can kill for something, are you also ready to die for that reason? Which of these reasons would you be willing to give your own life . . . dead . . . buried . . . gone for?"

Jack raises his hand. "Cool. You' mom. You' mom."

"Wait . . . wait . . . wait. . . ." I tap the blue marker on the desk. "Let's go down the whole list. I brought in a list of names yesterday to show to my staff—a list of twenty-seven people—mostly young, black men—Hispanic men—killed since January first in the city." The room goes uncomfortably silent. "Dead. Gone. And the year is only halfway done."

The irony makes me shudder. Twenty-seven people murdered in the city this year and my boys—in fifteen minutes—rattle off twenty-seven, twenty-eight reasons to kill. One number explains the other.

"I want you . . . seriously look at this list. Which of these would you say, 'Yes. Yes. Absolutely, I would give my life for that reason'?"

"Hey, you only got one life." Troy has settled into the mood I have hoped the discussion would bring.

"Money." I point to the list. "Would you be willing to give your life—gone forever—over money?"

Theaster is quick with his no.

"Depends how much," says Kahlil.

"How much is your life worth, Kahlil? What would be the cutoff point . . . that you'd be willing to die for? Twenty-million?"

"No."

"Let's see your hands?" Almost every hand goes up. "Let's erase this reason. Not willing to die for money." I erase "money." "Okay. Would you be willing to give your life over a female?"

Loud laughter. Nickee shakes his head . . . the only one who has no answers today.

"It depends . . ." One of the boys isn't sure he wants "females" erased from the board. "It depends if she's got your baby."

"An' it depends what you're fightin over."

"Let's leave female up here with a couple of questions marks."

"Yeh. Not die for just a plain old female."

"How 'bout for drugs?"

A unanimous no.

"Not willing to die for drugs. Jealousy?"

"No." The list gets smaller.

"Willing to give your life for power?" I ask.

"For respect," says Gary.

"One vote here to die for respect. Death before dishonor. Remember—you're going to be dead . . . but you're gonna be respected."

The boys laugh.

"Flowers lying nicely over your grave . . . shoe-polish sign saying, 'In memory of Gary . . .' on your car's back window. Two people here vote yes—respect . . . die for respect.

"Family? We've got some hands here. Theaster, whom in your family would you die for?'

"My mom."

Jack raises his hand. "My dad."

"Everybody in my family." Troy is very sure.

I leave "family" on the board.

" 'Beat'—buyer drives away without paying?"

"What? . . . for twenty bucks? pssshhh . . . "

I erase "beat."

" 'Trash talk.' "

"No."

"Someone said a rude thing to you' mom."

"Yeh."

"You would be willing to die for that?" I ask.

The boys want to talk about this, but when the murmur of debate stops, the general feeling wobbles towards no—not be willing to die for someone saying a bad word to your mom.

"I beat 'em up," says Jack. "Not die."

"Willing to die for your gang?"

Sneers connect across the classroom.

"Not willing to die for your posse?" This answer catches me by surprise. No one votes to die for a posse. I have heard boys in this room swear lifelong brotherhood to posses like the Sons of Malcom X. The Three-Two posse. "Your posse not like a brother?"

"No. When they get shot and they die—'twan't that they want to die . . . ," says Jack. "Risk for your posse, maybe . . . not doin' it to die."

"No hands. Not one person here willing to die for their posse.

"Grit. Evil eye?"

We erase "grit" and "sneakers," "car" and "gold chain."

"You can get another pair of sneakers."

"Get 'nother car."

"Three—willing to die over a stickup." I mark down three votes.

" 'Snitch.' "

"Yeh."

"You willing to die over a snitch . . . a setup?" I ask.

"Well, someone's gonna die if they snitch." Laughter interrupts Jamie's answer. I have not one doubt.

"Five people—yes.

"Die over someone stealing your stash?"

"I rather live."

We are getting near the end of the list—most of our reasons to kill, erased. "Someone talking to your girl?"

"They can have her . . ." My eraser keeps moving.

"How about hurting your sister?"

"They're gonna die."

"Another vote—willing to die for your family."

Theaster raises his voice. "Don't erase the next one."

"Getting your sister pregnant?"

"If he getting ready to leave her—die!"

"Revenge?"

"Yeh. Matter fact . . ." Gary is unshakable. "The last three." Family. Respect. Female.

"Our list . . ." I look at the blue letters. ". . . five reasons—willing to die for these reasons."

"Not me." Kahlil is voting with his voice. "I rather die bein' on top of a girl than kill somebody."

The boys want to rank the list. I write at the top of the board: "Willing to die for this reason."

"Sounds as though family comes right at the top. Willing to die to protect family. Thirteen yes. One no." The no comes from Michael whose mother has refused even to attend his graduation from high school this spring.

"Die for a female? one . . . two . . . three . . .

"Die for respect? Four.

"For revenge? Three.

"Willing to give your life . . . would you give your life for a stickup? Wait . . . wait . . . wait. . . . The question isn't 'Would you defend yourself?' It's 'Would you give your life for revenge?'"

"Erase it."

That's it. Family, respect, and females. Heads nod across the room.

I pause and tap the marker on my chin to signal a change of theme. "Now I'm going to write a new word on the board."

Irrational.

"Do you know this word?" The question draws a blank.

"There's a normal person—regular person. Then there's an irrational person—a nut. Two lists. Normal, here. Nut, there. The two ways of looking at killing.

"A nut—a crazy person—kills for no good reason. Why do people kill?—How many on our list?"

"Twenty-eight."

"Why do people kill? An irrational person has twenty-eight reasons—or more—to kill. A nut.

"And how many left on the list—reasons you're willing to die for? Family . . . almost everybody here said family. A few of you said Respect. Female.

"Let me tell you what a normal person is willing to die—or even kill—for. A normal person's kill-die formula." The room is so quiet, I can hear the hum of the water fountain on the wall. "If your mom goes to the lake . . . your little sister . . . little brother sitting on the bank next to your mom . . . and some guy comes up with a gun . . . starts shooting. Your mom—or me, because I'm a mom—would be willing to die—some might even kill—to save the life of her little son or little daughter. Agree with that?"

"'Cause you mom gave them life." Jack and talk of his mom seem destined to begin and to end the discussion.

"That is normal human feeling. To die for something so important. There's a reason to die, and this baby that I brought into the world . . . that I fed . . . and walked the nighttime hours with her, and I made little dresses for her, and sent her off to school, and I cried over her report cards, and I worried about her boyfriends . . . Yes, I'd be willing to die for her. Some moms and dads might even say, kill—I'd be willing to kill—to save her. Self-defense. That is a normal response. The response of the regular, normal person."

"Yeh."

"Your life—the most precious thing you have. His life . . . the most precious thing he has. You don't take life without a good reason. For family . . . maybe. Self-defense.

"But there is another kind of person—this one doesn't kill for that reason. And that's the nut—the irrational man."

Why is this discussion coming so hard? Talking a roomful of boys out of killing. Why can't it just be "Thou shalt not kill"? The Ten Commandments. God says so . . . as my father said to me. There's an unfinished business feeling in the room. I don't feel the connect I usually get.

"The nut . . ." I feel uneasiness settle on the room.

"You've seen him." Half the hands go up. "The irrational person—the nut—pulls a gun in the school . . . on a crowded sidewalk . . . on a dare . . . all the reasons we started with our list . . . everybody's afraid of that person—you too. . . . The nut . . . shoots for no good reason . . . kills for sneakers or earrings or a stash . . . taking a life, the most precious thing you have. . . ."

The class ends with an eerie feeling of unfinished business.

Over my breakfast coffee two months later a morning headline holds my eye: "Camden youth is held in killing tied to gang": "At the August sentencing, authorities said, a member of the Sons of Malcolm X gang needed to restore his reputation in the gang after failing to help his comrades in a fight."

At 3:30 A.M., on Raritan Street, the papers says, they hand the boy a gun and tell him to shoot—just any man . . .

Reason to kill. Number 29: To restore your reputation with the gang.

Nickee . . . the silent one in Classroom 123.

9

LISTENING

One thing my mother taught me when I was growing up: We were to find a world in need of help and, with the help of God, do something about it. I often look back with wonder now to see how my mother's energy and values shaped my life. School Board. Home and School Association. League of Women, lobbying in the state legislature about schools and education. I packaged the memories and labeled them "my crabgrass-and-diaper-rash years." If there was an article to be written, I was at my typewriter. It was the League that had introduced me to politics and to the press, connecting with reporters and editors to spotlight the League's concerns. On the lovely brick patio by the lily pond behind our home, I was hostess to outdoor receptions to meet-the-candidates. I knew them all by their first names. They knew me by mine.

Word at the Children's Shelter said that "a Miss Goody-Two-Shoes" was coming from Haddonfield to run the place. Well, she could find out for herself.

My first night, the girls overdosed on drugs in the unlocked shelter for runaways while I attended a concert of the Philadelphia Orchestra in the Academy of Music.

I had been administrator for just eight hours.

The phone call said that three girls were vomiting at Kennedy Hospital. Love, gentleness, lofty grandeur of the Academy of Music, its gilded pillars and crystal chandeliers—it all crash-landed to a world of gagging and spitting girls getting their stomachs pumped!

I wanted to scream.

Just hours earlier, I had dreamed together with a tumble of these giggling teenagers—we would make a giant banner in the hallway at the top of the stairs: WELCOME TO CLOUD NINE (Cloud Nine was the name I had chosen for the shelter for runaway teens); we would decorate each bedroom door with a snapshot of the roommates. Fun and pajama parties and teenage stuff.

I would *love* them into being good.

Right! Rowdy girls and overdoses and vomit basins!

I had walked into a propeller, and the old guard watched with glee.

Two boys had run away during the new afternoon-swimming at the Catholic Youth Organization pool two miles away. Another boy terrorized two girls by invading the CYO women's locker room; the CYO closed the swimming pool to Youth Center residents forever after that. In the Shelter, boys flushed rags down the toilets, flooding human waste across the basement. They carved crosses and bleeding hearts, or their mother's name, into the bloody flesh on their hands or arms by rubbing through their skin the pencil erasers from the downstairs schoolroom.

In the Cloud Nine shelter, boys climbed through windows into girls' bedrooms; the bets were on that Previte would be a grandma—fast. One night as I drove my car out into the darkness of the parking lot, I saw blue flames—like a welder's torch—shooting through a second-floor window security screen of North Side Room 221. This was my Introduction to Escape Science 101, Lesson Number One: Depress the button of any aerosol can and light a match to the gas: You'll get an arc welder's flame. Melting security screens. Or lexan windows.

That night I banned aerosol cans forever from the Youth Center. Tough-guy officers watched.

>─◆─○─◆─◄

When I came to America, fourteen years old, in a second-floor classroom of the high school in Spring Arbor, Michigan, the social-studies teacher chalked "juvenile delinquent" onto the blackboard. I had never even heard the words. I could hardly imagine disobeying my father and mother. Or the law. In the Chefoo School in China, the worst I had ever heard of was "a cheeky brat." At our house we didn't even use words like *gee* or *gosh*. Daddy said "gee" was short for "Jesus" and "gosh" was short for "God," and in the Taylor family there would be no taking the name of Lord our God in vain.

When we arrived in America, my biggest curiosity on the Spring Arbor campus was about bodies coupled on the grass, hidden and kissing in the darkness under the giant trees that bordered the highway. That was about as delinquent as I could imagine. In China, I had never even seen a Chinese couple holding hands.

At the Youth Center, I was an *ingenue*—in a war.

Stubborn . . . STUBBORN . . . refusing to be pulled over the line of combat into the enemy camp. "I can't" was the enemy. Inside my head the gramophone needle was still stuck in its childhood groove: *A Taylor never says "I can't."*

No, no, NO! I would not pull up my roots—the Bible words of *love, joy, peace, long-suffering, gentleness.* . . . Not even in such an ugly world. I vowed I would hold the line. Hadn't the riots stopped? Hadn't the salaries increased?

I remember exactly when the tide began to turn.

I awoke one day to a different name. It had always been very formal: Mrs. Previte, this, and Mrs. Previte, that. Then one day an officer called me "Boss Lady." Another called me "Lady Boss." Another, "MTP."

It was my sign. New dreams elbowed my staff.

They saw gentleness harness power. Something happened when you looked at a boy as a package of energy and wonder, not as a criminal. *High expectations created power.* You could begin to hear the laughter of a human being. A touch, a smile, a word about his handwriting or his wrinkle-free bed always brought answering smiles and bashful pride, and a boy was finally willing to try because the praise had felt so good. Try one more time. *Listening* was sunshine opening new blossoms in a child's life—the power of wonder and hope. This bumping into dreams—I called it *hope*.

That was the *power*.

The reaching out to touch another's warmth—that was the start of hope. Like my daddy's reaching out his hand to me to say, "Mary, you can do it." Hope grew from reaching out—tiny and wobbly at first like a newborn with hands outstretched to someone there to catch her— but something that could grow.

Some officers raged—wasting hope on such bastard kids—as though hope could somehow be all used up. The turnabout came when officers wanted the Power for their own needs.

Claire's voice in the night through the phone by my bed—Claire, an officer, at three o'clock in the morning . . . Johnnie's been in an accident . . . her son . . . got a gun and says he's going to kill himself . . . hit-and-run . . . only a learner's permit . . . can't see the end of the road. And Mrs. Previte, can you fix it?

Claire's thank-you gift—the angel pedestaled on my file cabinet always reminded me of that night, talking to a boy I had never seen— a frightened teenager miles away—listening to a boy who had a gun and wanted to die. The blackness of the night . . . listening . . . listening . . . groping to reach a boy with a gun at his head . . . knowing the cost of my making a mistake—sending *Hope* across the phone line in the blackness. *Listening* created *Hope*.

Officer Woody sitting across the desk, talking about his last hours with his wife and partner, Barbara—the breast cancer, the chemotherapy, the pain, the raw flesh—and then the gift—asking God to let his wife die in his arms. Faith had an inner dimension to soothe the grief. Believing that God was there. *Listening* healed.

Or standing—another dark night—by Karen Ranjo's coffin—my holding hands with Bob, her husband, one of my officers. Knowing that standing there holding hands with an officer as he said good-bye was right. That's what it was—holding hands with a whole family of staff—Bernice with the ache—all the hopes she had poured into her daughter, being lost to alcohol. Fay facing the terror of a lump in her breast. Eugene, an anguished father tracking down his son sent off to war in Operation Desert Storm. John asking, Can you get me a job in Florida? Carlos, a job in California? Janet, permission to adopt the baby?

My officers. They came to my desk for favors—I called it *Hope*—that I could fix it. I listened first, then picked up the phone to an alcohol-treatment center, a decision-broker for adoptions, a youth official in Florida, the Pentagon. David Sexton, one of my assistants, always laughed that he wanted to stay close to me forever because God sheltered me and those around me with a divine umbrella.

And here I was, the holding, connecting hands to hope—that's why they came to the desk—Boss Lady, please . . . PLEASE connect me to *Hope*.

And when I looked—when I got self-conscious, I knew it would never work. Looking at the waves out there, I'd sink like Peter walking on the water toward Jesus. Out on this ocean, if you thought about the waves, you'd sink. You weren't the power. The power was the Hope flowing effortlessly through the pipeline—the hours of *listening* and letting the *Hope* flow through to touch the pain.

A new brick building with giant skylights rose across the ball field in the asparagus patch, with daffodils blooming beside the walk. Officers I coached passed their Civil Service tests and got protected in their jobs. Visitors came from New Orleans and Ohio and Pennsylvania and New York. The Public Defender came, shook his head, amazed, then went home and wrote letters to the county bar association and letters to the editor about miracle changes. He bought a guitar for D.J., a child of the street in the girls' wing, and signed on as a volunteer. And somewhere along the way the officers caped me with a billowing new "rep": "There ain't s__t this g_d d__n s.o.b. can't do."

>─┼─◀▸─○─◂▸─┼─◁

The whirlwind of the Youth Center's tradition swept almost everyone along: "Shut up. Sit down. Get in line." It had been the way of life, and everybody conformed.

Well, not quite everyone.

Bernice Gray started her life picking tobacco in fields south of Richmond, Virginia, listening to her father talk about respect and pride. Land and family was what the man preached. Bernice had four children of her own and had never practiced "Shut up. Sit down. Get in line." Bernice hooked kids by *listening* to them.

When I installed Bernice Gray conspicuously in the large office across from mine and turned her into a social worker, the scuttlebutt line picked up the message and rolled it over a thousand different ways: a black . . . a woman . . . a listener. An officer from the ranks now presiding in a conspicuous place—sent powerful—very powerful—signals.

The very first week I came to the Youth Center, old Monahan, the maintenance man, had told me about Bernice. Monahan told me about just about everyone. "Good woman," he wheezed. Bernice Gray knew the one reason she was at the center—and the only reason—to serve the teenagers. Without them and all their problems she had no job. She was as often sitting on a bed next to a youngster as she was pushing papers on her desk. When a boy or girl arrived, the first hour set the tone. It was first impressions. Any psychologist could tell you—you had seven seconds—that's how long it takes a stranger to form an opinion of you.

Then an interesting thing happened: People began discovering the power of listening. You could shout at a boy, and he wouldn't hear anything you said, no matter how upright and powerful you were. His eyes would slit into the "grit" look from the streets, and out of his mouth you'd be hit with his unprintable anger from the street. But if you listened to him, you saw it in his face, the surprise, the softening muscles unclenching near his ears. And sometimes his ears would open—not just for that day but for many days to come. It had to do with respect.

Officers figured out what was wanted and tested a new approach with youngsters. Listening rubbed off. Staff training schedules listed classes in Active Listening with role-play drills. Then they did it their own way, fresher and more engagingly, without the drill.

It wasn't that Bernice Gray didn't know about the behavior that brought teenagers to the center. She knew a boy's charges . . . maybe someone had been hurt . . . The "f___n' this . . ." and "f___n' that . . ." No remorse. . . . It was a youngster sitting there across from her . . . not a crime. And when the cursing slowed. . . .

"Well, how are ya feelin'?"

And the boy would look at Bernice as if she were coming off the wall. And suddenly the voice changed. "I'm okay. I'll be okay."

It was all in the way you asked . . . "Are you injured in any way—cuts, marks, sores, bruises—are you hungry?" The questions about address and family and school could wait.

>─+─◆>─•─O─<◆─+─<

Boys like this had a way of touching the two organs you trusted the most—your ear and your heart. You let a boy talk and get the stuff out. You didn't judge. Anyway, who made you the judge, lawyer, and punisher—you, who had never been a teenager changing the diaper of an abandoned old grandfather in an empty house—looking for a drug-addict mom, high, and lost somewhere in the burned-out streets of North Camden? And somewhere in the midst of the boy's tears,

Bernice had become "Mom." And the Youth Center had turned into a different place. In less than an hour.

Bernice, in all the years, had never been threatened. Never been hit. Never injured. The youngsters stood as guardian angels: If a new resident came in sporting an "attitude," Bernice's guardian angels were always there . . . "Don't you talk like that to her. That's my mom."

Listening set up trust that lasted for the duration of their stay. She could tell that she connected, that they didn't want to leave her office. No matter where they saw Bernice in the building after that, or on the streets, they always remembered that very first moment.

"Mrs. Gray, if I could have you for a mother, I would never get in trouble again. If my mom . . . if she could just *listen* to me, or if she'd talk to me—care about me. . . ." They told Bernice everything . . . a mom who could keep all their secrets . . . they didn't need to lie. The twelve-year-old prostitute from across the river in Philadelphia—the Youth Center got her at twelve and at thirteen . . . fourteen . . . a nubbin of a girl with her jaw broken open by her pimp because she hadn't earned the amount of money the man needed her to bring home to him that night.

The girl was proud—like a child bringing home a straight-A report card. "I'm his number-one ho'." Like this was a trophy to show off. Number-one ho'.

"You know what you just called yourself?" Bernice asked.

"Well, like . . . what's wrong with that? I like that . . ." To be a whore. As long as she was number one . . . Bernice listened to teenagers who had never been number-one *anything*.

How did you focus on pouring your faith into a child when you could hardly keep from clenching your teeth and balling your fist . . . spilling your rage at what you saw and heard?

You could get caught in the national shouting match: Society should condemn its offenders more and understand less. Or take the other side: Social adversity plays a key role in creating young criminals. A twelve-year-old prostitute sitting beside you, glowing with pride about being a pimp's "number-one ho'." How did you connect with a child as wounded as this baby was? You didn't know what to think, or whom to blame. You *listened*.

It was her marriage more than anything else that had directed her to her career. Morris Gray wanted Bernice to take the test to be a sheriff's officer in the jail. That's where he worked. But how could you hope to change women who were so grown? With children, you could make a difference. Bernice took the Civil Service test for girls' supervisor at the Children's Shelter, even though she had no idea where the Shelter was. On August 6, 1973, John Milton Slim appointed Bernice Gray as a girls' supervisor at the Children's Shelter at $3.25 per hour.

Now there was a new esprit, a sense of being a veteran of something; people acted as though they were members of a winning team, or pioneers who had made it across the mountains.

They were trained by officers who had been through the fire. Ray could get a recruit's heart racing as though he were fumbling with the shoelace that was choking a boy's throat. "Expect the unexpected— always—*always*," Ray would tell them. "*Always*" for Ray always sounded visceral. Ray was a shift commander. "When it's quiet, somepin's wrong. When it's loud, it might be coverin' up somepin' else. When it's not normal, when the status quo changes, somepin' is wrong. *Always* monitor."

Ray believed in setting the tone at roll call before his officers started the shift. Ray was a combat veteran—fourteen months of blood as a sergeant in Vietnam. Safety had a special meaning to Ray Ruiz. "Your job is to keep the place safe. Make kids want to do the right thing. These kids are here because they failed with society's rules. They failed in school. They broke the rules; that's why they're here. They want you to do right by 'em. Not laugh or smile when they do wrong an' say it's okay." That's what the place was all about, he said. Live by the code. *Make kids live by the code.*

The boys always knew when an officer didn't practice what he preached. Kids picked it up, didn't want to hear, "Do this . . . Do that" when the officer didn't live any of it himself. Kids knew if an officer used drugs on the street . . . hung out at bars. The "rep" always followed him into the center. So now you gonna tell me to follow the rules? The kids knew. You nothin' but a geezer. You gonna tell me what to do?

Cheating the kids was what it was. Hardly anyone had heroes any more. And, flat out, the boys wanted someone to look up to. Someone who earned respect and showed respect. The athlete. The family man. The officer who could teach them something. I hired them fresh out of college and athletic scholarships.

Officers on the front line, mostly men and women in their twenties and thirties, wouldn't have labeled themselves as liberal or conservative. But if you made up a list of pressing questions: Should the death penalty be legal? Should a morning prayer be allowed in the schools? Should abortion be banned? Should we raise taxes to trim the deficit? Their answers would be yes, yes, no, no. A third of them owned guns. They thought of themselves as right in line with a majority of Americans. It was right and proper to nudge still-yawning kids to attention at nine o'clock every morning when Whitney Houston sang the Star-Spangled Banner for opening exercises on the intercom, and the student of the week led the Pledge of Allegiance and read the daily schedule. Teenagers needed to be reminded about hands on the heart and being proud of America. Order and discipline and traditions. Half of these youngsters had never known a ritual.

Half of my team of officers were in church on Sunday morning. The other half were the youngbloods, adult delinquents, and single parents. There were interesting divisions of age and class at the Youth Center. It mostly went by generations.

The Youth Center drew people with a mission. There was an air; the people who worked at the Youth Center thought they were important; their stride was sure. The young ones got a bit of a swagger when they were asked where they worked, what they did.

No, no, not a baby-sitter, and, no, it wasn't hopeless—getting kids to change.

The first question was always, "Well, aren't you scared they gonna hurt you?"

And Officer Mark Johnson, a master athlete—football and track at Delaware State—he and Juan Colon were partners in the younger boys' unit—would sit the person down and talk about reshaping behavior. After safety, that was the number-one goal: to shape behavior.

Nobody wanted to believe that you turned most of the youngsters into straight-acting human beings while they were there. Not turned around forever. Yup, while they were there. Two weeks. Two months. Two years. You could never undo the damage of sixteen years in two weeks. *The instant result that the officers got came from expecting the best.* Kids walked quietly in line. They learned to look you in the eye. They asked permission before they got out of their seat in school or in the cafeteria. The halls were quiet. It was a miracle what happened to a kid when you expected the best. Hell-raisers. Boys who had killed. It was a giant gift—this business of letting him know how good he could be.

You worked with a boy. Small steps. Did not allow him to get away with anything. The boy came from a get-over world. He had it in his mind that he would game as many people as he could. You showed him that you cared about him by doing the right thing—all the time. Some people thought they were doing him a favor by allowing a kid like this to continue, letting him go.

Confronting his behavior was doing the right thing. Upbeat. With a feeling that you knew he could change. That's how it happened all through the day—an officer correcting street behavior and ten minutes later patting the boy on the back. "Good job, man."

Everyone knew: *Respect* was what made a place work. You *listened* to a kid when he was down, the look in his eyes. He always remembered that. A human being. Kids weren't much into making trouble for human beings. They mostly bothered the walking rule book who swaggered around with a jingling set of keys—the officer who threatened and embarrassed and tried to take their manhood. They always spotted the officer who was "eight an' skate."

"He don't really care about us." Kids tried to run that kinda person out of the place.

Advice for someone new on the line always started with what an officer remembered when he himself first came aboard.

Leo Gold trained new officers in Basic Training: "Know the rules. Know the kids. Watch the moods and attitudes. An attitude changes, bad telephone call from Mom, Grandmom passed away—somethin' like that, nothin' to do with the center at all. A girlfriend, oh, yes. Depressed . . . violent. . . ." Officers knew that watching kids, *listening* to kids was their top survival skill.

Frightened, shell-shocked youngsters were not like the well-scrubbed kid next door. Even home was not safe. Even Mom wasn't someone he could count on to save him.

>—⊷—O—⊶—<

Two-thirds of the Youth Center residents had seen a dead human body in their young lives. I took a survey. Almost all of them had heard gunshots outside their homes, had a family member involved with violence. Some had heard bullets whizzing by before they were old enough to go to school; half before they ever got to middle school. Nine out of ten had seen a weapon used—guns, they told me, knives, bats, pipes, sticks, Mace. Most had witnessed violence on the street. Half had seen it at school. One in four—in their homes.

These were not ordinary kids. You had to start with that. They were scared. Folks out there beyond the cities didn't much understand what it felt like, never knowing if you were safe.

Making a kid feel safe when he first came in was half the battle. It set the tone. The first thing a new resident thought of was: "'m I gonna room with someone else?"

"Will I take showers alone?"

"Is there some big kid in here gotta worry 'bout?"

"Can I call my mother . . . call my sister? . . ." Officers could predict the questions.

Some kids sat frozen. You could see the terror.

"Sit here." They didn't move. Eyes looking down at the floor. Officer Ernest Sheppard usually tried to cut the terror with a smile, using the admission questionnaire: "Have you been physically or sexually abused—an' I'm not talkin' 'bout your girlfriend?"

And the laugh would take the kid by surprise. Shep was twentyish and looked as though he definitely knew about girlfriends. And anyway, an officer who could laugh couldn't be all bad—this giant sitting next to you asking questions.

"My name is Shep. My job is not just make you feel safe, but *be* safe. I'm here to make sure that you're fed properly, taken care of properly, safe from physical harm—verbal harm." And a kid would look at Ernest—250 pounds of muscle.

"Oh, yeh. Okay?" Then maybe the frozen body would thaw . . . just a little. "How long 'm I gonna be here?"

"I wouldn't really know. Only the judge can tell you that."

The Lord is my shepherd. I shall not want . . . Thou preparest a table before me in the presence of my enemies. . . .

"You hungry?" is the first thing you'd ask a kid, every time. Let him eat while he's talking to you. Food always calmed them down. Cereal, if it was in the middle of the night. Other times, a good meal— that's what they needed. None of them arriving had eaten in a while—six, seven, eight hours, they hadn't eaten.

Shep knew. You had to tell kids that what they heard on the street wasn't true. "People owning people in this building is not true . . . getting their behinds tooken by another resident . . . gettin' beat up . . . just bein' owned by somebody . . . the monarch . . . no monarch here . . . That person you have to answer to all the time, that person you have to give sexual favors to, or give up your dinner, clothing, whatever that person wants—you have to do. Go-fer for that person. There's no such thing here. I'm here." The kid would size the man up. "My name is Shep. I'm here to keep you safe."

Yea, though I walk through the valley of the shadow of death, I will fear no evil. . . .

"My name is Shep."

. . . for thou art with me. . . .

"If someone's botherin' you . . . threatenin' you . . . there's always someone in the vicinity to help you—especially me. Any problem . . ."

Shep would let them know about all the people around to help: social workers, officers, teachers, nurse—and Mrs. Previte.

Surely, goodness and mercy shall follow me . . .

Feeling safe. Most kids didn't have access to that much help out on the street.

Shep was comfortable. He knew. You had to talk to the whole group as if you were comfortable. Old-timers knew the rule: Kids picked up if you weren't comfortable. Shep started every shift—in charge—with his afternoon meetings, expectations, going over the right behavior, consequences, repercussions. These boys raised on television and MTV—their attention span was just so long. You had to go over everything. Every day. And when he was done, a kid would chime in: "You heard what Shep said." That ended his afternoon meeting. In the older boys' unit—B-wing—3:00 to 11:00 shift—what Shep said was the Bible.

Structure. Structure. Structure.

You taught your boys and girls exactly what to expect. You tapped the wake-up call each day at ten minutes after seven. Assigned platoons to mop the unit floor and swab the bathroom sinks. Boys lined up the bars of soap beneath the metal mirrors. You trooped them off to school at nine o'clock in single file. You stood with them, your hand across your heart while Whitney Houston sang, "Oh, say, can you see . . ."

They settled down to schoolwork, workbooks marked already with lessons for the day: Reading, math, and law-related education. School must go on.

Structure. It was an unpredictable world beyond the doors. Here it was predictable. Structure was the security blanket.

So was consistency, control.

In the great "out there" of the street, there was no consistency. Things changed for them out there, day in, day out. Even meals. At my house, I took breakfast, lunch, and dinner for granted. These children didn't.

What happens to children who witness the violence of a war zone? Beirut or the West Bank. Chicago or L.A. Camden. Children of war.

Emerson and his roommate, Faheem, munch on hoagies as guests this month at the Board of Trustees' luncheon in the cafeteria. The chairman of the board—so middle-class, so suburban, so "college"— presses the boys with questions.

"When I was growing up," he says, "my father made me think about my future, what I would be. Do you think about the future?"

Faheem nods. "I do think about my future," he says quietly, "whether I'll be alive at twenty-one." The chairman of the Board of Trustees puts down his hoagie. Most of us felt safe when we were growing up. You have to switch gears when you sit talking to youngsters like Faheem and Emerson.

Faheem is sixteen—has no father and no mother. In how many months at the Youth Center—not one visitor. Emerson at fourteen sees his future as a choice between prison or death at the hands of gangs and drug dealers.

For two months after Emerson arrived, he hardly spoke. He carried terror in his bones. If he were a soldier, fresh from Vietnam, doctors would call his symptoms post-traumatic stress disorder. Can't concentrate in school. Can't sleep. Can't trust his world. Or visualize a future.

After twenty years, I still shudder.

"The good thing about this place," Faheem says, "safe—the staff won't let anyone hurt you."

>-+-+>-·O-<+-+-<

The Youth Center's college scholarship class is all about giving the gift of motivation for boys who do not hope, a time for touching college catalogs, turning the pages of dreams. They are youngsters from the world of AIDS and crack and family disintegration. Poverty. From schools that are paralyzed by fear. From child abuse and neighborhoods touched by teenage suicide. *These are boys who hunger for fathers.*

While Vernon talks, not one purple shoelace shuffles in the sneakers on the floor. Teenage ruffians in white T-shirts. Rapt. *Listening.* This is the Youth Center's *Officer* Vernon Boyd, Camden's Woodrow Wilson High School football captain, junior and senior year, All-South Jersey, football-scholarship winner to the University of Missouri, who these days holds his stopwatch in the Youth Center weight room counting his boys' heartbeats per minute under stress, teaching them new lessons about fitness. To boys who have never known their father, he preaches cleanliness and grooming and black pride.

I often see the wistfulness in a boy's eye—watching the men I surround them with—the fathers, the brothers, the coaches who scold and yell and comfort kids. Men to admire. Men they have never known. *If I could balance the scales*, I think to myself . . .

Vernon Boyd comes from the same streets and corners these boys have come from. The difference is that Vernon has a father. Heywood Boyd, a chef. And a catering business all his own. All man. A job. Dreams spread across their faces as Vernon talks. The boys all call him Vern. His college football scholarship, his college diploma all framed and hanging on the wall at home where you see it as soon as you walk in the door, college degree in hotel and restaurant management, an athlete from their streets, always reaching to be a carbon copy of his dad.

I look at the boys in this classroom, watching the men in college scholarship class—how they talk, the way they hold their bodies—noticing everything. A search for how to be a man.

>-+-<>-O-<>-+-<

A sixteen-year-old boy named Rick is guiding a visitor through the older boys' dormitories.

"Whom do you admire the most around here?"

"Johann Arnold." Rick doesn't even pause one second. "He's an officer."

"Why him?"

"Like the first day I was here . . ."

There's a pause. I wonder what a youngster who tries to kill his father is going to say. The beatings, the terror from a drunken dad.

"I told him, 'I'm here for something pretty bad. I'm going to be here a long time.' And Johann said, 'And I'm going to be right here with you.' " The look on the boy's face tells me everything I need to know: A man has planted love and trust. He has filled a boy's reservoir with respect. Johann Arnold shapes his boys by giving them his time and affection.

In my mind I picture a little boy struggling to plant his feet in the giant footsteps of a man.

A story like this is best told in living color. Rick is white. Johann Arnold is black, a minister, and an athlete.

>–+–◆–○–◆–+–◄

Five boys crowd together on the couches in my office, discussing success: The "big boys" in their lives are drug dealers.

"I got two pictures of success," says Winston. "One . . . like . . . go to school . . . college . . . graduate . . . get a good job. The other one that sticks in my mind . . . a big drug dealer. For real, man. *That's* success. You see all that money out there. Inside, you got all your mom and dad always taught you—school, education, what your teachers tell you. All the stuff they taught you is in the future. The money right here now is comin' to me. Direct—what you can touch."

>–+–◆–○–◆–+–◄

The five boys look up at the three-generation picture of my family on the wall in my office—Alice, my mother; Alice, my daughter; and me.

"In my house we had certain family sayings that had a lot to do with how we acted," I tell the boys. "Taylor family sayings . . . like *A Taylor never says, 'I can't.'*"

New thoughts need time to sink in: "A Taylor never says, 'I can't.'" I pause for emphasis as I talk to them.

"I figured I was really going to play get-over when I lost my hand. You know . . . *'I can't.'* Wouldn't have to do the dishes . . . *certainly* . . . *surely* not. My mother wouldn't even hear of anything like that. She says, 'Line right up there by the sink with everybody else and take your turn.' When I lost my hand, it was, 'Okay. You *don't* have to take piano lessons anymore. Now you can take *organ* lessons so you can play with one hand up here and two feet down there.'"

The boys laugh, looking at the picture of my mother on the wall, Alice Taylor, every inch the mountain-climbing, baby-delivering, wagon-riding pioneer.

"A Taylor never says 'I can't.'"

"Can you go back to the dishes, though . . . how you do dishes?" I have opened the door to the no-man's-land of talking about a missing hand, and the boys are tumbling over each other in their curiosity to walk in. With my story, I have given permission.

One hand . . . dishes . . . wallpapering . . . painting my house.

"You make this quilt?" The boys tugs on the blue-and-white scrap quilt draped across the couch.

I nod. "Our family saying was, 'A Taylor never says, *I can't.*'" I love their endless curiosity. "Nobody was *allowed* to say, 'I can't.' Family

stuff like that—it *makes* you do everything . . . tie my shoes . . .
yes . . ." The boys look down at my shoelaces.

"Would you show me how to tie your shoes with one hand?"
Winston leans over to look. "How *do* you tie your shoe with one
hand?"

I laugh as five boys lean forward on the couch.

"That seems impossible." Winston shakes his head. I always feel
amazed at the instant connect—one word about a missing hand and a
closed door opens to a thousand, pushing, boyish questions. Laughing
together. Real talk and instant bonding.

>─┼─◆>─○─◆─┼─◁

Officer Mark Johnson holds the college catalogs in his hand. He has
never thrown them away, these parts of his dream, brought them
today for the boys to see from his own memory file, passing them
along the circle. Gentle, eager hands touching another man's dream.

Mark's Rule Number One—his first advice—for every new officer
was "Never look at the kid as a criminal. Treat every one as a human.
A kid. Not a crime. You work with 'em." There was a faraway look in
his eyes, a look of remembering . . . the terror of one summer night . . .
his knees knocking in fear among the cobwebs in the culvert beneath
the road . . . a seventeen-year-old boy named Mark Johnson in a
courtroom in front of the judge.

He watches the boys turning pages in his college catalogs. "My
mom sat me down . . . said, 'You gettin' ready to mess you'self up for
life. You hang 'round you' friends. Doin' all this crazy nonsense. It
only take one time for you to mess you'self up for *life*."

"And it was that point, I cut my friends off. Made some new
friends. I lived every day in the gym. To this day I'm not sorry.

"'Cause all my friends have been locked up. Billy in jail for murder.
Eddie in jail right now for all kinda robberies—whole nine yards. The
point I'm tryin' to make, man, are the people you call your friends can
lead you down the wrong path."

>─┼─◆>─○─◆─┼─◁

At six feet, six-and-a-half inches, John Golaszewski, Supervising
Officer at the Youth Center, towers over every boy in college-
scholarship class. "I want to pose a question to you guys: What do you
think it is that makes the difference between the guy who goes to
school, gets a job, raises a family, helps everybody out versus the
person who gets locked away . . . gets in trouble?"

There's a long pause as John waits for an answer.

"A person who made it in life could be better loved by their
family. . . ."

"'Better loved by their family.' Anybody else? What's that one factor that causes people to turn their life around? What do you think it is?" John doesn't wait.

"It's having at least one person that's cared about you. Could be an athletic coach, Boy Scout leader, mother, grandmother, uncle, pastor. It could be anybody. Someone who's crazy about you."

John could kneel on the tiles of the Youth Center gym, sit on the floor, squat on the floor, aim the ball from anywhere in the gym and hit baskets—dead-eye. Everybody in the Youth Center knew about Big John and basketball.

Junior year, his team won the state championship. Senior year, All-South-Jersey first team with a player named Wayne Smalls from Camden, a guy named Charlie Wise from Lower Cape May, a guy named Joe Hickman from Woodstown, a guy named John Olive from Bishop Eustace, and John—John Golaszewski. He got a scholarship to a college in New Hampshire. Good-looking girls on campus, beautiful room, unlimited-expense-account-big-man-on-campus. At six feet, six-and-a-half inches, he was a very big man on campus. Back in 1974, it cost $8,700 a semester to go to Nathaniel Hawthorne College. Four-year degree, $69,000 plus books. John became N.A.I.A. College-All-American. Led the nation in free-throw shooting.

If you wanted to know what the boys really remembered about John's stories in college scholarship class, you stood the next day in Miss Brenda's or Miss Cathy's or Miss Mary Ann's classes and listened to the boys retelling the story of THE SHOT HEARD ROUND THE WORLD.

John's shot. . . .

They still talk about it in Gloucester City. Gloucester City had no mall. No McDonald's. No movie house. No activity center. What they did have was the best high school basketball team anybody could ever remember and the state championship game.

. . . Playing at Princeton University . . . 6,500 fans . . . Gloucester High playing East Rutherford . . . supposed to be the best team in the country. East Rutherford had a player—Les Caisson . . . supposed to be the best high school player in the country . . . Gloucester High winning the game . . . seven seconds left to go and John got the ball in the corner . . . and "Guess what?" John says. "Instead of holding the ball—I shoot it.

"All I had to do was *hold* the ball, and Gloucester High would win the state championship. . . ."

But John *shoots* the ball. . . . The ball hits the back of the rim. The big guy, a seven-footer, throws it the length of the court, and the ball goes in the net—and Gloucester High *loses* by *one* point. . . .

The classroom groans. Winston, a basketball star at a private school, puts his head down between his knees.

"Now let me tell you somethin'—6,500 people—My girl broke up with me that night—Someone tried to kill me that night. The whole school hates me. Guess who the head coach of the other team was. Ever hear of Dick Vitale? Sports announcer?

"He was the head coach of East Rutherford. The next day the newspaper said: *SHOT HEARD ROUND THE WORLD* . . . Right?"

This is the part the kids would repeat in class the next day:

"Next day I go into a pizza place in Gloucester City. Ordered a cheese steak. I'm real depressed. My girl left. The people hate me, people spittin' on me—throwin' apples 'n oranges at me . . . I'm sittin' in the place, eating my cheese steak, and this guy looks up to me and says, 'D'you hear about the Gloucester High game last night?'

"No, what happened, sir?"

"He said, 'Some big dumb Polack shot the ball at seven seconds, and Gloucester High lost the state championship.'

"So I pushed my sandwich away and just put my head down. He said, 'What's the matter, Son?'

"I said, 'Sir, *I'm* that dumb Polack.'"

Laughter interrupts John's story.

'It's haunted me. Even today, I don't even go to my high school reunion . . . 'fraid I'll get in a fight . . . someone square off. . . . Let me tell you something. Adversity pays off in your life. If we won that game, everyone would have forgotten who I am. I'm a famous person now."

The boys howl. "Let me tell you something. . . ." John keeps talking through the laughter. "One night about eleven years ago . . . I'm tryin' to get away from this, right? My coach retires—thirty years put in. Someone asks him, 'What's the worst thing that ever happened to you, Coach?'

"He says, 'Some guy wasn't thinkin' . . . blew the state championship. . . .' That haunted me for a while.

"Then one night at four o'clock in the morning, I'm sittin' up watchin' a Big Five panel on TV and they ask him, "Were you ever at a game in your life that you thought was over and the situation turned around? And sure enough, Dick Vitale, at four o'clock in the morning—me, the TV set, and Dick Vitale. 'Yeh. When I was back in high school, this big dumb guy shot the ball with seven seconds left to go and lost the game.'"

The clock above the classroom door ticks half an hour past closing time, but nobody moves. John has to wait for the laughter to die down. "But, fellas, we all make mistakes. My mind at that time was not focused properly on the game. And that's where a lotta you fellas are right now. You've chose wrong. You've listened to the wrong thing. But take advantage of that. I didn't let that shot ruin me. You know, I went further than anyone that was on that court—got a scholarship to college. We all make mistakes, but *what you do with what you're given is the answer.*

"The Bible says, *What Satan meant for evil, God meant for good.* . . . When something bad happens to you, turn it around."

As boys in the circle thumbed the pages of the college catalogs, we talked about grants and college loans, scholarships for art and music and academics, scholarships for sports, making *books* number one.

I felt the excitement as the boys walk down the hall. Miguel, the newest artist for *WHAT'S HAPPENING*, wants to talk about art scholarships.

It is sobering: The war is so huge, our outpost so small—one tiny battle station built in an asparagus patch, thirty-seven beds—in a bloody contest. Kids—dreams—dying all around. Sometimes it is hard to feel that what you do, Alice Taylor's daughter, means a plugged nickel in the whole kid-chomping maw of the war.

Jake trails me to my desk. "Can you help me get college catalogs?" he says. "My own?"

"Do you know which ones?"

"Duke and Florida State."

>—+—◆—○—◆—+—<

The big things, if you get them in place, everything falls into place. I look around. Is there any place better?

I saw dreams settle on a roomful of faces yesterday. Listening to John and Mark and Vern. These are kids who never dream.

They listened yesterday because what they heard was real. Big John's losing a state championship, seven seconds left to go. Vern's lying in bed crying because a blood clot in his leg, bumped from a chance with the St. Louis Cardinals. Mark in a cobwebbed culvert running from the police. I watched their faces. Kids who usually wiggle and carve their desks at school, make silly comments— yesterday they sat for an hour and a half. They barely moved. And suddenly their hands were waving. Yes, they wanted me to help them write away for college catalogs. And no, it wasn't just a passing show. Jake—can you believe it, Jake—the last one I'd have guessed . . . trailing me to my office. Florida State, he told me. And Duke. He wanted college catalogs, he said.

Maybe Duke and Florida State college catalogs can help sell dreams.

>—+—◆—○—◆—+—<

Today a scruffy thank-you note is posted over the office copier, covered with wobbly signatures from top to bottom—

Dear John, and Mark, and Vern,
I always wanted to go to college, but I never knew what I wanted to go for until I listened to you.

10

GOOD-BYE, TERRY

I watched them bury Terry Mata today just beyond the sheltering arms of a giant ginkgo tree in Pennsauken's Arlington Cemetery. Terry Luis Mata. Twenty years old. One of our own.

He was shot to death on Saturday by an unidentified gunman—a drive-by shooting—near the State Street Bridge in Camden. A spray of bullets that killed one brother and wounded another. José and Terry Mata. They had always been inseparable.

Is it twelve we've lost this year? Jamal. Gadget. Jason. Billy and Anna. Dan-C. Alex. I've lost track.... This time—Terry.

"Cheaper to educate them than to bury them," the medical examiner tells me. It costs anywhere from $25,000 to $50,000 to conduct a homicide investigation—a minimum $2,500 for an autopsy at the medical examiner's office.

I find myself reaching for memories, thumbing through old pages in behavior logbooks, reading almost-forgotten progress notes. Written in elegant blue ink or scruffly black ballpoint or broad felt-tipped turquoise marker, sometimes hardly legible, the sentences mark the giddy skidding slides of a boy reaching to become a man. A sixteen-year-old driving his life full throttle, first pressing down hard on the gas pedal, then the brake pedal, then the gas pedal, then the brake pedal—as though the car were hiccoughing.

I read the now-closed record from the loose-leaf pages. It's a progress report all right—of a remarkable Camden County Youth Center staff's taking a street boy and shaping him into someone new. In two-and-a-half months, I wonder, could we have done more?

6/1 New admission: Terry Mata, age 16—Room 166. Says he was beaten by narcotics cop. Told shift commander he had used some cocaine before being picked up. Watch for signs of drug withdrawal. John

6/3 He's trouble. Making dope deals in the unit. Says he will have the kids deal for him when they get out. I spoke to him three times about his foul mouth and threats. Pat

6/4 Terry had a very good day. Actually talked to resident Luis Santos about improving his behavior! *Gloria*

6/6 Terry is very sneaky young man. Watch him at all times. Use time-outs with him whenever he messes up. *Allan*

6/8 Terry can be a positive role model if staff will just sit down and encourage him. He has strong influence on other residents. Let's make it work in our favor. *Rob*

6/25 When I corrected his behavior at breakfast, Terry threatened me. "If that f_____g lady gives me another violation I'm gonna f__k her up before the day is over." (Two pages of Charlene's alarm-red longhand give details.) Violation. *Charlene*

7/1 Terry has improved considerably since his violations. Respectful and helpful with getting other Spanish-speaking residents to cooperate with the program. *Gwen*

7/2 Terry cried after he telephoned home. *Pat*

7/6 Certificate of Achievement—Earns Student of the Week Award.

7/7 Terry earns Level One Honors. Keep encouraging him. *Rob*

7/9 Terry got upset with Pat but did ask to go to his room to take his anger out on his pillow. *Veocia*

7/10 (A.M.) Outstanding day!—Terry is working very hard to help others follow the "manners" rules. Initiated some intelligent lunch-table conversation. *Gloria*

7/10 (P.M.) Terry blew up when I asked him to curb his foul language. Shoved supper table across the floor. Threatened to f__k me up. Restrained by Officer Wiggins. Then he calmed down and apologized. Capable of negative behavior! Smart mouth! Hot head! Loses temper easily. *Pat*

7/13 Terry is trying hard. Wants to be the leader of the wing. Encourage him to stay away from horseplay. *Jones*

7/14 Cooperative. Uses his Success Skills. *Estelle*

July 15

Dear Judge Robert Page:

I am pleased to write this letter of commendation for Terry Mata. He has advanced up the Youth Center ladder of honors to GOLD BAND LEVEL. He has been selected by all departments of the Youth Center because of his full participation in the program, his positive attitude, his excellent behavior, and his mastery of selected "success skills."

This young man is setting an excellent example for other residents.

Sincerely,
Mary T. Previte

7/18 Behavior very good. Is thinking before he acts. Great improvement. 360-degree turnaround! *Veocia*

7/20 Still doing very well. Continues to be proud of making HONOR LEVEL. *Gloria*

7/21 Went to court. Terry was sentenced to State Training School at Jamesburg. *Ray*

7/22 (A.M.) Very good attitude. Talked with me one-on-one about what happened in court and states he wasn't angry with anyone. This guy has really shown he is Honor status. *Estelle*

7/22 (P.M.) Doing GREAT!—even trying to get Rios to stop playing around. *Carlos*

7/25 Shows a lot of respect for staff. *Dorothy*

7/27 Terry's behavior has been consistently good in the last 2 1/2 weeks—a real positive role model in his ability to improve behavior and attitude. Deserves a lot of positive feedback for his achievement. *Gloria*

8/5 Showed signs of goodness today trying to talk to Long and Nieves and Rios about their attitude. *Pat*

8/11 Terry still on HONORS—GIVE LOTS OF BACK-UP COUNSELING! *Rob*

8/11 Really working at it. Sometimes you can see the strain. *Pat*

8/16 Terry's conversation is usually very violent or drug-related. He could be positive if he had someone to talk to who has goals to stay out of trouble. *Audrey*

8/17 Terry frequently does discuss things other than drugs or violence but seems to have very little support from family or friends outside the Youth Center for "straight"-type goals and plans for staying out of trouble. *Gloria*

8/18 RELEASED TO JAMESBURG. Behavior, attitude prior to leaving was Excellent. Cooperative. Pleasant. *Gloria*

>─┤─◆>─○─<◆├─<

The Congregacion Amor De Jesucristo shares the corner of Thirty-sixth and Federal with the Rosedale Bar, a graffiti-covered laundromat, and a garish green shack hawking fried chicken: *9-pc bucket w/3 ears of corn $6.99.* Arched window frames that once held sacred glass are boarded now with wood. We gather there for the procession to the cemetery.

I expect a line of gaudy cars. Drug barons and their gold. Glitzy rich. The Mazdas. Porsches. Cadillacs. Jeeps so popular with city drug lords. I look for the gaudy drug scene that my boys paint with their stories in every issue of *WHAT'S HAPPENING.*

It is none of that. I find, instead, a battered Chevrolet truck. A dented Ford with a much-used baby seat tucked in the back. A shiny black Camaro. The caravan leaves behind a group of mourners hastening to change a flat rear tire on the crumbling concrete of the church parking lot, hurrying to join the procession. The drug captains who recruit young boys to the dangerous front lines of grubby drug corners obviously don't show up to honor their fallen soldiers. These are the halting wheels of the poor, teenagers in Reeboks and Nikes and day-glo T-shirts, young girls with mewling babies strapped to their chests, an inching procession, maybe fifty cars, headlights on in the morning sun.

In Arlington Cemetery, white-gloved teenage boys in freshly printed T-shirts struggle with sorrow and unpracticed manliness to carry a coffin—a brother, a friend—to his final resting place. No one where I live would mourn the dead in white T-shirts newly painted with iridescent paint. But this feels right today. Terry would feel at home with teenage T-shirts, freshly printed from the Pennsauken Mart. Across the chest, the shirts show a chartreuse tombstone nestled in tufts of green grass, a rainbow of pink and blue arching overhead. Black letters mark the stone: *IN MEMORY OF TERRY MATA R.I.P.* Pallbearers are in T-shirts, new sneakers with stylishly loose laces, black dungarees, and snow-white gloves.

A young pastor prays his gentle Spanish prayers and reads words I do not understand. I am an English-speaking stranger, drawn by a common grief. Losing a child. Looking at boys I know with tear-stained faces above these mournful T-shirts. José, his older brother—the man-of-the-family today—takes the white gloves, gently, one-by-one, from the pallbearers, folds them slowly, and places them in a neat, white row across the coffin. A tiny mother, Carmen—I recognize her from faithful visits to see her sons at the Youth Center—gratefully held steady by her boys, places her single red carnation—wilting now—upon the casket. Parents aren't supposed to bury their children. We follow her. Long-stemmed red carnations heaped silently on neatly folded white gloves. No father comes to this cemetery today—just as he never came to see his boys on visiting nights.

José ignores us all, held by the magnet of his grief, like a monument beside the casket. Not so long ago he moved through our hallways with his brother. José and Terry—inseparable. Like twins. José went to the training school for boys. Terry followed. Always together. On the State Street Bridge on Saturday night they were shot together. One lived. One died.

José reaches his hands into the air—as though to "high-five" his brother with both palms—and finds only lonely, empty air. His hands form into desperate sobbing fists that beat down upon his thighs.

"Nah, man!"

He crumples down against the box separating him from his lost brother. A big brother sobbing the primal good-bye of a child.

They lower the casket. Nobody leaves. They fold up the faded canopy above the grave. No one moves.

A yellow forklift moves among mourners with their mournful T-shirts and drops the white concrete cover onto the vault. Still no one goes.

A battered truck backs up to the open grave and tips its load of dirt onto the lowered casket. Two old groundsmen rake it into a gentle mound. Slowly, one by one, the youngsters—all so young for such grown-up grief—carpet this new scar in the earth with their fresh flowers: the cross made of crimson roses, the giant yellow football chrysanthemums.

I reach down and pick up a wilting palm frond and a white carnation and walk with them slowly back to my car.

A fading bumper sticker in the procession catches my eye: *Only sick people need drugs.*

You can always tell when another youngster dies in Camden. Out comes the white shoe polish for painting their good-bye messages. Car windows turn into drive-by memorials to the dead. Caravans of cars leaving the funeral wake or cemetery split into groups, almost as if dispatched from some black-draped command post to every part of town. For maybe a month, white shoe-polish letters on their rear windows mourn the dead.

There's something about the simple sorrow of those white shoe-polish signs—like a child with a chubby fist crayoning a plaintive good-bye. I start to weep. *WE LOVE YOU. WE LOVE YOU.—IN MEMORY OF Terry.—WE LOVE YOU.—IN MEMORY OF Terry.—LOVE ALWAYS.—R.I.P.*

At the Youth Center, on my office window that lets me see the boys wave to me as they pass down the hall, I tape the palm leaf and the white carnations. I add a little note:

In Memory of Terry Mata, 20, buried today.

11

TEDDY BEAR

Electronic locks click shut behind the officers.

"The kid wouldn't spill a word." Two prosecutor's officers stand inside the Youth Center entrance shaking their heads. With them stands Dannie Porter, at 6:00 P.M., as I'm walking out the door. A boy just tiptoeing into fourteen years of age. A teenaged vault of information about a killer gang, the Sons of Malcom X. Fourteen years old, with padlocked lips. "Even put the boy's mom on the phone to talk to him—get him to cooperate. He still wouldn't talk."

A failed mission—for prosecutor's investigators who are used to winning.

Outsmarted tonight by Dannie Porter, with no grown-up hair sprouting yet on his body, not even peach fuzz on his chin. A member of a killer gang, for pity's sake, and no one can pry loose one word that might unscramble the mystery of the latest round of killings in the city—four killings in five hours.

Initiation rite? I ask. Kill to join? A test?

The investigators look at one another, almost surprised that I would ask—maybe I know too much—and change the subject.

"Kid looks you in the eye: 'I'm a soldier. If I die, I die.' Fourteen years old—'s a shame." The investigator shakes his head.

>⊷⊶⊙⊷⊶⊰

A spiderweb of fractured glass radiates across the B-wing plate-glass windows when I arrived at work this Monday morning. The window looks out on the fenced-in garden court. A failed escape attempt— 8:20 P.M. on a Sunday night. Alphonso and Enrique hurled a card table against the bullet-proof glass last night, trying for a breakout. These attempts—dreams to be free from the judge—happen several times a year. Repairs will cost five hundred dollars when Berlin Glass Company finally finds replacements for this maximum-security glass.

Two officers: One monitoring evening showers. One leaving the boys to use the toilet. One careless moment. Leaving the boys alone is always against the rules because it gives "a window of opportunity" for escape. Or some other kind of mischief.

Enrique and Alphonso want to escape. In Philadelphia, Alphonso has a criminal record thicker than the Doomsday Book and on this side of the river another one just as thick. Enrique's stomach was cramped from drug withdrawal when he arrived last week—the shakes, the diarrhea, the depression—coming down from cocaine, morphine, and opiates all at once. Enrique's mother died of AIDS last year. His father has HIV. The boy is just tired of *being*.

"Someone broke in on payday at my house and stole my father's disability check," Enrique tells the nurse. "If I be there with my gun, they wou'n't of did it."

I call the prosecutor about the spiderwebbed window, about the escape attempt. Piling new criminal charges on their records will make it worse for both these boys, who are looking sheepish and angry at us that their effort failed. But I have a rule: *There are always consequences.*

These boys live in a get-over world. In America's urban classrooms, jiving and surly students rule the turf. If they troop in late, they do. If they want to sleep in class, they do. If they want to ream the teacher out, they do. And terrified teachers let them do it. What teacher knows if a boy has a gun in his pocket? Or a girl, a razor blade. Who knows if her tires will be slashed in the parking lot, or her windshield broken?

Overstressed juvenile courts across the land battle some of America's toughest problems: drugs, disintegrating families, household violence. They have neither the money, the people, or the time to save most of the desperate young souls who pass through their doors.

Here in this place we hold the line: At the Youth Center we preach *consequences.* Morning and noon and night. Officers tell the boys: For everything you do, you'll pay a price. Good consequences. Bad consequences. *You* choose which. *Your* choice.

Youth Center teens are not victims of a strange disease that makes them stand on a corner, selling drugs—or toting a gun. They are not sick. Like everyone else, they choose. They choose the darker world that puts aside the rules, that tosses out self-discipline, and school, and manners, and following the law.

But this is a day I wonder if I myself talk enough to the boys about consequences. They boast that they get over on their schools, their moms, the judge. I wander through units every morning, listening to officers named John and Al and Gwen and Johann and Juan, talking consequences to boys at morning meeting. They set the tone for the day. But have the boys heard it enough from me?

A "locking-the-barn-door-after . . ." feeling sits on my shoulder as I ask officers Juan Colon and Mark Johnson and Laurie Scott to round up the C-wing boys. Underneath C-wing's cathedral ceiling, morning sunlight streams in to touch the blue and purple bedroom doors that circle the dayroom where I stand this morning. They pull the boys in from playing Ping-Pong and foosball. Dannie Porter is writing a letter on a yellow paper with wide blue lines. Thirteen- and fourteen- and fifteen-year-olds plunk down in rows before me on the denim cushions of the couches like a class of schoolboys. All I need is the school teacher's ruler and the chalk to complete the scene.

"How many of you know about my letters to the judge?" I ask. Three hands go up, requesting permission to speak.

"Brian."

"A letter to the judge when we go on honors."

"Right. I tell the judge that you've earned honors. Anyone know the names of the judges?"

All the hands go up: "Page." "Nardi." "The lady judge."

"Judge Linda Rosenzweig." I add her name.

"Green." "Orlando." "That funny name—Scardz . . ."

"Nah. He retired."

"When you get on honors, you earn a letter." I look across the couches. "Were you listening? Tell me the most important word— When you get on honors, you earn a letter."

Hands wave for permission to speak. A chorus just like little children. *"Earn."*

Teaching boys and girls every one of them—just like this—there are times like this I know I should have remained a teacher. There is not a feeling in the world like this—to hold the breathless energy of children's hearts cupped in my hands.

"Shall I tell you what my letter says to the judge?" Suddenly I get this eerie feeling that Dannie Porter's brown eyes have locked onto mine. He won't let go.

"Dear Judge Page," I quote from memory. "I am happy to inform you that Johnny Smith has achieved honors because of his cooperative attitude, his participation in our program, and his mastering selected 'success skills.'" Thirteen pairs of eyes follow my hand as I point to the wall behind me. I touch the giant poster where "success skills" are listed to help along the daily role plays after school: How to listen, How to ask permission, and How to follow instructions.

"I end the letter like this: 'Johnny Smith was voted on honors by representatives of the whole Youth Center staff. I am pleased to write that he is a positive role model for everyone here.'"

Everyone is listening. My eyes hold on to Dannie's. "A letter with your name on it—to the judge."

With words, I paint a picture of the courtroom. A tall raised platform behind the desk . . . a judge in a big black robe, looking down at them and their lawyer at the table below. They know the scene, every one of them—from being there themselves.

"A judge is pondering—thinking—back and forth—just about you.

Is this boy bad? Or is he good? Sort of like two columns. One column lists the reason why you're here—a column with your name and something bad." I motion my hand from top to bottom like a column. A few boys begin to squirm. "And now he's got my letter. My letter starts another column in the judge's mind. Something good. Something to balance." The words are coming out teacherish this morning. That's how I feel.

"Now listen to me. Bring your eyes right here. The new column— the good column—doesn't erase the thing you did." Very sober faces. I pause to let that thought sink in.

"Let's add another thing to Column Two—your good column." I look over at Officer Juan Colon. "Once in a while—when you've made a very big impression on someone like Officer Juan . . . very good behavior . . . very good at success skills . . . he'll go up to court and testify to the judge. Or Officer Gwen." Officer Gwen Walters has stepped into the group to listen. "I was in Judge Nardi's courtroom this year when Juan testified . . ."

". . . for Stan," Juan says. Stan is a C-wing resident.

I can see the great big giant wheels turning in their heads. "Now let me tell you, when one of your officers goes to court to speak for you, the judge is going to listen. Or one of your teachers. Or recreation staffer. It makes him think. Juan doesn't have to go, you know—goes because he *wants* to. Going-to-bat for someone." Some of these boys grew up without English in their households and most without books of any language in their homes. So today I'm choosing simple language. Simple words.

"And then there's me. Once in a great, great while I go to court to testify for someone. Only a few, few times. You see, I'm not the one who sees you every day and every hour—not like the officers. In order for me to testify, I have to know you very well . . . see you for a long, long time . . . be very impressed by you."

I sense that naming names will put a real, live boy into this speech. "Who knows Ricardo?"

Six hands go up.

"And Jimel . . ."

Three hands.

"And Rick . . ."

Six hands.

"Stan . . ."

Thirteen hands.

"This year I testified in court for each of these boys." No one is wiggling on the couches now. "What do you think happens when I testify in court?" I'm not really seeking an answer. "I've been here at the Youth Center such a long, long time. Helped to build this building that we're in. How old are you, Dannie?"

"Fourteen."

"Benjamin?"

"Fourteen."

"José?"

"Fifteen."

"Neikeith?"

"Fourteen." I name them every one—thirteen, fourteen, fifteen.

"I was here before every one of you was born. Every single one." I look across to the desk where Officer Juan Colon is standing. "I might have been here before even Officer Juan was born." Juan smiles his lopsided smile. And everyone laughs.

"And when I talk, the judges listen because I've been here such a long, long time. One thing else. I've always made sure that the judges know that I only tell the truth."

"Reputation," someone says.

"My reputation can go up there in Column Two. The good things you want the judge to know.

"But let me ask you. If I can talk to the judge about good things, can I also talk to him about bad?"

For a roomful of squirmers, I have held them spellbound for all of ten unbroken minutes. No one has to answer. Heads begin to nod.

"I want to help good things to happen for every one of you here— but good things are something you have to *earn*. You do good things, you earn something good. You do bad things, you earn something bad."

It is time for second-period class.

At suppertime when I'm distributing the spring issue of WHAT'S HAPPENING to eager hands, Dannie Porter waves me down.

"'n I talk to you?" he asks.

The boy stands quietly by the blue swivel chair in front of my desk, waiting to be invited to sit down. Nice manners. I make a mental note. His fingers are fidgeting.

"Sit down, Dannie."

"Uh, I wanted to talk about your . . ." The boy reaches for the right word. "I'm not sure if I should say 'lecture' this morning."

"Conversation?"

". . . conversation this morning. About writing a letter to the judge. I'm here for something pretty serious. I guess you'd say I need all the help I can get."

"Want to tell me?"

"Gun charge."

"Gun with a body?"

"They sayin' maybe—but I ain't shoot nobody. If they find a body on this gun . . . could be talkin' to try me as an adult."

Gun with a body is a phrase the youngsters taught me—gun that's been used to shoot someone.

"Serious . . ." In New Jersey, even a fourteen-year-old charged with a serious crime may be tried as an adult.

I heard guns with bodies are cheap, I tell the boy.

"But this one weren't cheap—paid 400 dollars for it. Nine millimeter. Could be as much as 900 dollars."

Dannie is fourteen, sitting across from me, measuring the size of the gun with his hands. A 9mm is an automatic weapon that shoots 16 rounds.

"I livin' on my own, me and my brother in a house—you know Bennett that was here? . . ."

Bennett is a member of the Sons of Malcolm X. They are posse brothers, living in a posse house. I refuse to give even a flicker of recognition.

"My father owns the house—lets us live there."

"Birth father?"

"No. Sort-of-father. Malcolm. Once in a while he come around. We have to take care of his cats in the house. Bennett keep messin' up and forgettin' to take care of the cats."

"Two boys alone in this house? Who cooks?"

"We ain't cook."

The boy is waiting for a reaction. He doesn't have long to wait because I feel angry. A fourteen-year-old living alone in a posse house!

I am sick of children's knowing their father's name but not his face. Sick of babies' dying before their first birthday. Sick of girls' dreaming of being hairdressers and ending up as whores.

"No," I say. I want to shake him because there's no one else in the room to shake. *No* sends a message about values—I want him to see that his world is not all right.

"No," I tell him. "Fourteen is about having a mom and a family that loves you—talks to you, listens to you, cooks for you, cares about you." I think back. I wore pigtails down my back when I was fourteen. The boy is listening. "Fourteen is about someone taking care of you. Asking you about school every day. Fourteen is about digging worms for fishing and shooting basketballs on the corner."

It's the war of the worlds—the big-man world of guns and drugs and money against a lady that's pulling him back to a kid world of moms and hugs. My childhood stuffed doll from China is propped up on the file cabinet behind me. Birds' nests. A turtle shell. The penny-for-a-chewing-gum-ball machine on the shelf.

How do you pull a child back to the child's world where he belongs? This boy needs to see that someone cares about such things.

"Two boys in a house—no one cooking for them—no one taking care of them—no mom loving them. No!" I'm surprised at how angry my voice sounds. "No!"

My voice softens to bring us back to a child's world. "Tell me about home. Who lives at home?"

"My mom. Three sisters. My brother. When I been away for days, my mom ask me where I been."

I can imagine. "What's nice about home?"

"My teddy bear." That catches me by surprise—the transformation to being a boy. The gun-metal look of a man melts to the smile of a boy.

"I have a teddy bear, too," I say softly. "I shaved its fur off when I was little, and it never grew back. And I poked its glass eyes till one eye got lost in the stuffing inside its head. And, you know something nice? When my mother died in Michigan—maybe three years ago, my daughter put my teddy bear in my suitcase and when I got there for my mother's funeral, I found my teddy bear."

We are two children talking. Mary and Dannie. "You keep your bear on your bed?" I ask.

"On the shelf in my room."

"Mine has a knitted scarf around its neck. My daughter, Alice, knitted it for my bear."

We are bonded, this child and I, with a secret walkie-talkie between our hearts. A boy still round with baby fat has let me tiptoe into his childhood where no one else in the Youth Center can ever go. Our secret hideaway of children—where a boy and a girl can safely talk about teddy bears.

"What else is nice at home? Your mom cook for you?"

"Chicken. Macaroni-and-cheese . . ."

I can't get it out of my head—this image—a boy with steely eyes who tells the interrogators, "I'm a soldier. If I die, I die." A few days past his fourteenth birthday. The same boy who shares teddy bears with me.

I wish the power of this moment in my office could drag him forever from his grown-up world of guns. But I know better.

"Can I write a story?" He pulls the squeaking blue swivel chair around the desk by my typewriter. I type the words as he speaks.

GANGSTER WORLD—I CAN'T GET OUT
by DANNIE, age 14

I experienced being a gangster. I experienced being a drug dealer. But I never really experienced being a kid that went to school, getting into sports, doing homework. Ordinary kid kinda stuff.

Shootin people. Bein in a grown-up world. Either goin to jail. Or get killed. That's not a world for kids.

I can't get out.

An epitaph all chiseled in stone at fourteen years of age: I can't get out. I want to weep.

I have heard his message before: *I can't get out.* The no-win choice between prison or death at the hands of gangs and drug dealers in the war zones of the inner city. No place to hide. No place to escape.

>─┼◆>─O─<┼─<

It spooked him . . . knowing that he would die.

Mondo was trapped. Seventeen years old, he had already been raped and stabbed. He was one of only a handful of teenagers in a world of grown-up pushers in East Camden's thriving drug lane called "The Alleyway." He stood there watching them break this guy's legs inside The Alleyway—seven guys beating the poor sucker with a baseball bat. Young, maybe twenty-three—'cause he wanted to go back to Puerto Rico. . . .

When you signed on in The Alleyway, they told you . . . *Sign on forever.* You can't get out. They told everybody that. The big guy's right-hand man was the guy that handled everything, all the shift changes, gave everybody their days. All sat down . . . inside the parkin' lot. . . . He would come with the schedule for them to work. That's when he reminded them . . . "You can't get out."

"For good"—that's what it was . . . "You gonna work for me, you gonna work for good. If you get caught, you get caught—but I get you outa trouble." The boy knew that Number Two was talking bail and big-name defense lawyers—the best—all bought by big-time drug money and the mob. With his own eyes Mondo had seen it all. Street insurance to prevent newly rich, young sellers from breaking away to start competing sets. "You leave, you get shot. Legs gonna get broken. . . ."

At first he hadn't believed it, but there he stood watching them break this guy's legs. . . .

"Damn!" he said softly. "Believe it. . . ." That's when he knew that he would never get out alive.

He had tried to leave . . . stopped working for a while . . . didn't sell drugs over there for a bit . . . and they kept coming by his house . . . telling him he had to go to work. . . .

Even when the Drug Taskforce arrested him and the judge assigned him to a program hours away, Mondo still could not feel safe. He was scared to be away from that place and already two months away from there, and he still thought they would come there and kill him in that place.

The Alleyway at Morse and Boyd streets is a tightly run business with schedules and benefits and rules.

"Can't have a lotta people hangin' out back there. There's only gotta be the trappers sittin' there. Nobody can trap for us. We have to keep the noise down. Accept only tens and twenties from customers.

No ones. That's basically it. An' if the cops come, we can't run into the houses, not where they hold the ounces of cocaine at. Hide it on the ground somewhere or up in the garages . . . on the steps . . .

"We get our schedules in the afternoon. Time. Place. Corner. And it change once a month. Everybody in there only have one day a week 'cause it's a lotta people.

"When I used to work on Sunday, I used to make over $1,500 . . . for myself. . . ."

"In one Sunday-night shift—in *twelve* hours?" I try not to sound incredulous. When I started teaching how-many-years-ago in Kansas, my salary for an entire year was not $1,500! One shift? I ask the boy. "So how much must a street soldier collect in order to make $1,500?"

"Maybe $3000 . . . $4000," he says. "Our package . . . the $200 package—we got ten bags in a package—we gotta turn in $150, keep $50 for ourself on each bundle." He says The Alleyway rewards its sellers with one fourth of the take. Each posse has different standards.

"So you did one day a week. One day or one night?"

"Sunday night. Five or six customers . . . like every three minutes."

"Lining up . . ."

"Pretty much a lotta people there. These drugs they got there . . . is better than any other drug in Camden . . . cocaine. It's really pure. And customers really liked it and . . . so they would keep comin' back an' buyin' it . . . all right . . . and it made The Alleyway more stronger . . . a lotta people would come once they heard about it. Alleyway . . . red bag . . . twenty-dollar bag . . . half gram o' cocaine." The boy measures with his thumb and finger.

I try to create the picture in my mind. "About an inch—in a little red plastic bag."

"Mm-hm. . . . When we bag it up, we burn it to seal it."

I wonder about who it is that is being destroyed. A teenage drug dealer like Mondo will earn more money than he can from any legitimate job within his reach. But every one of the boys tells me about the risks: prison, serious injury, or death. Shootouts with rival gangs or with the police. A boy with pockets bulging with drug earnings is a target for the stick-up boys.

"I thought these two guys was comin' behind me to rob me. Walkin' over the Tenth Street bridge. Twelve, one o'clock. Dark." Tears brim in Mondo's eyes.

"Grabbed me on the shoulder. Gun in his hand. I told 'em I didn't have no money. Threw them what I had."

In the big tall weeds they raped him. One held him down while the other got his stuff off. Then the other. He couldn't see their faces.

"Don't turn around or I kill you." Gun to his head. Holding him down.

Why him?

Only two boys in all these years have taken me by the hand and led me into the violence of a boy's being raped. Young boys struggling among darkened weeds and bushes. With boys or girls I listen, hushed, to the pain.

He was crying. Too scared to shout. Fourteen years old against two grown men. He wanted to kill them. For taking his respect.

"I went home an' got a gun. But they was gone. Drove 'round two hours lookin' for them.

"You never forget. You know 'round any corner it could happen again. Sometime when I walk outside, I see his face.

"Always know I will be killed one day out there. Warring off an' on. Now I always have three, four guys . . . everywhere I go. . . ."

Tables in Cathy Fraser's classroom are jumbled with glue and glitter and fat magic markers to make twenty-four-inch, cut-out Easter eggs. Norberto rests his head on the table, his dark curls spilling over his hands.

"You don't want to make one?" Cathy asks.

"I ain't really celebrate Christmas and Easter," he says. At seventeen, the boy is all bones stretched from teenage growing. Cathy recalls the schoolroom lesson on heroes.

"Who's the most inspirational person in your life?" she asks the class. "Someone you admire."

"I ain't really have no one like that," Norberto says under his breath.

"Well, how about someone that has helped you in your life—now—anybody?"

"I'm the leak in my family," he says.

"The leak?"

"You know—the one nobody cares about."

"Can you think of anybody at all—that cares about you?" Cathy asks.

"Well . . ." Norberto looks up at Cathy standing beside him. ". . . the people here have helped me, they care about me."

Ronnie glues tissue paper on his egg, tuft by tuft by tuft, rows of pink and green and blue giving it three dimensions. Do we ever graduate from first grade? Over and over, going back to the beginning—for these children, sometimes a kinder, gentler chapter in the stories of their lives. Teenage fingers and glue and tissue paper and sparkle paint. Remembering.

Denise at the next table is sprinkling glitter over a dribble of glue marking the shape of a butterfly. "I'm not gonna put mine up," she says. "Embarrassing." *Embarrassing* is Denise's word. Denise told me this week about not being a virgin anymore, about her friend's being raped in a bathroom in her Camden school by an intruder with a red T-shirt. She has already told me, "I ain't gonna go in front of all them people in the Guard of Honor for my basketball. It's embarrassing . . . front of all them boys. Embarrassing." Our highest award, the Guard of Honor, is a Philadelphia 76ers' basketball. Celebrity-signed. Hugs and handshakes across the whole gym, wall to wall, and the award basketball at the end of the line. Flashing Polaroid camera lights.

Norberto signals to Cathy. "Miss Cathy, can I do one?"

The boy's hand is awkward with the fat yellow marker, coloring a big yellow chick holding purple flowers. "You got any cotton balls?" he asks. Above his yellow chick, he floats puffs of white cotton clouds overhead and crowns the finished egg with a pom-pom of flowered lavender ribbon. Cathy and Norberto admire his masterpiece.

On Cathy's IN MEMORY OF . . . bulletin board, Dannie has added a yellow tombstone.

IN MEMORY OF MY DAD MALCOLM X.

My dad was a good man. He spoke what he felt.
He was born a trooper. He died a soldier.
Allah-U-Akbar (God's the greatest.)
I am a Son of Malcolm X. I love my dad.
As-Salaamu-Alakuim
Born 1925. Died 1965.
He was converted to Islam.
Signed, Dannie X.

A day later, I still feel tugged about teaching consequences. I'm not sure why. Perhaps I am still angry about the broken windows. Angry at myself for not pushing the message enough. I hate to fail. It has become a morning ritual—at that one bend in the highway on my way to work the rush of pictures in my head—what secret message will connect me with a child today to make a new channel for hope? Will it be Emerson that puts his arm around me as I pass him in the cafeteria, or Safima that reaches for my hand? What new story or artwork in the schoolrooms will leave me surprised by joy? The affection. The childish delight. The waving hands that tell me we're friends—I want to believe they've been saved forever.

And then a spiderwebbed window. Yesterday I talked to C-wing. Today it will be B-wing.

The older boys each has a copy of *WHAT'S HAPPENING*, the student newspaper, clutched in his hand—delivered to them at lunchtime.

"Shall I tell you about Pablo?" I ask them, pointing to the front page. I read the headline lettered crudely above a row of tombstones:

PICKING OUT THE WRITING ON MY TOMBSTONE by Pablo, 17. "You know what Pablo's first story was for me?"

The boys are sitting in two rows on the couches in B-wing—all looking up at me. "Pablo was fifteen then—wrote me a story about his playhouse, a kid's hideout in Pennsauken, a beat-up couch along the river, that no one knew about. A hideout all his own. That was two years ago. Story about a kid's hideout. Then Pablo's in trouble again, and back he comes. This time his story's different—about a bullet in his shoulder from a drive-by shooting and a mom trying to scare him into being good—you've already read it—right? Pablo . . . on his way to Jamesburg Training School that day when I sat him down to write—ten minutes before the sheriff's officers came.

"No kid stories anymore. It's seventeen years old and guns and drive-bys and a mom all crying—she's telling him to go to the funeral parlor to pick out his funeral stuff. Moms. Right? Trying to hold you back from trouble?" The boys all nod. My boys from the street invent madonna moms that are very close to God. Not one eye moves from mine.

"Then there's the next story—not yet printed. Another one from Pablo. His cousin dying in his arms. 'Not really a cousin' is what Pablo told me—'more like a brother'—dying from battery acid poisoned in his veins. Two kids this year have told me about murder by battery acid."

I know that I am dispensing life or death. And so do they.

"Where does it end? From an ordinary kid with a hideaway on the river to a seventeen-year-old hit in a drive-by, his cousin dying in his arms.

"Tell me. Inside your group, what percent is shot or dead or in jail?" No one answers.

I'm usually gentle with these youngsters. Today I'm angry. And that's a change. Angry at a world that kills its children. But in this room I know I'm looking into faces of how-many youngsters whom I know will die before they're grown. "Come on. How many . . . shot, or dead, or in jail?"

"Seventy percent," says Kareem, who is heading for state training school tomorrow.

"Get real," says Nickee. "More 'n that." Nickee's best friend was the victim of the latest gruesome killing. Eight bullets pumped into him, body set on fire.

"You know what? We sit in my office, you and I. You write these stories. Sit tight together. Talk real. Then six months to two years later—I open the daily newspaper at breakfast. And the headline tells me you're dead. Rasheed. A two-inch story on an inside page of the *Philadelphia Inquirer* told me that Rasheed is dead. At breakfast. With my cup of coffee. Three gunmen mowed him down at his kitchen table, loading cocaine into crack vials at 5:30 A.M.

"Rasheed. I knew it couldn't be my Rasheed. He told me he was going straight. No more drugs. Stopped selling drugs for a job at the laundromat. Sat by my chair, knees almost touching, and told me so. Quit drugs.

"You know what I did? I rushed here to work that day. I saw the newspaper. Snatched out old issues of *WHAT'S HAPPENING*—four years back. Maybe I got the name wrong. Maybe I did." A very long pause. "I didn't. It was Rasheed.

"And I should have seen it coming. You know what his stories told me? 'Sneakers cost $100, a pair of jeans $40 or $50. Nobody wants to wait. So they sell drugs.' Nobody wants to wait. That's it, isn't it? Nobody wants to wait.

"Someone told me that Rasheed had become a 'Big Boy'" (a Big Boy brokers out the drugs to small-time dealers). I go on. "Big deal. Big Boy. What good does that do him now that he is dead? A dead Big Boy."

"And then there was Terry, another of my boys, killed in a drive-by shooting before last year's snow. I watched his brothers lay white gloves atop his coffin, pile the flowers on . . . everyone wearing T-shirts. . . ." I move my hand across my chest . . . "In memory of Terry. . . . Watched his mom crying, brothers holding her up, piling the dirt and flowers on the grave and nobody moves. How do you say good-bye? He was just a kid. Dirt and flowers on top of him in the graveyard. Just a kid.

"I brought a flower home from his graveside and taped it up in my office window. The one from the hall, you know the window—the one you pass. Wrote a sign . . . IN MEMORY OF TERRY MATA. BURIED TODAY.

"And you know what? I came to work one morning and found that someone had taken down my flower and sign. Know why? Not even two weeks after they buried Terry Mata, his brothers were back. Not even two weeks—hardly time to get the tears wiped off their faces . . . not two weeks after they piled dirt and flowers on their brother— locked up right here again. Boys who sat on that very couch where you are sitting now."

I look across at Officer John Wiggins. "Am I telling the truth, John?"

"True."

The room is silent.

"Am I telling the truth?"

"The truth." A tousled head nods.

"For every act there is a consequence. You choose. Your conse-quence." I hold up my pointer finger. "The finger that types a good letter about you to the judge is the very same finger that yesterday dialed the numbers on the phone. This finger—this one right here. . . ." I lift it high. "It calls the prosecutor to file a complaint about a broken window." I point across to the spiderweb cracks on the plate-glass window still unrepaired in the dayroom. An escape attempt. This finger.

"I'm here to help you if I can. But if you hurt my staff or hurt my building, I WILL HURT YOU."

The silence of death.

"If you hurt my staff or hurt my building, I WILL HURT YOU."

Word of my speech runs through the building like wildfire. Two boys, Enrique and Alphonso, get extra charges added to their list of crimes.

"You and your little talk with the kids . . ." Officer John Wiggins intercepts me late in the day at the door of the gym, "It's kinda like— preacher being there all week at church, feedin' the flock . . . preacher. They won't hardly listen to him, but when the evangelist comes through, that's when everybody starts movin' . . . doin' the right thing."

This week I am the evangelist.

It's late in the day, but Dannie wants to talk to me.

"In a way I was happy. In a way I's sad . . . ," he says. I can feel the boy seeking out a special friend to tell a secret. ". . . My number-one girl just told me she's pregnant. I know it's mine." This is the fourteen-year-old who this week talked to me of teddy bears and Mom's macaroni-and-cheese.

"Bein' a dad. Havin' a baby so small. Like how do you play with a baby? It's gonna be a boy. I wanted a girl."

Oh, please, God, no! Not another fourteen-year-old father! In Camden, births to teens—173 per 1000—are more than double the state average. Children tumbling into gangs and drugs and alcohol and violence and too-early sex to find what they cannot find at home. Who tells a child like this that men should not father children until they are able and willing to be responsible for the *consequences* of childbearing?

A week later I return to the Youth Center from a week's holiday away. Dannie Porter is gone—now far beyond my reach. Moved upstate to start serving time at Jamesburg Training School.

I feel the breath slipping sadly through my lips, a tightness closing around my heart. My teddy-bear boy. In a day, a week, a month—not time enough to change the horrors of his lifetime. We barely touched.

>─┼─◇─┼─◇─┼─◁

Cathy Fraser stands at my door, in her hands a giant cardboard Easter egg, wrapped with wondrous lavender ribbon and soft with cotton clouds.

"Norberto's," she says. "First prize for Most Original." Winner's ribbons, purple and red and green, hang from the bottom of the egg.

I think about a gangling boy whose head is topped with curls, who calls himself "a leak." A boy who sat so still when I was talking to all the boys. I never knew what messages were sticking in Norberto's mind.

"Someone I admire?" he asked Miss Cathy in her classroom how many days ago. "I ain't never had no one like that."

"He left today," she says. "He wanted you to have his egg."

12

OFFICERS

Morning sunlight streams through the skylights in the ceiling, making the TV picture in B-wing hard to see. Officer John Wiggins turns off the television set in the dayroom, where half of his boys are already seated watching morning cartoons while the rest now finish their chores.

Sixteen boys, sixteen- seventeen-years old, crowd the seating that rims the room. The room is spartan, as the dayrooms are in every unit. Two heavy oak couches with denim covers face the television set. County carpenters have made them comfortable but massive to survive the adolescent storms that arrive so regularly from the street. A couch like this would survive a generation, maybe two, in a family room. Here it will last perhaps a year. Benches of polished oak rim the walls. One might expect to find such benches in a summer camp, except these are anchored with steel to the floor. The wood is surprisingly clear of carvings and teenage gouging. So are the dayroom walls. Pocket knives and pens and pencils are stored away with jewelry at admission. Yet somehow—behind closed bedroom doors— the rulebook never wins. In the fifteen bedrooms that open from the dayroom, carvings mark walls and windows—even ceilings—with street loyalties. *East State Geech. Hilltop was here. 28th $ for ever. Eutaw. Gumby—North Side. 45 Kings Down Town.*

Here slept "Tiger" and "Scarface." "Smoov" proclaims his love for "Pooh dog." It doesn't matter that "Smoov" will get a violation for writing on the wall. "Smoov" has left his mark. And so have dozens of passions of the heart. *Mayra + Jose ever - Nat n Marcie .A* thousand boys and girls a year walk through these halls. Bedroom walls tell a thousand stories: *Get ready to die Rose Street. . . . Watch your back . . . 1 by 1 . . . Trust me . . . Rich kids don't die . . . God I'm sorry. Forgive me please.*

The dayroom floor is clean but bare, even the toughness of its sand-toned epoxy finish abraded by thousands of wiggling sneakers. Most of the sneakers here cost more than seventy-five dollars a pair these days, and scrubbing the sneakers with a washcloth is a morning ritual more important than brushing the teeth.

From their seats, the boys in B-wing can see the posters that decorate the bedroom walls of boys who have made it all the way to honors. Room 172 has covered every inch with black pride: basketball posters of Julius Irving—"Dr. J,"—L. L. Cool, Malcolm X. The shelf above the boy's bed has a massive red copy of the *Qur'an* of Islam, tucked next to a gold Champion sweatshirt, a black knit Timberland hat.

In the honor room next door, the boy has posted above his bed the front page of the *Courier Post* with the headline: A MATTER OF LIFE AND DEATH, a newspaper story about the all-time record for killings in Camden this year. The boy who sleeps beneath the clipping is charged with murder. In the next room a poster forms the centerpiece: "God and I make a great team," surrounded from floor to ceiling with magazine ads of Quad sport dirt bikes, Suzuki motorcycles, pinups of scantily clad girls.

8:45 A.M. The daily morning meeting starts in B-wing. Some of the boys this morning are "old heads," months of morning meetings under their belts. Some are uncertain, fresh from the street.

"Good morning, young gentlemen."

"Good morning."

For Perry, it's important to show that he doesn't care. He stretches out his leg with his head almost pillowed on the back of the couch. The room is quiet. Eyes focus on officer-partners, John Wiggins and Johann Arnold, who stand flanking the TV set in front of the boys.

"Everybody is expected to do certain things."

John stands relaxed in his turquoise-and-gray jogging suit, letting the thought sink in. Slow-drawling, laid-back comfort flows when Officer John Wiggins speaks. The voice never jars, and neither does the way he walks—always honey in slow motion.

"When I first came here to work, I was expected to do certain things as an officer. Uh. Expectations." He focuses his gaze on the boys before him on the front row, the veterans of the unit. "When you guys first came in here, what were you expecting it to be like? Did it meet your expectations? Was it more than what you thought it was?" John piles the questions on, waiting for the boys to warm to the topic.

No one moves. At the end of the couch a boy rubs sleep from his eyes.

John is always patient. "You know, me being a preacher's son, people always expecting me to be a nice guy. Not so. Can't always be like that. Don't want to disappoint nobody. That's just the way life is. People always expect a preacher's kid to be up here." John stretches high with his hand. "It don't work like that.

"When I came here to work first time, I expected you guys . . . you know . . ." he pauses as though he's reaching for just the right word

". . . a bunch of hard-headed guys, guys you couldn't get along with. But most you guys proved me wrong. I feel like most you guys *aren't* knuckleheads. I said *most*, not all. Majority you guys are not what people expect you to be . . . comin' off the street." John pauses.

"First time you got locked up . . . got out the police van—"

Jamie Thornton interrupts. "John, we got school today?" The boy has trouble sitting still. He hates speeches and he's fidgeting.

"Yeah. We expect to talk about that, too. That you like to go to school." He looks at his partner. John and Johann map their strategy each morning before they awaken the boys. "Am I right, Johann?"

"That's correct." Across the room, as though on cue, Officer Johann Arnold picks up the discussion. "Thornton, how long 'go you get here? 'Bout two years ago?" He picks the boy that most begs for attention and fun. Calling on Jamie Thornton first—by name—will make Jamie's day. Two weeks is the average stay for boys in the room. Thornton has been here for months.

"Johann, stop playin'." Thornton beams.

"That right?"

"You tryin' put me on the spot."

"We expect it out of you." Johann looks at Thornton. The officer is teasing. "We expect you to do what you do. If you didn't do it—if you didn't do it, Thornton, we wouldn't think you were Thornton."

"Ain't been here no two years."

"How much?"

"Nothin' like that . . ."

"Three years ago?"

"See . . . ," seizing the joke. Laughter from the group.

Johann keeps pushing. "When you came here, what was it like? First time. . . ."

"No two years." Thornton pretends to nurse his wounded feelings, smiling all the while. "I don't know, man. Was too long ago. I forgot."

"Okay."

"Did you expect to have cable TV?" John asks.

"Yup."

Snorts from around the room. "Be serious."

"Nah, man." Thornton is soaking up the attention, rubbing his moustache.

"Gordon, don't pay attention to what Thornton's talkin'. Serious, man. What did you expect? I want to know . . ."

"Boring."

"Boring." Johann is like an echo.

"Jail, man. You expect it to be like jail." Thornton's voice rises, aiming to be point man in every discussion.

"Bars on the windows and doors."

"Was that the word out on the street?" Johann asks. "Like a jail? That the word?"

"They said it was Kiddie City."

"They did?"

"Yeah."

"La-la land." A boy on the couch rubs his head.

"La-la land?"

"So your expectations—as a jail or as La-la land." John Wiggins leans against the wall.

"It's a jail, though."

"You not free," Johann says.

"Ain't no jail. Ain't no bars. Ain't no bats. Ain't no guns." Gordon is preoccupied with guns. In quiet moments he boasts to the boys about his arsenal of guns on the street—sawed-off shotguns, 9mm, Tech 9s.

"Gordon, you 'spect guys to be beatin' up each other?" Johann asks.

"'Spect to fight. 'Spect it on the street. 'Spect it in here." This is a boy who wears a bulletproof vest to his high school.

"You expect to have a fight once in a while."

"Yep."

"Did you expect the officers here to have uniforms on?"

"Yeah."

"Yup."

"You did?" The officer seems surprised.

"Yeah."

"With sticks. Badges? All that?"

"Just uniforms."

"Just the uniforms."

"Yeah."

"And handcuffs and all that?"

"Mace."

"Mace! You kiddin'?" Johann Arnold hasn't thought of that.

"Don't drop the soap. My friend told me that."

"Rumors. My friend tol' me the same thing."

"Take your manhood."

"My friend bin here . . . said it ain't like that."

"How 'bout you, Paul?" John draws the boy out. "What did you expect?"

"All you walkin' round with food hang ouch your pockets. You know what I'm sayin'?" The tone is affectionate. Two sides of this morning conversation can poke fun.

"Food hangin' out the pockets?"

A shout of laughter across the room.

"Well, that's an important thing." Johann Arnold jumps in: "Did you expect to be fed every . . . three times a day?"

"Yeah."

"What kinda food did you expect?" The boys laugh. Johann keeps threading the word *expect* into the conversation. Setting expectations is what morning meeting is about.

"Wait a minute," Johann protests. "I'm serious . . . having three square meals a day . . . that's important to me." Johann Arnold measures fifty-one inches of muscle around the chest. The biggest chest on the staff, the boys will tell you. Maybe fifty-one-and-a-half inches—70 to 80 push-ups at a time . . . 50 to 60 sit-ups . . . "What kinda food?" he asks again. ". . . Sloppy? . . . You, know—is the food better than you expected?"

"Yeah. Better than I expected."

"I knew what it was gonna be like anyway."

"Yeah?" says Johann. "Heard something on the bricks?"

"'Cause my sisters an' brothers had been here."

"Oh, okay. So you heard from sisters and brothers that this place was . . ." Johann stands propped against the officers' desk. Success skills are posted on the wall above his shoulder: *How to listen. How to ask permission. How to follow instructions. How to deal with someone else's anger.* "Well, was it bad?"

Shrugs.

"Didn't 'spect nothin'."

"Expectations," John says. "You don't expect me to do anything more for you than I do for Harris who just came over from C-wing."

"Nah."

"'Cause you want everybody to be treated equal."

"Yeah."

"I'm tellin' you . . ."

Officer Johann Arnold looks over at John. "Now when you first came from court, when you saw John Wiggins for the first time. (Laughter from the boys.) Now, come on, man . . . when you saw this man for the first time, what did you expect him to be like?" Everyone laughs. John is a bear of a man.

"Hungry."

"Hungry." Johann laughs. "Don't get in trouble now. Don't get in trouble." The boys know the partnership between the two men who anchor B-wing on the morning shift. The men are tight.

"First came in here?"

"Yeah."

"John was mean."

"He was mean?" Mock surprise ripples up to Johann's red hair. John Wiggins is mean like Santa Claus.

"Lookin' . . . the look on his face . . ."

"That's your perception." Wiggins rises to his own defense.

"Man, he laughin' and he jokin', but he know the real deal."

John attracts the "old head" boys with the adoration of high-school athletes for their coach. Today John can be calling one of his boys "Brother Jamie"; tomorrow, showing them smuggled photographs he

himself snapped in Martin Luther King's church. "Just sit back . . .
long as you cooperate . . . don't give nobody a hard time . . . do what
you s'pose to do," John says. ". . . That what you expect? Masters, I
ain't heard nothin' from you."

"I ain't 'spect to be goin' to school every day," the boy says.

"I didn't 'spect that neither." Groups of school-age boys cluster on
Camden corners every school day, truants and dropouts from school.
Out on the streets, most of the boys have had problems with school.

"Did you expect the teachers to be . . . you know, helpful?"

"Pssshew . . . no."

"I didn't 'spect to be on honors . . . nothin' like that . . . chill an'
all . . ." Thornton sits dressed all proud in black—Los Angeles
Raiders all the way—his badge of honor for being on honors.

"Do you think this place can spoil a person?" Johann asks.

Santee, who has been fading into the wall in the back of the room,
pushes to speak. "You come here . . . you know 'bout ever'bod' here
from the streets. Most ever'bod' from the same part of town . . . you
know . . ."

"That make you feel better?" Johann asks.

"Yeah." Santee bobs his knee up and down on the bench. "If you
don't know someone . . . they don't help you—you by yourself. . . .
You know what I'm saying?"

"Locking horns?" the officer asks.

"Johann's right," the boy says. "Hold your hand. Officers . . . that's
what they do." He has wrung out a little truth.

"Comfortable." Johann Arnold has reached the bottom line.

"Safety. Is that important?" A chorus of agreement. Tough boys are
talking about feeling safe in very strange territory. The first way to
connect with a boy. Make him feel safe.

"You guys know I don't 'llow any fightin'. And John don't 'llow any
fightin' in here. An' no profanity. Vulgar language instigates fighting
and violence. That's why I don't allow cursing. That's not a safe
environment. It'll set something off. I'm not gonna 'llow it." Officer
Johann Arnold knows that talk like this will take the pressure off. The
weak boy always feels he has to prove his manhood. "You don't have
to fight here, because I'm here. You'll see me. Around the day, I'll do
my security checks. I'll walk in the bathroom . . . walk in your
rooms."

Officer John Wiggins has turned serious. "The reason this place is
not what you thought is because you guys cooperate. When we come
here, day to day, that's what we expect you-all guys to do. It's
expectations. In the morning time, I tell Weston to do something . . .
he don't say, 'I won't do it.' Hey, I don't expect that. You expect from
me. I expect from you.

"The reason this place is what it is, we respect ourselves. I respect
myself. And I respect you guys. Respect. Expectations. If I didn't

respect myself, I'd let you guys do pretty much what you want to do. And we'd have chaos all day long. We don't 'llow that to go. We have expectations.''

The boys are looking for someone—officers, parents, teachers—to set limits and impose discipline. Without walls to bounce against, the boys seem lost. The officers have pulled the boys into the expectations for every day: Listen. Follow instructions. Ask permission.

>—•—◦—•—<

New officers were lucky. The older people from whom they learned weren't just anybody—they were the last of the old-timers, full of stories of the old days, who knew everything about lockups. If you were interested and sincere, they'd tell you—about counting every spoon and fork after every meal because no one wanted a smuggled fork stabbed in his eye. Ray Ruiz would tell about the day he caught the boy in midair in the South Side shower room—sleeves of his sweatshirt tied around his neck. Showers—there was no way you could be too careful in monitoring the showers and bathroom. Naked bodies. In lockups that was the biggest trouble spot. Sometimes the old-timers—like Bernice Gray—would tell me that the new officers didn't understand—not really, not where we had come from.

Sometimes new training programs tried to teach with videos, but the old-timers knew that one story by word of mouth is worth a thousand pictures. A video creates one lonely image; a story gives birth to a thousand images in a roomful of brains. Leo Gold could talk about the night that Michael White plotted a mass escape. "Vibes" talked the loudest when something was up . . . bad vibes that prickled down your spine . . . too quiet . . . too noisy . . . a missing screw. Leo looked up during his security check at the start of the shift and saw the gap-toothed air vent missing all its slats over the drinking fountain in the older boys' unit.

You searched inch by inch on a night like that—in mattresses, under sinks—your fingertips knew that they didn't dare miss one nook or cranny—until you had a pillowcaseful of metal slats ripped from the grille covering the ceiling air duct. Spears, shanks twelve inches long, sharpened to points on both ends. Steel rings ripped out from bedroom smoke detectors . . . contraband—officers used words like that—*contraband*—an officer's worst nightmare. Mark Bare once found a ten-inch kitchen knife in the sole of a sneaker on a boy he was admitting. At a time like that you wondered if the transporting police officer had ever bothered to search. On this spooked night, two solid hours of searching . . . inch by inch . . . fifteen bedrooms . . . pillows and mattresses . . . five sinks . . . three showers . . . two hoppers . . . two urinals . . . TV room . . . dayroom . . . chairs . . . tables . . . and not one clue where all the stuff was hidden.

Ten years later Leo could still describe six of the boys locking arms

... shoulders ... kicking their legs ... swaying with the tom-tom chant in the TV room—

> *We're knock-ing out staff*
> *And we're leav-ing to-night.*
> *We're knock-ing out staff*
> *And we're leav-ing to-night.*

The lockdown. Keeping boys in eyeball range and no one between Leo's back and the wall. His adrenaline pumping survival. Looking so cool. Leo was such a liar with his looks. Leo's stories about vampire roaches in the crumbling old building could break up a class. Roaches and breathing mouldy air in the old building had given Leo more trouble than the boys.

To the new officers, Leo preached about building solid relationships. On this deadly night, this boy at his back, grabbing the back of Leo's shirt, they had the weapons ... and the word ... the boys had already said "the word"—*Kill ... kill the officers* ... So why didn't the kid take Leo down? A kid standing there at Leo's back ... wide open for a clean shot ...

"You walk on shift and hear them say they're gonna kill you. ..." Leo trained new officers at the state Corrections Officers Training Academy in Trenton. "... The relationship you build with a resident—the rapport—can save your life. Kids watch you if they see you as a person that will help them and listen to them when they need someone to talk to ... look at you as a good person ... seek out your help. In these situations then they will respond to you. You build a relationship with your youngsters—respect, communication." Leo would look at his recruits, "You won't have to battle with them."

"Huh?" The hands would wave.

Then Leo would get the debate: "Leo, it's against the rules at our place to build a relationship ... make a connect."

"No?" Leo never got ruffled.

And then he'd get the no-smile stuff ... officers from other youth centers ... just enforce the rules ... just provide security ... hands-off the programs ...

Leo always hammered away ... "Teach a kid some new skill ..." always big on teaching a kid ... reading ... shooting baskets ... doing dips in the weight room ...

"Not allowed. No relationships. Not in classrooms or the units. No input." ... Words like *strictly custodial function* ...

And Leo would shake his head. Anybody that worked in the "big house" knew—one officer to fifty or a hundred men; or a youth center—one officer to eight ruffians. You survive only on relationship.

Crisis-intervention classes always brought out the dirty linen: Officers had their lists of dangerous partners. Never a name—no one ever liked to "rat" with names. But everyone could describe the "kind of" officer they hoped they'd never have to work with. You'd see your name posted as partner to someone who didn't know how to handle the crew, and you'd groan. Your gut talked when you were teamed with a dangerous officer. Eight hours of going it alone or fighting fires. The most dangerous was the one who spent a shift always challenging the boys, setting the girls up in no-win situations. Threatening, trying to embarrass them. It was usually a mouse trying to act like a lion. And it never worked. The boys saw someone trying to take their manhood. That's when a unit got dangerous.

Or the partner that forgot to check the kid on suicide watch and wandered in and out . . . wouldn't back you up with his word or physical presence. You shouldn't have to tell a guy: "Don't just sit there, man. I need some help."

If fifteen or thirty kids decided to go off, you wouldn't be safe. Teamwork, support was what the job was about. The only way it worked.

"Only a lock between you and . . ." Juan Colon could remember way back when ". . . two or three officers against thirty boys. Almost double capacity. Kids on the mattresses on the floor . . . on the shelves.

". . . Kickin' . . . bangin' . . . you actually thought the doors are comin' off the hinges . . . the kickin' an' bangin' . . . an' the noise level . . ."

It was the noise that overwhelmed you. Ominous echoes off the walls and doors and ceiling—that's what really frightened you the most.

Being alert. Teamwork . . . that's what you wanted in a partner. Support.

Everyone knew. Respect was what made a place work. You listened to a kid when he was down. You saw it in his eyes. He always remembered that. A human being. Kids weren't much into making trouble for human beings. They mostly bothered the walking rule book who swaggered around with a jingling set of keys . . . the officer who threatened and embarrassed and tried to take their manhood. Officers often brought the baggage of their lives to work. The one who didn't know how to get along with anyone outside the walls didn't get a change of heart when he walked inside the unit. The boys always spotted the officer who was there just to put in eight hours and leave. Eight 'n' skate.

"She don't really care about us." Kids tried to run that kinda person outa the place.

Tough officers hated just as much to be teamed with a wimp. You had to worry about the ones who trusted too much.

"The kids'll want everything." Shift commanders warned new officers: "Be able to say no. Don't let the kids dictate to you."

Volunteers or college interns usually fell into that trap . . . "Poor

little darlings . . ." believing everything a kid would say to them . . .
The ones who brought in *Playboy* magazine to buddy up to a kid . . .
Bleeding hearts who believed that the kids would do the right thing all
the time . . .

"Get-over kids . . . remember that. You can't give away the whole
store . . . whispering in a kid's ear . . . giving him extras . . ." You
couldn't put yourself on the same level as a kid. That was a buddy-
buddy trap. And it was always dangerous. Because the day would
surely come when you couldn't give a boy just what he expected, and
then he'd blow.

There was also the "hidden officer." You got to recognize him . . .
hear no evil, see no evil, tell no evil. . . . You knew a "hidden officer"
when you worked with one. Just a body . . . didn't speak . . . "didn't
say nothin' to the boys . . ." is how an officer might describe it.
"Lunchtime . . . kids sittin' right there at the table with a man . . . and
the boys call across to another table to me—to ask if they can get
up. . . . Kids don't even see that officer there. . . ." You had to worry
about working with an invisible man. A good officer was none of that.

>-+-<>-○-<+-+-<

Being a good officer was like watching tractor pulls or bog racing.
Noisy, messy—and if you got too close—hands-on, as you had to once
in a while—some of it would get on you.

Jorge Consuelo had gone off before. The boy could spit for an hour
nonstop. And you'd wonder where he could manufacture all that
saliva. Fifteen years old, worrying about his mother. After six weeks
he had finally told Officer John Wiggins the secret—a giant jump of
trust to tell an officer that "our mother's in prison.". . . Something
like that sat like a lump beneath your heart and never went away, and
anytime anyone said anything about someone's mother—"Hey,
mother f____r," something would break all over again. You tried to
push the picture out of the corners of your mind . . . your mother
sitting in prison or jail somewhere in an orange jumpsuit . . . a
prisoner number on the pocket over her heart. Mothers were supposed
to be like the madonna in the Easter verses posted on your bedroom
wall . . . haloes and white lilies and downcast eyes . . . or like Miss
Mary Ann Zeiser, Jorge's teacher at the Youth Center.

Someone talkin' 'bout "doing it" to your mom . . . The catsup hit
Officer John Wiggins on the side of his face, spilling like blood down
his jaw, leaving an ugly stain down his jacket.

An incident always happened fast—often without warning—here,
at the end of lunch in a crowded cafeteria, the boy pouring catsup into
a pint carton of milk and pinching the carton closed—like an
unopened pint of milk—like an April Fool's prank—someone opens
the carton of milk at supper to take a drink and out comes catsup . . .

Everyone who saw it knew John wasn't going to look the other way. . . . John didn't ever look the other way. . . .

"Jorge."

John was picking up the dirty napkins from the table, pointing to the tampered milk carton filled with catsup . . . and the boy's back stiffening—a lose-face look . . . the lowered eyes . . . the flush on his face, "I-guess-I-got-caught" rage in front of all his boys—and no, he didn't do it . . . and there was John telling the boy, "I would appreciate it, Jorge, if you didn't take me for a sucker." He had *seen* Jorge do it. And then Jorge picked up the chair—that was the one dangerous moment—the frozen moment of choice—big boys, every one of them grown as men, with Jorge there beside them, wavering between picking up a chair or picking up the catsup. . . . It was a save-face thing. And half the boys knew that if the boy picked up a chair, they'd have to take him out. . . . It was a "John's-my-man" kinda thing "and I'd have to take Consuelo out if he hit John with a chair. . . ."

And that's when the catsup hit John in the face.

When you thought about it later, you kept hearing Jorge say over and over again . . . "Don't call my mom no names, don't be callin' my mother no names . . ." and everybody knew that Officer John Wiggins was not about disrespecting his boys. . . . Some kids would kill if you called their mom a name. . . . Jorge was that type of kid, with a real thing 'bout his mom. . . . None of it made sense. John was the one who voted yes for Jorge at the Thursday afternoon vote—which boys were going to be voted up to getting increased privileges. John never forgot where his boys came from. You went to bat for your boys when they showed that they were trying. Jorge was trying, and Officer John Wiggins believed in giving a boy a chance.

You remembered things when it was all over. "Word is bond . . . ," Jorge was shouting down in the gym that he was gonna punch athletic director Melvin McClinton in his f____n' face . . . because he was "tired of the system. . . ." Jorge had wanted to play badminton, and Melvin had told him to wait until the basketball game was finished. . . . The fuse was always short with boys like this . . . couldn't wait . . . wanted everything right now. You saw it a thousand ways . . . gold chains and earrings had become a teen health hazard. . . . You want a gold chain? You snatch it now—kill for it. . . . You want a hat? You steal it now, which was what got them to the Youth Center in the first place. No brakes.

In the classroom, Mary Ann Zeiser stood by Jorge's elbow and graded his arithmetic minutes after he had finished the page. He was loud. He was boisterous. And he begged for her attention. Jorge loved Miss Mary Ann—blonde curls, motherliness, skill, and love all bundled into one. Miss Mary Ann had this look—that if she held you, you would feel sheltered in the softness . . . her smile . . . her body . . .

her heart . . . forever. She would let Jorge sit doing his math because he could always shine in math . . . Miss Mary Ann always saw dignity in a kid. Out loud in front of the boy, she told everybody about Jorge and his fractions . . . about the love poems he wrote. There was the day Miss Mary Ann asked him about the qualities of Student of the week.

"Well . . . all 'at chew (that you) have to be is teacher's pet."

And Miss Mary Ann was desperately trying not to laugh . . . Jorge standing there by the foosball game, his hat turned sideways on his head . . . a kid that probably only a mother could love . . . who had probably never been thought of by any other teacher as anything worthwhile, standing there really believing that he was the teacher's pet.

And he was. Miss Mary Ann, who had three teenagers of her own, always said, "The badder they are, the more I love them."

Mary Ann Zeiser had stumbled quite by accident into his pain about his mother, Jorge having written something on the board without permission one morning, something funny . . . Mary Ann's blue eyes pinning him to the wall.

"I'm gonna tell your mother on you."

And he looked across at her, "My mother's in prison . . ." The ragged murmur of heartache . . .

Certain people you just reached out to. . . . The Friday that Miss Mary Ann baked them a cheesecake and a cherry pie because everybody had been good all week, Jorge took the whole cherry pie, like a kid who had never had anything of his own in his whole life. And all the class was saying, "That whole pie's not yours." And Jorge said, yes, it was. It was all his—daring anybody to come near his pie.

Miss Mary Ann had to remind the boy—fifteen years old—about sharing, like you would teach manners to a little kid—like, "Jimmy, share your Tootsie Roll with Billy." So Jorge shared a couple of pieces. Everybody else had cheesecake while Jorge ate the whole half of a cherry pie and took his goody bag of cherry pie back to B-wing—sort of like a trophy or a love letter to show off that someone cared about him.

You could never quite know the feeling, the boy had told Officer Al Thomas—having no one to go to. . . . Didn't ever see his parents . . . didn't know where they were . . . not even where to reach them on the telephone. . . . When it was phone time, Jorge phoned a house in Camden where someone said there were girls—no one he knew . . . just a "Let's pretend" that he really did have someone he belonged to to call on the phone. . . . Officers knew a poor kid who didn't belong to anyone—it hit you harder than the loneliness of the poor little rich kids . . . the generic trophies to be patted in the morning, kissed at night, taken on trips during vacation, and assembled, well-dressed, with glowing complexions and preppy turtlenecks for Christmas photos.... Those were abandoned kids, too, but those the Youth Center hardly ever got. When rich kids rebelled, they were sent to military schools, prep schools, far away so they wouldn't be an inconvenience to Dad and Mom. Your heart never quite got touched so much by the poor little rich kid, but Jorge—six weeks and the boy had had no visitors....

"Any friends?"

"All locked up."

"Older brother?"

"Somewhere in Pennsylvania...." Al had been taking Jorge to his room for a five-minute time-out after the fuss in the gymnasium....

"You can't do anything to me that my family hasn't already done to me...." Someone, fifteen years ago, had made a baby, who knows where, in a car ... a van ... under a tree ... tagged him with a name—Jorge, and then forgot about him. You wondered where all the pocks and scars came from on the boy's face. It wasn't the face of a fifteen-year-old. It was hard, more like thirty-five....

Even a hard-nosed officer like Al got soft when a boy started talking about sleeping on porches and eating out of dumpsters. It made you think—a boy of America eating out of dumpsters!

Visiting nights Jorge would be talking loudly so that everybody would hear—about his mom coming to visit. And you knew that the boy's mom was locked away in jail somewhere and would never come to visit, and you saw it often enough from boys who got no visits, looking at the clock ... waiting for the summon of their name ... saying, yes, for sure, their mom was waiting for them in the cafeteria. You knew it was all a sad game of Let's Pretend, that they would be getting visits like everybody else ... and no one ever ... ever ... called Jorge's name to come to the cafeteria on visiting nights.

"I want to spend my life in jail," the boy told Al. In an awful way, down in the pit of your stomach, you understood.

In a moment away from his boys, Al would talk about his boys seeing their parents all "drugged up" ... seeing strange men parade through the house to have sex with their moms ... the addict woman who told Al that she traded her eleven-year-old daughter by the hour to men for a hit of cocaine. Al was constantly pushing back the boys who were trying to hook him up with their mother or their sister. It was a scheming kind of thing to connect their family to a decent man. Just this Tuesday at visiting hour, Masters had introduced Al to his mom. Al knew the deal ... and, no, no, no, Al wasn't into that....

After an incident, before even one day had passed after the catsup incident, everyone would swap these mental pictures of the boy—like trying to find the real Jorge, fists balled up in towels like boxing gloves fashioned from rags. No man here was big enough to take him out, Jorge said that—to "Big John" Golaszewski ... six-feet-six-and-a-half ... 350 pounds.... It made you know that the boy wasn't thinking right—mattress all ripped up and pillow shredded on the floor. Big John was the shift commander that night, talking straight to the boy. Hey, the judge had given Jorge a holiday furlough, and Jorge had given the judge a thank-you by going AWOL. What kind of thinking was that? John said maybe Jorge should stop blaming everybody in the world and start looking at the choices he was making.

After that, Jorge stuck to Big John like a burr to a horse's tail . . . a guy that would talk straight to a kid like a father . . . would hold him in a restraint till he calmed down and would not hurt him.

Officer John Wiggins could tell the boys about the ruffian streets of North Philadelphia across the river where he grew up. John knew about neighborhoods where there were no supermarkets, no day-care centers, where emergency rooms served as the family doctor by default. John remembered the day he got his ear ripped off, a bloody piece of meat dangling down his neck held on by a thread of skin. He and his boys had kept ringing the doorbell at the Couples Club at Thirtieth and Cumberland streets, a prank, until someone had lost all patience and had hurled a stick at them—a stick with a jagged nail on the end.

It wasn't the kind of story you expected to hear from a preacher's son. And the part that everyone remembered most was that John's brother was more worried about what his mom was going to do to them for sneaking out when she had told them to stay inside—more worried about that than John's bloody, dangling ear. Mrs. Wiggins, five-feet one inch, was not above pinning a son to the floor with her foot on his chest to let him know that she meant business. The neighborhood was still brick row houses then, where a neighbor could sit safely out on the porch. People knew each other, but it began to change. Old-timers moved out. The Wiggins family moved across the river to New Jersey and built a house in the rural suburbs. John's father became the pastor of a church. When you saw boys being shot at in the neighborhood, sawed-off shotguns at the head . . .

Maybe that was why every Sunday morning, John sits at the organ in the Emmanuel Church of God in Christ in Lawnside, shaking the pews with the majesty of his music, all the stops out. Or Wednesday evenings, practicing with the church choir. Instead of sitting in jail. Boys he knew in North Philadelphia were now in jail.

The Youth Center gave John the son he didn't have—always a string of boys wanting to know about his life, what made him what he was: "John, do you get drunk?" "What does your wife look like?" "When you gonna bring in a picture?" "What you gonna do tonight when you leave here?"

Whenever John was reassigned for a shift with the younger boys in C-wing, his B-wing boys accused him, "Man, you sold us out." There was always—always—some boy in the unit that said he wanted to be like John.

It was the kind of thing that made you understand why a person would want to be an officer. There were a hundred stories of how officers got to the Youth Center. The Federal Prison System had tried to recruit Leo Gold to switch to working with adults—Leo had first been assigned to the Youth Center as a college intern—but the way Leo saw it, adults were "drones" by comparison to kids and energy and basketball. You had a chance of turning a boy around. Leo didn't hesitate one minute when I offered him a job as an officer at the Youth Center right out of college.

Janet Graddy grew up in Camden and had monitored the recreation center across the street from her house, starting when she was nine years old and had never stopped working with youngsters—even in Germany when she organized youth activities for military dependents on a military base. When Youth Center school was canceled because of the snow, Janet would corner her A-wing boys and girls with games of Black Magic or line them up like Cub Scouts and Brownies, slapping their knees with games of Zoomie-Zoomie. When Wanda gave birth to a little girl during her stay at the Youth Center, it was Janet who adopted the baby.

Robbie Reid, unit manager for the older boys, knew from the start that he wanted to work with young black kids. Around the country, one in four young black men is in some way supervised by the criminal justice system. Yes, you knew the boys were belligerent, cussin'-teachers-out, no-way apple-for-the-teacher boys, and yet you would watch the boys blossom under the wings of the officers in your unit. . . . Nickee padding behind John Wiggins like a puppy following a boy . . . officers treating the boys like their sons . . . getting their hearts wrapped around youngsters with names like Santee and Jorge, Saleed, and Rick . . . pouring themselves into them . . . then sending them back to the streets, the grubby, man-eating streets with no place to play except a broken milk crate tacked to a telephone pole—where boys went that didn't go to school, that didn't have parents who made them go, or maybe didn't have parents at all—knowing the boys would more than likely return. Robbie Reid wanted to pour into them what he got from his own childhood.

Robbie was born the fifth of twelve children. A preacher's son, he never remembered when he wasn't looking after brothers and sisters and Sunday school and youth recreation groups. When he thought about it afterward—government cheese and Spam and powdered milk—he realized that they were probably poor, but *he* had always thought that they were rich.

Robbie went off to college and became football All-American in

NCAA, a running back chosen for the All-State team. He had started
at the Youth Center as a recreation leader, moved up to officer, and
finally to social worker and unit manager of B-wing. By contrast, the
boys he chose to work with at the Youth Center lived daily
catastrophes—had never once had parents and teachers like his.

When I hired officers, I scoured the world for men and women like
this.

><+>·-O-·<+>·<

John Wiggins didn't think that putting a boy on punishment did
much good. There were better ways. Most officers who worked with
him had an understanding about that: If they lined up "bad guy" and
"good guy" roles, people would place John's peg in the "good guy"
slot, but John always preferred to call himself a "middle-of-the-road
guy." He wanted his boys to see officers supporting each other.

Johann Arnold and John Wiggins started every shift with a look at
whom they had to work with. Some officers started a shift: "This kid,
he'll be a pain in the behind." Johann and John started right up front:
"We'll take care of him. He won't be that much of a problem." They
both preferred to start a shift with, "Hey—it's not gonna be a
problem." You could be working with an officer who was always
saying, "Oh, shucks, this guy is gonna be a problem," and you would
spend the shift dealing with this guy's problem. Officer attitude was
what made or broke a shift. People would come in and say, "Hey, we
just gonna have a terrible day." And you ended up having a terrible
day.

Even if you had thirty boys instead of the fifteen you were supposed
to have—you fixed it in your head—improvised—made things the
best that you could. Most of the time a kid came and told you if he
was having a problem—someone poking him in the line, saying stuff
to him in the wing—"Hey, yo, I'm-a get you." Or "I'm down with so-
an-so . . ." making the kid feel intimidated. Filtered it to Robbie Reid
or the officers. You always let the boys know who was in control . . .
every move . . . every step . . . someone trying to intimidate someone
. . . you took the pressure off that kid—"Hey, if you have a problem
you come and deal with the staff." You let the bully know—"Hey,
we're not gonna let that happen."

Johann and John jumped right on it—sat them right down—had a
meeting, waited until they got quiet. You never tried to shout over top
of them. The boys knew that you were sitting there waiting for them
to get quiet. It always worked out.

Once in a lifetime, you had a partner you loved like a brother. John
Wiggins had once had a partner like that—John Wiggins and Carlos
Pacheco. They liked the same things—played basketball with the
kids—both of them athletes. You got to know each other's back-
grounds, how the other worked.

Carlos was laid back; John was assertive. They knew without saying anything. John knew how Carlos operated; Carlos knew how John operated. Some people got jealous—two officers getting that close. For that matter, two *men* getting that close. It was rare, their talking like school chums throughout the shift. They didn't associate familywise, but when Carlos moved to California, John phoned him a lot, chalked up a phone bill. Carlos said John was closer than a brother.

John Wiggins liked the boys. He'd tell you in a minute—this one could be a comedian somewhere, that one an athlete, this one an artist . . . talented kids that could make it somewhere if they had a chance. John's cheeks would bunch up with dimples on both sides when he told stories about his boys . . . "Comical . . . you watch 'em and see some of things they do. Sit 'round and tell stuff happened out on the street . . . Nickee here . . . one his buddies . . . problem with this stepfather . . . tied some typa rope around his hands to a telephone pole till the cops come.

"You sat around just listening. The best time to get a lotta stuff on your boys was when they were just sitting round . . . in the gym . . . start telling you stuff. . . . 'I 'member few years ago when I was growin' up . . .' and they start rattlin' off . . . anything . . . girls . . . when they first got locked up . . . Jorge telling about his mom being locked up. Maybe the boy was trying to explain why he always acted the way he did. Half the stuff they said it caught you by surprise . . . stories growin' up—like Nickee hanging out with buddies on the street—first time gettin' drunk."

John started calling his boys "the Bartles and James boys." They laughed about it. Nickee Weston would say to John, "You remind me a lot of me," and John always reminded them, "Hey, you get out, you can come back and be an officer just like me!"

John wore his jewelry—the gold chain, the gold rope by his watch. You didn't have to be selling drugs to make money. John's New Orleans Saints cap had the peak pointing down the back. John didn't get bent outa shape over his clothes. He walked very relaxed, very sure that the boys were watching him every minute, purposely doing something to see if he was watching. John invented his own scripture and verse: "When they know that you watchin' . . . the good an' the bad . . . they feel that they got your attention. An' if they feel like you ain't watchin . . . they feel like you don't want to be bothered with them."

John told his boys, "We're the closest thing that you have to a father right now while you're in here. . . ."

The catsup in the crowded lunchtime cafeteria . . .
"I'd appreciate it if you didn't take me for a sucker. . . ." John

Wiggins had been right beside Jorge, and "sucker" sounded too much like something else . . . maybe like "mother f____r."

Jorge was shaking. "Hey, man, don't be callin' my mother names"—the boy's hand still on the chair and every eye in the crowded cafeteria on the boy. Jorge didn't fight when the shift commander and Officer Bill Hughes escorted him, a come-along hold, one on each side, from the cafeteria.

Social worker, Robbie Reid, and Jorge sorted the whole thing out, sitting on Jorge's bed in Room 168—a boy on honors sending a bad message . . . squirting catsup on an officer in front of all the boys. No one was a better mediator than Robbie, and, yes, John had always gone to bat for the boy. Jorge needed to apologize, so Robbie summoned John.

"I didn't mean to get you in the face."

"Whatch ya mean to do? Get me in the heart?"

Jorge looked up at John. And Robbie started laughing. Something had happened in that room—nothing that you could completely understand. Whatever the contest had been, you knew that John had won.

"A nice little conversation" was the way John described the post-Catsup Conference in Jorge's bedroom when it was all over. John gave Jorge a violation, for twenty-four hours, assigning him to spend his free time in his room. Even John, who smiled for days about the catsup caper and who didn't much like to give his boys violations, knew that you couldn't let a boy get away with raising a hand to an officer. Next time it might not be catsup.

>—◆>—◦—<◆—<

A hand raised on an officer is rare, so Jorge and the catsup is the talk of officers and residents. Johann Arnold had been off for the day when the incident happened.

"I went home and got my pizza . . . extra sauce," John says to his partner the next day. John eats for comfort.

Johann Arnold says the Lord made his partnership with John. Johann, the preacher; John, the preacher's son, the organist in his father's church. Certainly none of their boys would doubt that it is true.

"Yo', kitchen!" John Wiggins calls across the room to the cook now turning stacks of pancakes. "Keep the catsup off the table today. Ban the automatic weapons."

In fewer than twenty-four hours, officers are already calling John "the catsup man."

"Hey, Tartan man."

"Tartan man?"

"Yeh, Tartan catsup."

Johann Arnold comforts his partner. "You got the vest on, man." If

the boys were awake and listening, a vest would mean the bullet-proof
vest that many of them wear to school or on the streets. But Johann
and John swap references from the Bible on their shift. The vest today
is quoted from Ephesians 6. "The whole armor of God," says Johann.
Truth . . . righteousness . . . faith . . . peace . . ."

With four B-wing boys scheduled for court this morning, the
officers move through the rooms, prodding boys to dress and groom.
The boys move slowly, still in a fog of sleep, a fashion parade of
leather 8-Ball jackets, black Looney-Tunes T-shirts, and one-hundred-
dollar sneakers swaggering down the hallway to await the sheriff's
van, among them Jorge Consuelo, the youth who sprayed Officer John
Wiggins with catsup.

"Today, everybody's a brother . . . ," John mumbles. "We vote
today." Thursday is vote day—officers and unit manager Robbie Reid,
voting which boys move up to higher honors, which boys move down.
Everybody will be on good behavior today. John turns to Nickee
Weston, "You know, my daughter ready to come an' get you." (John's
daughter is six years old.) "How come you didn't protect me?"

"She smell the catsup?"

Wiggins nods. "Hey, Johann, you see that Bartles and James? The B
and J boys?" This week a bottle of homemade brew is the talk of B-
wing—B-wing, now dubbed "the B and J boys," a painless way of
achieving some intimacy. A contraband bottle has been discovered
wrapped in a jogging suit on the floor of the locked clothing closet, a
plastic soda bottle full of water and orange peels and chunks of bread
for yeast.

"C'mon, B and J, let's mop the floor." For days everyone has joked
about who made the hooch. It sits on my desk for everyone to see as
the week's "show-and-tell." Everybody knows . . . nobody knows.

Johann nudges the boys. "Anyone for social worker, nurse? Wanta
see anybody today?" He notes names on his list. Beds made, counters
tidied, and floors all mopped, the boys settle down to the day's
morning meeting.

"We are in the horizon of a new day . . ." Johann's opening sounds
like the invocation prayer of this week's Sunday service at his church.
". . . New steps you have never taken . . ." These boys from the street
listen almost with a hush of reverence to the deity. Like triumphal
wake-up calls of a pipe organ and sun streaming through stained-glass
windows to start the day. Like Moses or Martin Luther King or Maya
Angelou: "Lift up your eyes upon this day breaking for you . . ."

There is a scripture preached by corrections and detention officers
that says: "Be tough. Don't ever, ever, show them that you're
human," the idea being that tough kids will go for kindness the way a
lion goes for a wounded hunter. Johann Arnold never subscribed to
that theory. The law of the jungle, he says, is what brought the boys
here. Officer Johann Arnold lives by another precept: Make the boys

safe so they can be kids. Set high standards and mete out respect and discipline.

"A new horizon. Some people think you are zeroes," he tells the boys. "Let me tell you. I start every one of you out at one hundred. I don't start you out at zero and you work your way up. I start you with a hundred points. You don't have to do nothin'. You're there. You're all right. Right now. Don't have to prove nothin' to me or nobody else."

It is hard to beat a team like this—Johann and John. The men know these boys need values—values best taught by living models.

"Now, soon as I got in the door today, you told me John got sprayed by catsup."

The unit still feels uneasy about the catsup, and John needs to reassure his boys. "My little thing with Consuelo—we got it all squared away. Nice little conversation. Typa guy you can talk to . . . clear up misunderstandings. I understand about bad days. I hope you only have bad days only once in six months." He stands this morning in front of boys who will shoot a man for soiling their brand-new sneakers. He looks into twenty-four pairs of eyes. It's no big deal, he says, about his sweatsuit . . . already washed. ". . . ain't the typa guy to get bent outa shape about my clothes. . . ."

John closes the catsup incident by making it a "bad day" glitch, a "misunderstanding" put to bed. His B and J boys are calm. As the boys line-up for school at the B-wing door, John has already spotted a bully, and he takes the boy aside and whispers in his ear, "I want you to stay away from Watson and Perez today. I've got my eyes on you."

Three days later Jorge Consuelo leaves the center. Mary Ann Zeiser waits for him by the door.

"Can I have a hug?"

The boy looks, as if to see if anyone is watching.

For just a few seconds he holds her, the scars of his face pressed on the golden curls—like his mother's head.

As much as you tried to be the same with everybody . . . Mary Ann says to herself. . . .

She will miss this boy.

13

TANGLED HEARTS

They had paraded through her heart— little girls who had been raped by their fathers, hustlers, junkies, alcoholics, runaways, transvestite boys who wanted to wear their pantyhose and lipstick when they went to court to stand in front of the judge. They ranged from nine-year-olds to those who had already crossed the line to adults, from illiterates to teenagers who excelled in school but flunked in life; from boys with heads shaved bald or tufted like a Mohawk or with limp tresses straggling down their backs. They were boys tutored enough to say, "Yes, sir," "No, sir," and "Excuse me," and two minutes later would knock the snot out of anyone who looked at them wrong. Boys with angry eyes. Sad eyes.

They came from families where a father, a mother, a brother were in prison; from families who sent their children out to steal to get something to eat; sons and daughters of doctors and lawyers and judges in the palaces of Cherry Hill; from families where their mothers and grandmothers dispatched their children to the corner to sell drugs; children who had no homes but slept in unlocked cars; children who arrived with bruises and cuts—bullets still bedded in their flesh; those whose socks were rotting on their feet.

America, America, God shed His grace on thee . . .

Bernice Gray didn't want to be social worker anymore. In one week, two weeks, how in God's name could you get teenagers like this to face the realities of their lives? She would move to the midnight shift as shift commander, safe from teenagers who could tangle with her heart. For eight years, she had loved this straggling procession of youngsters who rarely knew how to love.

How many years ago, when Bernice was struggling with her own husband's addiction to alcohol and why he didn't love his children the way her own father had loved her, old Doctor Kahn in Camden had given Bernice a piece of wisdom that she never forgot: "If you haven't been loved, you don't know how." Morris Gray had grown up in foster homes where he had learned to keep the world an arm's length away. He didn't know how. Just like the Youth Center youngsters.

You could never, never be bored with these boys and girls. You'd

discover you loved their humor, their sparkle, their potential, but you
could never shake off the pain. You'd listen to a fourteen-year-old girl
whose mother was putting her up for adoption.

"When your mother doesn't want you, and your father doesn't want
you, no g_d d__n body wants you. Why didn't she just have an
abortion? Why didn't she just let me die that way?" Fourteen years
old. Mixed: Indian-white. No shoes. Shorts. A halter. No clothes. In
six months, not one visit, and the summer would turn to winter, and
Bernice and the women officers would chip together and buy the girl a
coat. Bernice had taken the child up the road to Pine Hill to her
mother, but her mother had a white man now and wanted no
memories of her dark-skinned child and the girl's Indian father.
Children had a way of getting in the way of new love affairs.

Bernice was tough as beautiful nails. She said she had finally
learned not to take the children's problems to her heart. I wasn't sure.
Heart problems, blood pressure, had put Bernice in the hospital three
times that year.

For eight years he had looked beyond dirty clothing, smelly breath,
and dirty sneakers, always looking for the hurt inside. Where did this
boy come from? Where did he want to go? Sometimes not combing the
hair—the dirty clothes Bernice told officers, that was a boy's way of
saying, "Look at me. Somebody PLEASE look at me." She wanted
officers to teach the boys to comb their hair and brush their teeth in
the mornings, to wash their hands after they used the toilet. These
youngsters needed basic stuff. The stacks of soiled underclothes in the
laundry room showed that some kids didn't even wipe.

If officers never saw the real person under a thousand coats of
protective armor, a thousand boys and girls a year, Bernice had looked
beneath the crust at the rawness. She had felt the pain.

To map Bernice's role at the new Youth Center was to map the
center's rebirth from chrysalis to butterfly. There were those who had
hated every change from dungeon to the spotlight of national awards,
trails of visitors coming to our doors. Bernice had never needed to side
with any group; she said that she didn't need to come to work to get
her loving. Some people resented that the woman wasn't a joiner.
Taking a child's humanness away, girls in shapeless house dresses—
Bernice had not joined any of it in her heart. They had had their turn.

It was Bernice and her friend Dorothy Thomas who against all
orders had unlocked the doors to let freeholder Lewis Katz come in—
in 1973, the year that fourteen-year-old George Dunbar hanged
himself. Dorothy had once worked as a domestic in Lewis Katz's
home. Bernice always told me woman-to-woman that my coming was
"a breath of fresh air," opening doors that people were refusing to open
before. Bernice had harnessed teenage energy to change the place,
watching them blossom with gifts of responsibility: creating the
Cloud Nine Shelter student council, appointing student welcomers for

boys and girls just coming in, student inspectors in charge of daily Clean-and-Tidy checks of all the bedrooms. The student inspection team was a hundred times tougher in their inspections than the staff ever was.

The state caseworker would be returning a runaway to Atco, preaching all the way that the boy had to give his family another chance, and one hour later the boy was being picked up by the police, walking back miles and miles to go to the Youth Center's Cloud Nine Shelter. You had to understand, he said. At Cloud Nine, he was the boy who welcomed each new resident.

Now here, on a day in May when the whole world was turning new and green with spring, Bernice was asking me to change her role—not to be a social worker anymore—to bury herself in the silence and peace of the midnight shift.

I have blocked it all out. Did she write it in a note? Did she sit across the glass-topped desk? Like a memory that hurts too much, that I wanted to bury somewhere, not one detail remains in my mind.

Bernice Gray was my alter ego. I anchored the Youth Center. Bernice anchored the shelter at Cloud Nine across the street. She held youthworkers spellbound in her training sessions on incest and child abuse and child prostitution. She joined me on television talk shows. When we chopped down and split the logs of the giant tulip poplar hit by lightning at my house, Bernice joined the crowd at the Saturday log splitting, lunching on cornbread and ribs and black-eyed peas around my dining room table. We shared a belief in children.

Together we knew that in this place if we held a teenager in our hands—some mother's child for one day, one week, one month, awaiting a trial, a youngster in the growingest time of his life—we would surround him with opportunities to learn. It was time to stop the chorus of it's-not-my-job. Of course it was our job. *Shaping America is everybody's job.* Turning children around had to start somewhere. So why not start with us?

From my first day at the Youth Center, Bernice had cheered me on.

I had known from the beginning that in the great Out There, there was an angry horde of Philistines who didn't believe this place was for reaching kids. I didn't need to take a poll or put my finger to the wind. There was a roar of sentiment across the land that youth centers like this were for holding—or better yet, for starting the punishment quickly!

I came home from national conferences with tales of America's children still being locked in pretrial detention cells twenty-three hours a day—solitary confinement before they had even stood before a judge for his word of *innocent* or *guilty*! In my own state, there were metal rings on cell walls in detention for stringing up a youngster by the wrists. Stealing a child's rights in America—you could still get by with it. Teenagers didn't know the law, and neither did their parents.

Moms were poor; they could barely survive. Dads? You didn't even have to ask. And no one blinked an eye.

To punish or to teach? To hold or to help them grow? The questions were gussied up with fancy words by judges, police, and youth workers as the "philosophy debate."

You walked in the front door of any youth center in America and knew before the door clicked, locked, behind you which philosophy ruled the children there—the smell, the colors, the sounds, the air, the expressions on the faces of the children and the staff.

I had lost a partner. Again.

Teenagers sleep softly in the darkness of the midnight shift, like babies pressed to their mother's breast. Here and there in the younger boys' wing, a boy curls in a ball under the white warmth of his blanket, sucking his thumb. Officers in sweatsuits and sneakers walk softly on room checks and headcounts, logging the suicide watch, washing the midnight laundry. A lone boy arrives in the night.

There is peace

>—◆—○—◆—◄

Claude Seligman's hand-sketched picture hangs above the bricks and barn beams that form my bookcase on my office wall. Claude drew it for me before he left.

A picture drawn by a boy who wanted to die.

I ponder about that picture—the hand of man stretched out and reaching for the hand of God. All framed in black. Copied from Michelangelo. The hand of God reaching for the man's.

Reaching. That's how I think of it now.

Claude's sketch is the centerpiece of my "story wall"—surrounded by Stanley's sketch of a Great Dane; D. J.'s horses; her nude; a six-inch strip of red-white-and-blue ribbon from the ribbon-cutting that opened the new Youth Center; and Stevie's graduation picture, always splashed with sunshine from the skylight high above a jungle of plants. Stevie from Day One. I collect memories and stories. Sometimes when I get deep with a child, we stand in front of my "story wall." The pictures talk.

The first time I saw Claude Seligman, he was lying like a dead body on the North Side floor under the fan in the old building. In the hallway. A transistor radio was by his ear. Claude didn't move.

A phone call from the court had warned me about the boy: A very disturbed seventeen-year-old coming in for armed robbery. The phone call said the boy was wrapped in a death wish . . . get a psychologist on standby.

Claude Seligman had arrived with military boots laced to his knees, and after he had spent days lying on the floor, he switched to sitting, numb, a statue on the edge of his bed—drawing for hours. He wouldn't speak. Drawing, sketching nothing but guns. Black, brooding guns . . . guns . . . guns. Black metal, stiff with death. Claude's whole life was preoccupied with guns. Linda Portwood, the social worker, could usually connect with a boy in a few minutes. She did it by listening. With Claude, it took days. There was only silence for Linda to listen to.

When he finally talked, you could listen to the boy's story and wonder if he had ever really lived. Bouncing around with so many relatives, so many parts of the country. Claude always seemed puzzled when you asked him what place he called home. In the tenth grade he had dropped out of high school and just roamed. Born in Toledo, Ohio, to a broken family, he was the father-protector of his little brother, Jimmy. Jimmy, he said, was his big job . . . the centerpiece of his life. Jimmy. He would be a father to Jimmy. If Claude had never had a father, Jimmy would have one in Claude.

Then Jimmy ran away from home. Jimmy and cops and court.

That was the problem. Claude said he failed at every job he had ever touched. School, family, love affairs. Failed with Jimmy, too.

He was weary. Weary of hands that reached and never touched. Of hearts that reached for hope and never . . . never . . .

Claude began to think of death. Almost one in five American high school students has planned to take his own life; one in twelve has attempted to kill himself.[1]

With Claude, maybe he would use a gun.

Guns were his life. Maybe guns could also be his death—death in a blaze of glory. Guns . . . death . . . peace . . . the ultimate success . . .

On a summer morning in July, he decided to rob a bank. Planned in one short hour . . . the perfect suicide. It would look like an armed robbery. Armed robbery of a bank. Like Bonnie and Clyde in the movie, going out in a hail of bullets . . . pulling the gun . . . cocking the trigger. And the cops would have to shoot. The girlfriend who had just walked out on him would get the message.

In the blind alley behind the Third National Bank in Camden, the kid who had robbed the bank and the cop who had chased him there . . . leveling their guns at one another in point-blank range. *BAM. BAM. BAM.*

But neither fired.

The Camden cop who faced him down didn't believe in playing Dick Tracy, or Kojak. Not taking a man's life if he could help it.

Claude saw it as another failure.

Linda Portwood, the Youth Center social worker, sat on his bed next to the boy for days in total silence until he felt safe to talk. Sat and admired his drawings. Turned the pages. "You're very good," she told him. A trail of North Side boys lined up to his room, attracted by

---

[1]Center for Disease Control.

Claude's notebook full of guns. Linda had a way with boys. They opened up. In the old musty building, Linda Portwood commissioned him the Youth Center Artist in Residence.

Color flowed from his fingers. When Linda finally coaxed him away from his bed, Claude painted giant red and yellow and blue balloons around the building's entrance halls. And when he was done with the balloons, for days he painted blue and red supergraphics, zooming, like happy directional markers pointing students to the schoolroom. The institutional beiges and creams disappeared. This thin, blue-eyed blond dressed in Army-surplus greens always so military looking, Claude had made the walls talk. The school and office wing suddenly alive with color for teenagers.

He could color the walls with magic but never his own life. Claude never smiled. Black thoughts. Dark moods. He was paralyzed by darkness. Like a boy burying his head under a giant pillow day and night. No sunlight. No fresh air. Only darkness.

One day Claude, paintbrush in hand, plopped down in the red stuffed chair next o my desk. As usual, his pant legs were stuffed into his laced-up boots.

"I have a picture for you." He handed me a roll of white sketch paper. "I drew it for your wall." He waited while I unrolled it. I could see that he had more on his mind than giving me the drawing.

"You think the judge would let me go to Upward Bound?"

Upward Bound at the community college two miles away was a catch-up program for promising students who had fallen behind. Upward Bound became the first steps that led to Claude's release on probation. He wanted to be a policeman, he said. Claude the Cop. He started college.

He would come to the campus for therapy, stopping in to visit. "I had another fight with my girl," he told me one day. He had come back to finish painting his murals. We talked as we painted together. There was the day he told me he blew out his girlfriend's door with a shotgun. "She locked me out," he told me.

Guns still. I shuddered.

Then there was the day he told me that he had dropped out of college. Too much stress right now, he said.

Painting supergraphics on the hallway wall, we talked about easing up . . . giving himself time.

Linda Portwood would not give up on Claude. Linda was a Quaker from the open spaces of America's Midwest. Like mine, her mission was to save the world by reaching its kids. We were partners. Weeks turned into months. Through handyman jobs he did at her house, painting and fix-up, she kept in touch with the boy. It allowed them to talk. And now he could talk about his pain. Little pieces at a time. Simple things like, Should I get up? Should I eat lunch? It was all too much.

Suddenly the calls and visits stopped. Linda ached with worry. "No calls. No visits."

We were standing in the hallway outside her office when the telephone rang. I saw her pick it up to speak. Linda started to weep.

She didn't have to say. I knew. He had done it with a gun.

Hanging above the bookcase on my wall is the picture that Claude drew for me before he left. Before he killed himself. I look at it every day. All framed in black. Copied from Michelangelo, the hand of man stretched out to reach the hand of God.

And then I look away.

Claude . . . and the hands of a thousand boys and girls a year . . . Sometimes our hands reach out . . . but never touch.

Not long after that, Linda resigned and took a job as a counselor with the Family Court.

▷━◁▸━◦━◂◁━◃

Bernice moved into the quiet of the midnight shift. For a week she anchored herself over porcelain, her body retching every night, adjusting to staying awake through eight hours of darkness.

HUNGRY GHOSTS

With my morning cup of coffee every morning, I read about America's hungry ghosts. It's a daily parade downplayed in two- and three-inch stories—almost ordinary, almost routine—in local papers.

**TEENAGERS ROBBED OF JEWELRY
BY THREE GIRLS WIELDING A RAZOR**

**CAMDEN PIZZA DELIVERYMAN
REPORTS BEING ROBBED OF $380**

**CAMDEN GIRL, 15, IS RAPED
WHILE TAKING SHORTCUT HOME**

**THREE MEN BEAT, ROB VICTIM
TO GAIN $27 AND SNEAKERS**

**EAST CAMDEN WOMAN ROBBED
OF JEWELRY OUTSIDE HER HOME**

**GIRL SPRAYED IN FACE
WITH CHEMICAL, ROBBED**

**N. CAMDEN MAN, 25, ATTACKED,
ROBBED OF LEATHER JACKET**

**THREATS OF VIOLENCE,
SHAKE HOLY-NAME CONGREGATION**

**EAST CAMDEN MAN TELLS POLICE
OF ATTACK BY SIX CHILDREN**

**CAMDEN WOMAN ROBBED
OF GOLD EARRINGS BY YOUTHS**

**PENNSAUKEN MAN STABBED
OUTSIDE EAST CAMDEN TAVERN**

**WOMAN GRABBED, THEN ROBBED
OF $350 ON EAST CAMDEN CORNER**

Saleed reminds me of hungry ghosts from my childhood in China. *A hungry ghost is a neglected spirit. A spirit bent on revenge. The spirit of someone who dies without leaving children. If you do not feed their spirits, if you launch them alone, the Chinese say, launch them into the Other World . . . unprotected . . . unnurtured . . . unsupported with the bonding of family rituals—these hungry ghosts come back to haunt you—with mischief and terrible paybacks.*

The Chinese pour time and money into pacifying these spirits. At the annual Festival of Hungry Ghosts under blossoming peach trees, I have watched my Chinese friends offer mandarin oranges, almond cookies, bottles of wine, red cans of Chinese Coca Cola, poured out on the mounded graves to appease the hungry ghosts. In elaborate family rituals they burn bundles of paper money, dispatch it up in flames and smoke. Red firecrackers by the hundreds explode over the ancestral graves to bribe the spirits to go away—all painstaking rituals to keep the ghosts from creating disaster.

Saleed is one of Camden's hungry ghosts—a drug dealer. Fifteen years old. Youth gangs today are better armed than their predecessors. Switchblades and baseball bats have been replaced by AK-47 and Uzi assault weapons. Police arrested him—this time—as he swooped down with his "little crew" on Woodrow Wilson High School for a payback shootout.

"Our posse ain't mess with small guns—mainly AK-47s and Uzis. I watched a guy get blown away this summer—I was standing maybe four feet away—three white dudes from out the city in their car. That's mostly who comes to buy our stuff. White dudes. He was trying to stiff our man, drivin' away fast without payin'. Three of them injured, killed—I don't really know. Our big guy told us 'Don't go out on the street for a few days.'"

Soured drug deals and gang violence—Saleed says he feels no remorse.

"People respect us—they's maybe 200 members of our Black Posse on Twenty-fourth Street. Don't nobody bother us. We don't bother them. Shootings is maybe only two times a year—mainly over gang rivalry or someone tryin' to stiff us."

A hungry ghost. Only ten years old and he was already a witness to violence: brutal fists in his own home. Saleed was born in 1976, amidst America's euphoria of celebrating its two-hundredth birthday. Gun salutes, firecrackers, parades to celebrate the birth of the one land in this world where all men are created equal.

Not quite equal.

"I learned to tie my sneakers by myself," Saleed says. "The streets have been my father and my mother."

In the quiet suburb where I live, new puppies at curbside get more instruction—"Heel" and "Stay" and "Go"—than Saleed ever got.

"Crossin' the street—red lights, yellow lights—" Saleed tells me, "I learned to cross them by myself watchin' people do it." No one to hold a mittened hand at the red light. No pat on the back. No hand on the shoulder.

"This old guy stopped me on the street when I was coughin' in the rain one day—ask me if I was okay. I was maybe ten. Right then and there he took me to the doctor. I was runnin' a fever, and the doctor gave me some cough syrup.

"I wished this old guy was my father. My father was in prison."

"Your mother?"

His mouth freezes. I have moved off-limits. His mother is a drug addict, my social worker tells me. That tells me as much about her son as it does of her: Young children of an addict mother suffer rock-bottom poverty, homelessness, and usually a total lack of supervision. They are robbed of childhood. Instant adults. Trying to take care of Mom. Raising little brothers and sisters. "They ain't too much we can do but try to keep the lights on and pay the rent."

Saleed's words stumble along with long pauses in between. "Alone . . . they ain't a feelin' in the world like bein' alone. Eleven years old . . . abandoned . . . father in prison . . . mother gone."

It is a child's ultimate fear—being abandoned by a parent. He looks out at a dangerous world he can never learn to trust.

"When it came time to eat, there was nobody there to feed me.

"What was I s'pose to do? Be hungry?

"Dog food. Trash cans. Just to eat, I did things I wish I never did.

"Was I gonna go to school in rags? I got clothes from wherever I got 'em from. Alone and abandoned. That's how I lived."

Saleed is one of a growing tribe of children who raise themselves on America's streets. They are children robbed of their childhood. They steal. They sell their bodies—sell drugs—to manage a life of daily catastrophes.

"You can steal from the trashcans when you be hungry," Saleed goes on. "You can't steal no hug. Someone has to give it. I sometimes wished for a whuppin' when I needed one."

Off and on since he was eleven years old, the Youth Center has been cupping its sheltering hands around this boy. He stumbled into our family of lost souls, escorted by sheriff's officers, a child caught with drugs. We raised him. He has been our son. He is fifteen now. Our officers Dot Stanton and Gwen Walters, and his teacher, Brenda Reid, have been his mothers.

To create a family for himself on Thanksgiving Day—a furlough—he wandered over to Dot Stanton's house. Miss Dot.

"I never did go home," he says. "Just hung round the streets." A cheese steak on the street was his Thanksgiving dinner.

Saleed has no family traditions, no good memories of turkeys, or ham, or a grandpa's family stories.

I try to imagine: Never remember making gingerbread men from tubs of dough in the kitchen sink? Never remember sausage-and-rice stuffing in the Thanksgiving turkey? I can't even imagine the loss in my life—to be robbed of years of memories in my heart from family Thanksgiving and Christmas. Gaping holes where love should be.

Back in college when I was learning how to be a teacher, professors pounded into the heads of every one of us that we should teach children to be masters of their destiny. Not victims of fate. Now I sit looking at Saleed. Master of his own destiny. Sure. Not one teacher, not one teacher-training textbook told me about boys like Saleed.

"I never sat on Santa's lap when I was a kid," he tells me, "but I always had a wish—for a family that care—a mom, a dad, a grandpop, a grandmom."

Saleed's words haunt me through the Christmas holidays. Childhood pictures shape us: We become who we are, all our troubles, all our passions, all the things that are bound to come up and face us— from these childhood memories. *Memories are the family album that tell us who we are.* This boy has no good memories, no traditions, no rituals to glue him to a family, nothing to glue him to mainstream America. He belongs to no one.

As Martin Luther King's holiday approaches, Saleed posts his own "I Have A Dream" essay on the bulletin board in the school corridor:

"I have a dream that one day I have a family of my own and have a peaceful life."

The boy has never come close.

"No matter how much I wished . . . no way. I never knew one 'together' family—they was all messed up with drugs, abuse, kids gettin' no attention." To give himself a brother, he tapes a snapshot of a teenager over his bed, his Youth Center teacher Brenda Reid's son.

Saleed doesn't know how to play. Yes, there was a small park at the end of the street, but no one he knew played there. In the city, a lonely park is a danger zone, the hunting ground for drug addicts, prostitutes, and thieves. All the boy's friends were in the drug trade. At fifteen, he still didn't know how to ride a bicycle. When he wanted to dream, he sneaked away alone to the lighthouse along the Cooper River Park, the next town over—a boy's lonely hideaway.

Raiding trash cans was kid stuff. Selling marijuana on the Twenty-fourth Street drug strip was grown-up business that put food in his stomach and clothes on his back. He was ten.

The two-hundred-member Black Posse that owned the Twenty-fourth Street drug trade imposed no initiation rituals—no muggings or shootings or killings to prove his worth to the posse. He just blended in.

Anyway, Saleed had cousins in the group, so he got invited to join. In America's cities, homeless children turn up in gang neighborhoods, wanting to join. The gang opens its arms and lets them in. Joining a drug gang gives economic survival—and much, much more. It gives homeboy love. Like Saleed, they find a home—a family that will kill for them.

"You can make $4000—$5000 a day sellin'. Cocaine. Marijuana. We worked in shifts. The Big Guy had maybe seven, eight of us sellin' after school, from 4 to 12.

"School—I definitely go to school. I want to be someone. I have this dream of being a psychiatrist. Good at talkin'. Relatin' to people. 'Cept for maybe Thursdays and Fridays, I make myself go to school."

"Not Thursdays and Fridays?"

"That's money day. Payday for a lot of people."

I ask him about the girls who don't have money for drugs.

"You mean the geezers? (A geezer is an addict—a scrawny, starving addict.) Trade them drugs for sex—her house, your house, any 'bandoned house nearby. Could be a girl fifteen, or a woman forty." He pauses.

"Blow jobs. But most ever'body use a condom these days." He was twelve, he says, when he started trading drugs for sex. Not often, he says. Not sex every day. His preferences these days are Nikes, jean suits, 1.8 Toyotas.

Saleed has raised himself. But consider who has shaped him: By the time he is eighteen years old, he will have watched 26,000 murders on television, he will know about high-school football stars in North Jersey shoving baseball bats and broomhandles into the vagina of a retarded girl with an IQ of sixty-four. He will be part of a tough crowd who prefer to listen to rap tales of drive-by shootings, gang violence, and stealing O.P.P. (other people's property).[1]

Children are the prime consumers of violent TV images: They also commit the majority of violent crimes in the United States. Stomp, crush, kill—the steps to what they want. Numbed by TV knifings, shootings, and rapes.

A boy who wonders if he himself will be alive tomorrow, Saleed is dangerous. He is not awed by death or injury. He has never had a life, never known gentleness. He wears a fearlessness that gives him power in a world shaped by guns, shootings, violence. Throughout the Youth Center, his voice bellows above everybody else's. He faces down every challenge, nose to nose. He sets his goal to reign as undisputed king of the jungle.

Officers pen urgent warnings in the Behavior Logbook: WATCH SALEED!

From the first day he was admitted in the fall, Saleed made a vow when he passed my door: "I ain't never gonna go into your office. Never. It be nicer than anythin' I have in my entire house."

---

[1]Jonathan Kozol, *Savage Inequalities*, 1991.

So I was surprised when he thrust his head into my office after lunch one day.

"'n I talk to you?" He sat down in the squeaking blue swivel chair across from my desk, uncomfortable about recanting his vow.

"You write a letter for me to the judge?" He has this way of cocking his head and looking at me through the corner of his eye. "'m goin' to court on Monday." For good boys, my letters have a reputation—they aim to balance the scales of justice in their favor.

We talked for half an hour—of ugly streets and beautiful dreams—before he looked over his left shoulder to the artwork mounted on colored construction paper on the long wall above my bookcase.

"Kids draw those pictures?"

It was time for Saleed to meet what I call my "story wall," where every single picture has a story. He pointed to the large penciled poster in the center, mounted on black posterboard—Michelangelo's hand of man reaching for the hand of God.

"Claude drew that for me before he left."

"Draw good."

"He's dead now. Blew his brains out with a gun."

"For real?" Saleed got up and looked at the small signature penciled neatly in the corner.

"Larry did that one." I pointed to a yellowing sketch of a Great Dane. "Larry's dead. Stabbed in the eye in a drug bust in California after he left here. One of my boys—from Cherry Hill. Father's a doctor."

"That one with the horses . . ." I pointed to a picture etched in pastels. "That's from D. J. The last time she stopped by she had just had her third baby—each one by a different man." I thought of a blue-eyed girl with golden hair, playing her guitar. "She said she'd been on drugs," I said. "The baby was born missing some fingers."

"And this is Stevie. That's his graduation picture. His mom brought it to me when he graduated from junior college. Made the Dean's list." I always keep Stevie where the sunlight streams over him from the skylight, a beautiful black youth with a face full of hope.

They teach you tricks and techniques in this business to help you survive: Remain emotionally detached. Call them clients. For me it never worked. Saleed was not a client. He was my child, a boy all tangled in my heart. On top of that I was pouring my best into him. When I poured my best, I expected to win. But nothing about the boy in front of me told me I would win. I felt my eyes beginning to brim. Maybe the first time I'd felt tears so close in front of one of my boys. Would I myself have come up short without the special attention—yes, and love—of people around me? In this boy's life, every set of brakes has failed—family, school, neighborhood. Until he met Youth Center volunteers, the Reverend and Mrs. Cooper, church was nothing.

"When you get ready to go to college, Saleed, you come to me and I'll write a letter. College. You have it in you." We were both looking up at Stevie. "Don't play get-over for a letter to the judge when you haven't earned it."

Spitting out food at mealtime in the cafeteria till his officers banned him from eating with the group, shouting down the nurse in health class, bullying. He knew that I knew.

But I couldn't let him quit.

Life can be tough. But it's a lot tougher when I try to change other people—shape them into my image of what they ought to be. How do you force a boy to look at reality when it's the last thing he wants to do?

I knew the answer: You don't. Because you can't.

A boy decides to change only when change is better than the hell he's constructed around him. He has to hit rock bottom. I wasn't sure Saleed was there—bottomed out, hopeless in the pit of his stomach, desperate for something else . . . knowing . . . impossible to sink any deeper.

"I can't cotton the rough edges your life has given you. I wish I could. Cotton and cushion away all the bad parts. Make everything that's happened to you go away. Give you a mother and father. I will never know how that felt to grow up the way you did.

"I don't know if you will turn it around or not. You can. I don't know if you will. But I tell you, I believe that things you believe in can come true." I motioned to the drawings. "Every one of those people up on that wall sat in that chair where you're sitting. In this room, it's easy to be good. Every one of them . . . we dreamed together—just like you and me together. We talked deep."

I ached with hope for this boy. Everything Saleed had ever done he had accomplished on his own.

My voice softened so he'd have to concentrate. We both looked up to the story wall. "Claude is dead . . . Larry is dead . . . D.J. is gone. Stevie's a college graduate."

Elie Wiesel, Holocaust survivor and Nobel laureate, once said: "One must not cry here. If you begin, you will not stop. If only the walls could speak, if only the trees and clouds could testify."

Reaching into a drawer by my typewriter, I pulled out a paper headlined "_____'s Dream" and assigned him to fill in the page, writing "Saleed's Dream." "Write me the steps you have to take to make your dream come true."

"I gonna go back to school," he said, reaching for my paper. "Serious. Catch up in school. Be somebody."

I saw fragile hope.

In January, Saleed gets a rival in B-wing—Daniel. Daniel has been returning off and on since the age of twelve. We have raised both of these boys. Saleed and Daniel. They have been our sons.

"You're back?"

"It was a mistake this time," Daniel tells me with all his usual charm. Except for the snapshot posted over his bed—of him and his handgun—I think of him as a teddy bear.

"My girl at home ... we was gonna get married January first. She say she prayin' for me to step outa darkness into sunshine." In B-wing, he preaches cooperation and good behavior, charms the boys into his orbit.

Saleed is another story. On every shift, his behavior is a series of ups and downs.

In the cafeteria on a sub-zero January night, a chubby ten-year-old in a new, red, Christmas sweatsuit sits eating dinner with the older boys. Up the street from a mile or so away, a frustrated stepfather has been bent on teaching his hookey-playing son a lesson with an hour-long visit to the Youth Center. For a child, this is Scared Straight, an inside look at what happens to boys in real trouble. The boy is playing with his mashed potatoes, his voice frozen in a whisper.

Most of the boys are acting tough, winking at each other across the table as they raise the noise level in the cafeteria. Boldfaced overacting. In my office down the hall I listen in amazement: Saleed's voice—gentle, almost soft.

"School's gonna help you," he tells the child, competing against the hum of the dishwasher in the kitchen. Almost like a streetwise bully cupping a puppy in his grisly hands: It's a picture that haunts me as I drive home.

"It's okay to be 'in' with the group, try to impress them, but you gotta stay in school." The voice is almost fatherly. That's what haunts me. This boy who is always ready to fight, who walks in a perpetual "I-dare-you-touch-me" stance, who swoops his crew down on a public high school for a payback shootout—tonight he's gentle.

"Just a little kid. In a kinda way, he was me," Saleed says later. "In a way I felt kinda bad. Guys tryin' to scare him. I try on a reg'lar level 'splain to him 'bout school. He was listenin' to me, asking me all kinda questions. . . ."

"Old heads" and young boys represent an important institution in the traditional black community. At the dinner table, Saleed has settled in as an "old head," passing on to a young boy his wisdom of school and family and respect. "Old heads" help young boys to become men. Saleed has started preaching the message of "Do something with your life."

The father reaching out to a little boy: How do we capture this side of him and make it stick? How do we get a "hard core" teenager to build his self-esteem by helping someone else?

After school the next day, I invite Ageem back from his home up the street for a private conversation with Saleed in my office. I watch them settle on the couch—at one end, Saleed, a wiry teenager who never was a child, and at the other, a lively ten-year-old, chubby from cheeseburgers and too much television, a babyface with growing pains at home and school. Saleed has something to give this child.

To leave the boys alone on the couch, I busy myself with paperwork at my desk. I break the ice. "Ageem's a pretty name."

"It means *prince*."

"Swahili?"

"I don't know. Something like that."

Saleed has his chinos rolled up to just below his knees, showing legs misshaped by childhood malnutrition. He looks with admiration at the child's stonewashed green dungarees.

"Just went to school today chillin'?" Saleed asks.

"Uh-huh."

Ageem settles at the far end of the couch, within easy reach of my bird's nest and the Play-doh fort.

"You have fun in school? What you do today?"

"Music. Eat lunch. Do my work. Have some tests."

"Have some tests?"

"I got good grades on my tests."

"Yeh? What you get?"

"I got 85 in language, I got 92 on math, and B on my spellin' test."

"Smart, huh? So you do know how to do the work. Why you keep messin' up in school?"

"I don't mess up no more."

"One day and you don't mess up no more."

"One day here—that was a good one day. Yeh, two hours can change your whole life."

"Two hours can't change yo' whole life."

"It did. It did."

"You don't want to come here, huh?"

"To visit you. But not to come here."

Saleed abruptly changes the subject. "How you think it feel if you ain't got no mom or dad?"

"Sad? Alone?"

"Don't you think you can make it without yo' mom an' dad?"

"No."

"Why not?"

"'Cause. Nobody would be there to take care of me."

"You don't know how to take care of yo'self?" Saleed shakes his head. "That's good." The voices are so soft that I can hardly hear them. But I can sense Saleed's disbelief. A child who survived alone from dog food and trashcans—long before he was ten, he sits grasping to understand a pampered childhood.

Ageem thinks Saleed should understand the obvious. "But I don't know how to cook yet."

"Oooh . . . you don't know how to cook. That's the only thing, yeh?"

"No," Ageem's voice squeaks. "It's just I don't have no money. And I don't know how to cook."

"Ahhh. You ain't got no money. Don't know how to cook."

"No one to fix me cheeseburgers."

Saleed shakes his head, as though in wonder. "Cheeseburgers! Can't live without no cheeseburgers, huh? You 'preciate yo' mom and dad, don't you? I'm sure he loves you like his real son."

"Um-hmm. I'm going to the Sixers' game, Monday."

"Goin' to the Sixers' game!" For a fleeting moment, Saleed loses his "old head" dignity. This is kid-to-kid talk—the tone of one boy gasping enviously about the other's rare baseball cards. "Tchhh! Ain't NEVER been to a Sixers' game. Ain't too many kids been to a Sixers' game. Why yo' dad takin' you? 'Cause you ast him?"

"Uh-uh." He shakes his head. "Surprise me."

"Yeh?" A kid attending a professional basketball game in Philadelphia? Saleed ponders the wonder of it then launches into a monologue.

"Somethin' you gotta learn, everybody in the world not born with silver spoons in their mouth. Some had no spoons at all. A lotta them made it, because they wanted to."

I get the feeling that Saleed is talking to himself now.

"'Cause you grew up with nothin', that don't mean you gotta die with nothin'. You had no family; make a family. You had no education; get one. Can't read; learn to read. You can't sit there and say, 'I'm messed up 'cause my family was messed up.' That's wrong. You messed up because you wanta be messed up. If they was messed up, then that shoulda be your example not to be messed up. You don't wanta be the same way your father was—high, drunk . . . whatever . . . abusive. You gotta concentrate on what you wanta be in life. Concentrate on your goals.

"I never really had no mom and dad . . . to ask them questions. They was never around. Had to grow up, learn by myself. That's hard. to do.

"You gotta lot of opportunity, good background, gotta good family. You can be whatever you wanta be. What you gotta do is want to be it. You always got someone behind you to help you out.

"When you got a mom and dad, you gotta 'preciate it, 'cause you only get one mom and dad. And once they gone, you by yo'self. Only get one. You have 'em once, you try to take advantage of that, try to keep 'em as long as you can."

Saleed's voice is the deep bass of a grown man. I find it hard to believe I am listening to a fifteen-year-old.

"You never disrespect your mom and dad, 'cause they the ones who put you here. And you try to pray every day. You pray?"

Ageem has snuggled closer on the couch to Saleed. "My dad taught me how to pray."

"That's good. See, my dad never teach me how to pray. I had to teach myself . . . watch other people . . . that's how I picked it up. Now you know how to pray, you should pray every day for your sister, your dad, and some people you know that need help and wish them better in life.

"Everybody don't have it like you—'body don't have no jacket like this—'body have no pants like this. Don't everybody go to Sixers' game. People don't have no money to afford it, nobody to take them.

"You have advantage over a lot of people. You should always try to keep that advantage. When you lose it, it's gone—you can make the best outa it, but you still can't get it back.

"School gives you ways to better yourself when you grow up. That's why you should always have yo' mind in school.

"Play. You can play, laugh, joke in school—but never get to the point where you ain't followin' directions.

"Like the way you was readin' that stuff yesterday in our unit after dinner, that surprise me."

Ageem's eyes won't leave Saleed's.

"Ain't too many people in all them boys that can read like you did. You didn't mispronounce no words. I was really impressed. 'Daag! He know all them words.' That show that you take time to listen to the teacher, what she sayin'. You was readin' those things like you was in high school. I was like . . . Daag! And the other kids . . . like, 'you see the way he was readin' that?'

"School ain't the problem gonna get you locked up here. Doin' a crime *is*. And not listenin', or followin' instruction, or not askin' permission." Saleed lists the Youth Center's daily "success skills" again.

"A person that don't know nothin' can't get no job, can't support a family. You want a family?"

"Uh-huh."

"Want kids, don't you? Married and everythin'?"

"Uh-huh."

"Ever'body do. Some people—once they have a family, they don't know how they gonna support them. A lotta kids, they got kids and they ain't supportin' them. And that's just the next generation is gonna live a worser life than the generation before—as messed up as I was, 'cause for a kid to grow up with nobody supportin' them, the kid might as well not been born."

Saleed keeps coming back to his own story. "How you think kids feel that don't get the help you got?"

"Lost?"

"They do feel lost. They are lost. When you by yourself, they ain't any feelin' in the world like that—bein' by yourself. Nobody to love you. Nothin'. Psssh! Come holidays, Christmas, and stuff. Ain't nobody gettin' you nothin'. Ain't nobody 'round you. What you gonna do?" The boy doesn't really expect an answer. "They's nothin' you can do. Live without. That's how I grew up.

"Come holidays—wasn't nobody round to buy me nothin', so I guess I didn't have nothin'.

"Didn't have nothin' for Christmas, birthday. Never got nothin' for my birthday. You always get somethin' for your birthday, don't you?"

Ageem nods.

"People out there wish they had it like you. They don't. So that's why you always gotta take advantage of what you got." He pauses. "Why they send you here to visit?"

"School."

"I don't see nothin' wrong with you. Honor roll and stuff."

"The first day of school I got caught."

"Got caught what? Cursin'?" Saleed struggles to keep incredulity from spreading across his face. Cursing in the schoolyard looks almost like sainthood compared to his own intercepted plan for a shoot-out at the high school.

". . . guy cursed at me. I cursed at him back."

"What they do?"

"I had to stand up against the wall."

"In the corner?"

"No. Outside—made me stand up against the wall until the teacher came."

"Crazy, huh? That's the only thing you be doin'?

Ageem looks over to me. "Saleed's nice! He talks to me and stuff."

"What do you think Saleed's gonna turn out to be?" I ask.

"Nice. A doctor. A computer expert."

"Saleed had some advice for you. Do you have any advice for him?"

"Stay outa trouble. Stay in school. Go to college. Get a job. Be good so he won't have to come back here."

Saleed isn't sure the child has absorbed the message. "You gotta remember, man, that education get you far in life. . . . Education not gonna come lookin' for you. *You* gotta look for it. Once you find it, you gotta put it to your advantage. Too many people is dyin' 'cause they didn't know how to take care of theirself. . . . They always thought that someone was gonna be there to take care of them. They don't know how to read, write, do math—get a job, so they can't make money, so they rob, steal, and get killed, or end up in jail.

"People like her . . ." he nods over to me ". . . she help people. Everything she says will always be in my head."

He moves into kid talk. "If somebody hits you, that don't mean you gotta hit 'em back. Tell somebody he hit you. Let them deal with it. Walk off. 'Cause hittin' you ain't gonna hurt you. Gettin' suspended from school will hurt you."

As we walk to the front entrance, Ageem ticks off Saleed's lessons for me: "I gotta stay in school. Joke whenever but not too seriously, because you gotta get your work done first." He looks up at me.

"Am I allowed back for another visit?"

"Well, if you do come back for another visit you have to report to Saleed how you're doing."

The child walks into winter sunshine streaming into the lobby. Saleed walks into the gym and starts shooting baskets with the team. The lock clicks shut behind him.

I walk back to my office, thinking about Saleed's story in the last issue of *WHAT'S HAPPENING*.

TELL ME WHEN I'M WRONG
by SALEED, age 15

When nobody say nothin to you when you be doin somethin wrong—
is the same as not bein wanted. Givin up on you. Wishin you wasn't around.

The way I grew up, people see me do wrong, don't say nothin. Just keep walkin.

I got the message.

What happens to boys like Saleed who feel no hope at fifteen years of age? I hear the answer as a warning for America.

Two weeks later, the panic alarm shrieks its "get-help" summons, shattering the quiet of a routine Monday afternoon. At two o'clock the blue alarm light flashes over the classroom door. I feel myself bracing for what I already know.

Saleed.

Backup officers converge to help those assigned to classroom 123, escorting Saleed, one on each side, to his unit. The boy's white T-shirt is ripped across his chest, exposing bare flesh.

Fists have exploded in the schoolroom. Ripping clothes. Hurtled youngsters cowering for safety along the walls. Tables and chairs toppling. In the law of the jungle, there is room for only one king. Saleed or Daniel. The final standoff.

"You have any miracles?" Robbie Reid, B-unit social worker, asks me. "Daniel and Saleed. Two kids got bruised just now—checked by the nurse. It's been coming."

Saleed, like an abandoned street dog, curling his lip, baring his teeth—wild, untamed—has been out-finessed by Daniel, a pussycat lion with dangerous claws, who smiles his way to the crown.

Robbie and I struggle with options. Can we move him? To the girls' wing? Younger boys' wing? Saleed is just too aggressive.

"Right now five guys in his wing want a piece of him. We can't keep them together." Even in a crisis, Robbie Reid talks softly. "Too dangerous."

"Where is he now?"

"Locked in his room. This thing's not over. Not at all."

Slowly I pick up the phone and arrange a transfer to another center—a trade with neighboring Atlantic County—swapping boys: Saleed for someone else's problem child.

When the sheriff's officers lead the boy away in handcuffs, I cannot bring myself to watch. I can only remember his words:

"Everybody in the world not born with silver spoons in their mouth. Some have no spoons in their mouth."

I have seen a hungry ghost.

>─◆>─O─<◆─<

A child reaches for a mother who isn't there. A father who is gone. Reaches for family memories. Creates his holiday feasts from dog food and garbage cans. While away a holiday, wandering deserted streets. He dreams of family traditions that—for him—do not exist. Americans create puppies and kittens fantasies of childhood. Children like Saleed live a reality that is viciously different. For today, the payback is a dangerous classroom skirmish. I shudder about tomorrow.

We have had a 350 percent increase in births to single mothers in the last thirty years. Divorce is soaring, and more than half of divorced fathers do not see their children. Boys raised without caring and involved fathers are at a higher risk for violent and antisocial behavior.[2]

Shift commander John Golaszewski senses my mood. " 'Raise up a child in the way he should go, and when he is old he will not depart from it.' Sad. Saleed just didn't get any raising." His tone closes the door on hope.

On this cold day in January I watch officers shepherd a defeated boy in a shredded T-shirt. He walks blindly past a hallway bulletin-board posted with his own hand-lettered dream: *I have a dream that someday I have a family of my own and have a peaceful life.*

---

[2]Myriam Miedzian, "Why Johnny Might Grow Up Violent and Sexist (interview), *TIME* magazine (September 16, 1991), p. 18.

15

BONEMEAL

The two men slip almost curiously into the chairs across from my desk. Ron Helmer, the assistant prosecutor, and his chief investigator. A drive from the courthouse. If the watercolors and chalk and pencil drawings on the wall beside him catch him by surprise, I cannot tell. It is student art mounted on red and green and blue posterboard, to catch a visitor's eye. But Ron Helmer is always business. Strictly business. He wants a handle on everything.

"The kid in court—Luis . . ."

Luis, I think to myself. *A special trip by the prosecutor—down-county—to talk to me. Not unheard of, maybe once a year. . . .*

"We figured the boy was coached by a hotshot attorney," he says. "Stopped down to check it out." It's easy to see why Ron Helmer got the top job in the juvenile crime division of the prosecutor's office; his hands-on approach to hooligans and crime leaves nothing to chance. By day he faces down young criminals in the courtroom. By night he talks law and order to neighborhood groups. Most lawyers hate kiddie court in preference for the big stuff. Ron Helmer knows that youth crime is the big stuff. Young people commit the violence. Young people are the victims. Across America about half of all violent crime is committed by youth—and 80 percent of the time, their victim is another youth. About 1,800 adolescents will die this year of violence. Over 100,000 will be treated for violence-related injuries.[1]

I prop my feet up on the stool under my desk to listen while he starts an imitation of Luis in court.

"This kid in front of the judge . . ." Helmer's hand shoots up as though waving for permission, "raises his hand and tells the judge, 'Success Skill Number One—How to Listen' . . . something like that . . ." The man studies the wooden sign on the letter-in, letter-out bin on my desk: *It is better to build boys than to rebuild men.*

I look up at the ceiling and smile. You never know about these kids.

---

[1] "Youth Violence As A Public Health Issue," JDC CLEARINGHOUSE, October 30, 1992.

Luis is the Youth Center's star pupil—a school dropout from a house where no one but him speaks English. No one quite figured how the boy got hooked on "success skills." Maybe it was the dream of being something different. A boy getting hooked on "being somebody" was a giant victory. We were all made poorer by kids who couldn't or wouldn't become contributing members of society.

There were opportunities in the Great Beyond—to go to school, to take a starter job. But poor kids like Luis were usually reluctant or unable to reach for them. Ignoring opportunities—just sitting there— the experts who knew about these things called it the "culture of poverty," turning their backs on the American way of moving up. Now here was a book that Luis could hold in his hand to show him the way. A road map. Luis spent his quiet time in his room at night, back propped up on the desk, knees on his chin so he could look out the windows to the trees beyond the gully. Dog-eared pages marked the "success skills" he was learning: How to listen, How to follow instructions, How to ask permission. You dream of success stories like this. They don't come often.

"How to listen. Did he tell you all four steps?" I ask. Role plays in the boy's paperback, role plays break every skill into easy steps. In residence units the skills are posted in giant letters on posterboard. Blueprints for success. Giant cue cards for the daily role plays after school.

The prosecuter shakes his head, "Complaining to the judge that I didn't follow the rules. . . . Get that." Even Helmer laughs about that—a juvenile delinquent accusing the prosecutor in court. He nods at his investigator. "I didn't follow the rules . . . complaining to the judge that I had interrupted him . . . didn't wait my turn to speak."

"Skill Number One, Step Number Three . . ."—I reach for the paperback book on my shelf—"is 'wait your turn to speak.'" It is no hotshot lawyer that had coached the boy. I know. My officers taught Luis.

Most of the youngsters cannot even imagine the world we dream for them. Luis goes home from court—takes home his "success skills" paperback with him. Says he needs to teach his mom.

How do ideas come to you that change your life?

Sometimes you bump into them and know at that moment you must have them for your own. That's how it was with Structured Learning Training (SLT).

I don't even know the girl's name. The one who grabbed me and held me speechless with something called SLT. She walked me up the stone steps, over the stone bridge with the white picket fence that spanned the lazy murmur of water rippling into a pond. There were apple trees behind the campus. Nothing about it felt like a corrections center—the South Lansing Center for girls—maybe because it had once been a Jehovah's Witness religious center in the Finger Lakes region of lower New York. The stone amphitheater under the trees within reach of the trickle of the brook had once heard the faithful called to God. Today parents and girls crowded the stone seats in the Center's graduation ceremonies. I couldn't take my eyes off the girl. This chubby young tour guide, showing me around, a sparkling adolescent, like the-girl-next-door. She could smile. She could look me in the eye and hold me with her gaze. Like a well-trained publicist for South Lansing, she could fascinate me with success charts on the wall, the goal charts, the charts for exercise and weights. She was pointing. This was the starkly bare bedroom for an entry-level girl. And this was the bedroom cluttered with adolescent treasures of a girl who had earned it all, a girl in control of her own life. I watched teenage exuberance, a girl from a finishing school. Except she wasn't.

She was an end-of-the-line delinquent girl, sentenced and doing time. I watched quite fascinated. I knew all about delinquent girls. Every youth worker I have ever known votes with every finger, every thumb, and every toe that she'd rather work with a teenage boy than with a teenage girl in trouble. The "chivalry factor" damned the girls. The world of judges and police was a world of middle-class men who kept giving bad little girls a break until they had turned into hellcats that no one wanted to touch. That's who arrived at the South Lansing Center, most of them sentenced from the ghettos of New York state— New York City, Albany, Syracuse, Buffalo. The toughest of the tough, they had "bombed out" everywhere else for hitting people, running away. Most had already been in seven different residential settings before they got to this campus. Not one cream puff in the place. Yet here was this girl. My tour guide.

I felt my brain lock onto "receive," wanting for my own youngsters whatever had made this girl so poised and disciplined and confident. I sat the administrator down to learn the secret. The South Lansing Center had held this girl in arm's-length discipline. Like placing a bit in a young filly's mouth—South Lansing did it with all their girls— until she learned to respond to the world of rules. They had tamed her and taught her, step-by-step, these simple skills with hours to practice every day.

Goals to reach. It was an inch-by-inch plan that left not one thing to chance.

Watching that girl was my defining moment. Like the ancient story of Saul of Tarsus being hit by the light from God on the road to Damascus. Seeing a delinquent girl turned into something new. From the South Lansing Center I held in my hand the paperback with a road map for success for my youngsters: *Skill-Streaming the Adolescent.*[2]

---

[2]Arnold Goldstein, Robert P. Sprafkin, N. Jane Gershaw, Paul Klein, *Skill-Streaming the Adolescent*, Research Press.

Fifty skills for teenagers mapped out in tiny steps. Steps even a child could learn.

Fall and tulips always remind me of the year we launched Structured Learning Training—"success skills"—at the Youth Center. The officers became the instructors—like cheerleaders—after school, leading the role plays, two by two, teaching youngsters How to listen, How to follow instructions, How to ask permission.

I had a picture in my head of a poised young tour guide walking confidently before me like a teacher's aide. I couldn't get the girl out of my head. But how would I ever give that image to my staff?

My mother believed in painting pictures in people's heads. Maybe some people call it imagination; my mother called it *vision* and always quoted from the book of Proverbs: "Where there is no vision, the people perish." She taught me to talk in pictures.

I sat in the classroom in front of my officers, holding a tulip bulb in my hand, backed by the image in my head. I can't think now of one warden, not one other youth center administrator in all the land, who would launch a massive turnaround of his institution—holding a tulip bulb. It was weird, all right. But I had learned that pictures work. In a crowded casino theater in Atlantic City I could talk into a microphone to seven hundred Rotarians with a message we all need to hear: "You can change the shape of your mountain," I would say.

And I could make seven hundred businessmen see a solitary old shepherd—one man—on a godforsaken mountainside, planting acorns one at a time—oak trees springing up upon the mountain, once a lonely place. Giant branches sheltering little villages where children played on shaded country pathways along the mountainside. And the Rotarians would see it all deep in their hearts: They could change the shape of their mountain. With one little acorn in my hand—I could make the Rotarians believe. They could see the picture in their heads.

Fall is for planting tulips. Every September they arrived at my house by parcel post from Van Bourgondien's—big cardboard boxes punched with breathing holes.

"Can you guess?" I asked my officers. "Doesn't look like much." I took the bulb between my fingers and held it up. "Unpromising . . . small . . . brown . . . lump . . ."

A garlic? someone guessed.

I wanted to make an impact, so I said the words again quite slowly.

"In the palm of my hand an unpromising . . . *small* . . . *brown* . . . *lump*."

Then I paused 'til the words sank in.

"But what this really is," I said, "is the most beautiful red emperor tulip I have ever seen. Glorious red, on a tall, proud stem."

Every fall in my unpromising soil at home, I planted three hundred lumps like this one. Not one of them looked like much. In fact, I used to think that nothing would grow in my gravelly garden all choked with ivy, giant trees crowding out the sun, roots stealing the rain, exhaust fumes so heavy from the highway that the lily pond behind the house got covered with an oily scum. The most unpromising growing environment for a flower. Unpromising, some said, hopeless . . .

But a neighbor once told me that if I planted my bulb with a handful of bonemeal, even this small brown lump would grow into something beautiful.

In front of the officers I held up an almost-empty, five-pound bag of bonemeal and let the crumbly powder filter through my fingers.

"So every fall I plant three hundred unpromising small brown lumps, each with a handful of bonemeal. And in April and May my garden dances with three hundred of the most glorious red tulips I have ever seen. People passing by our house just stop to look. . . ."

In their eyes—their silence—I felt the connect.

"In our hands, the power to turn unpromising lumps into something tall and proud and beautiful."

The hush of that room was the start. The vision.

The Youth Center bonemeal was "success skills." Structured Learning Training, the textbook called it. Kids called it SLT. New skills don't grow from dreams alone. They grow from careful instruction and frequent practice. For six months we trained officers and staff how to teach "success skills." For seven months after officers started teaching SLT when the school day ended, and they role played with youngsters two-by-two, the Youth Center never used locked isolation even once. It wasn't just the skills that made the difference: Officer-cheerleaders were coaching them for success. Grown-ups sending a message to the future. There were still those who longed for the old days of lock-'em-up-and-throw-away-the-key. But the results spoke for themselves.

When a boy or girl first arrived, he had no privileges. That's how the Youth Center reined him in: No staying up after eight o'clock. No wearing his own clothes. No decorating his bedroom walls with posters. To earn every privilege, his picture mounted on a star in the Youth Center's Hall of Fame, everyone was measured by one measuring stick: How well have you learned and demonstrated "success skills"? It was old-fashioned: like heaven and hell. Responsibility. Accountability. Sin. How well do you listen, follow instructions, ask permission? For every act there was a consequence.

I felt convinced that I had the power to shape my world. Not one boy or girl—in my whole life—had ever said "f__k you" to me. But what about my officers—the men and women who faced down street toughs every day? The "attitudes." The see-if-you-can-make-me challenges. Not everyone hired to work with rotten kids wants them to succeed. They had to see for themselves.

Week after week, we had loaded the van with officers and staff stoked with picnic lunches and thermos jugs to cut the cost and sent them on overnight trips to South Lansing Center in New York. A picnic with a purpose. To roam the halls. To wander into residence units. To eat in the cafeteria. To see youngsters in the gym. To talk with youth workers. When each vanload returned, I printed their astonished reactions in my Memos to Staff.

Control, control, control, and *order*—my officers buzzed the words to anyone who would listen. They had found a new kind of control—a youngster listening to an instructor who had given him the gift of success.

My officers had seen the Promised Land.

It took me years to learn the lesson of my life: Loving a child is not enough. *Order and discipline and control rank equally with love if a boy or girl is going to learn.* Any teacher or mother will tell you: No child learns anything good when the school or classroom or home is out of control. Disorder and unruliness freeze the brain: the teacher's brain. The student's brain. The parent's brain. These teenagers came from schools where classrooms were "the educational equivalent of a meltdown," as I heard one teacher say. Across the land we had created a frightening world in which no one was in charge: A youngster put down a foot to find solid ground and found only unpredictable ooze.

We had to start with order where the children lived. Order in the schoolrooms. Order in the cafeteria. In every residence unit, in simple words, we posted simple expectations. That was the structured part of Structured Learning Training.

How to act in the classroom—steps one, two, three . . .

How to act in the gym—one, two, three . . . How to act in the cafeteria . . . How to move in the halls . . . I could walk into Cathy Fraser's classroom in the morning and see her sitting beside her newest student, reading the page of classroom expectations: Ask permission before you get out of your seat. Raise your hand to ask permission before you speak . . .

Children are very much creatures of habit. They thrive on routine, unvarying, benumbing, comfortable routine. And I was the tyrant, but one without tyranny. "You walk in here, and you know exactly what it's going to be like." Day Twenty or Day Two Hundred was the same as Day One. Comfortingly predictable routine. Officers kept it simple, and they kept it the same.

In morning meetings every day, the officers preached friendly reminders of correct behavior. Before his line of boys or girls moved through the halls, the officer reminded them of how to act. If someone broke the rule, the group came back. They started once again—until everyone got it right. The rule was always: *To teach is easier than to punish.*

The Youth Center had a motivator most schools never have: The youngsters knew that I could—and did—write letters to the judge about their good behavior.

On a hot August morning—the annual Deep-Cleaning Day before the school year starts—with me in French braids, red T-shirt, and denim walking shorts—shift commanders, officers, social workers, and youngsters arm themselves with scrubbing brushes, sponges—even scouring pads—and serious-smelling green detergent in plastic buckets. The ancient old building where we started—above the hospital morgue—is a faraway memory. That mouldering monument to sorrow had never felt clean or fit for youngsters.

How many years now have we been in this sparkling place—bricks and tiles and epoxy finishes and schoolroom colors? Lauren and I reach, cramped together in one C-wing shower stall, scrubbing off soap marks splashed from a thousand kids a year from the gray brick tile stall.

"You gonna pay us for doing this?" he asks.

My eyebrows wrinkle in mock surprise. "Pay you?" His question arrests my soapy scrub brush in mid air. "I'll tell you what. Do you want one dollar—or a letter to the judge?"

The reaction comes so fast that it's like the shower stall has been bugged with secret microphones. Out of nowhere, a mob of C-wing boys with warm water and soap suds and hands wrinkled like prunes is high-fiving around me over the thought of good letters to the judge. And before the day ends, a copy of a serious-looking letter slips quietly across a very clean floor under each bedroom door—on official Youth Center stationery—with each young scrubber's name in bold letters typed across the top.

Boys fall asleep on this night with "Dear Judge Page . . ." letters propped proud by their pillows. For most, the first letter of commendation they have ever had.

Cops say things straight up better than almost anyone else. I saw one take a buddy by the arm one day—lean toward him. "Look," he says in a confidential tone. "I know what I'm talking about. Good management is the best answer. It's the only answer. The difference between a good cop and a bad cop is a matter of what's expected from the top. That's all."

It was the English teacher in me that plucked the thought from Ralph Waldo Emerson and stuck it in my brain: "An institution is the elongated shadow of one man."

I was the Youth Center. I visited classrooms every day; commented on handwriting; fussed with the proper sounds over a youngster struggling to add or subtract fractions and whispered in his ear that I had always had a terrible time with math; admired his success. I admired classroom bulletin boards, marked in my memory each newly earned certificate of achievement. Perhaps I couldn't find last week's budget status report in the heap of papers on my desk—or the copy of the county's latest policy on filing widgets in triplicate, but I knew exactly where to find Tamika's latest paragraph posted on the wall outside Mary Ann Zeiser's classroom—the one that said she has a crackhead mom—a mom that never, ever, really understands. The page was topped with wobbly words in pencil: *What I wish I could tell my mother.* Together we wrote stories for the student newspaper, side by side. I inspected every bedroom every day, leaving Post-it stickers with notes on every door. I sat on piles of scuffed, blue exercise mats in the gym and listened to youngsters shouting in the latest game of bombardment.

Tamika put her arm around me as I walked by her table in the lunchroom when I stopped to see what was on the lunch menu for the day. I was never surprised. She always slipped her arm around me. The child had been beaten a lot—the scars and cuts even on her face.

I touched. Shoulders, hands, heads so desperately needing to be touched and patted with words and smiles and hands. I was a way station for youngsters looking for something to cling to.

Every team, every close-knit group, has one character that becomes its hub. She need not be the brightest, fastest, most athletic, most talented. She does not have to be the best. What she is, is the one whose soul defines the group.

Off my playing field, I lived quietly. I made quilts. I ran in the morning before the world woke up. On Saturdays in the springtime, I planted Vidalia onions in my community garden patch. Volunteer pink-and-white spider plants grew in a jungle among my Big Boy tomatoes. While I was at work, birds raided the seeds from the giant black center of the sunflower, its golden face following the daily march of the sun across the sky.

My quiet world.

But on the Youth Center playing field, the field was mine.

Words jumped out at me in strange places—in airplane magazines, on radio talk shows, in museums, at America's monuments in Washington, D.C.—words that hit the heart. I turned them into giant cloth banners on the Youth Center's talking walls, banners fluttering along the corridors a hundred times a day as boys and girls walked by—bright red and green and yellow:

> *Hold fast to dreams, for if dreams die,*
> *Hope is a broken-winged bird that cannot fly.*

No matter how far you've gone down the wrong road, turn back.

Give a boy a fish, and he'll eat for a day. Teach a boy to fish, and he'll eat for a lifetime.

No matter how tall your grandfather was, you've got to do your own growing.

No man is defeated until he starts blaming other people for his mistakes.

Whatever you can do—or dream you can—begin it.

And outside the staff lounge, a giant blue banner: *The difficult, we do in a day. The impossible takes a little longer.*

The words are from Langston Hughes, United States Seabees, Goethe, Irish and Turkish proverbs, coaches Vince Lombardi and John Wooden. We would make even the walls shout hope to boys and girls who had never hoped.

I saw a picture once of a man striding in his boots across the grass, trailed by a string of little boys, like carbon copies in lockstep strides, all following him. I could never get that photograph out of my head. When I saw my officers, my teachers, my recreation team—in my head I saw them taking giant steps, trailed by a thousand boys and girls a year, planting boyish, girlish feet in grown-up footprints. Footprints made by my officers. Footprints to mark paths that change the world.

>-◄►-O-◄►-◄

The color of the doors inside the Youth Center spoke to him first. The building talked.

Pink doors . . . blue doors . . . nice windows . . . got more windows than East Camden Middle School . . . nice rug . . .

When Camden Police Detective Lenny Hall escorted Ricardo Fontanez in handcuffs into the Youth Center, the boy's tongue was dry with fear.

The trip from Camden in the van was the first time the boy had ever been handcuffed. The bite of metal around the wrists. Weepy, prickly terror around his heart.

I thought it be bars and all . . . like prison . . . jail . . .

A tiny metal key unlocked the cuffs, and shift commander Ray Ruiz led the boy down the corridor into the area for younger boys.

. . . *Paper Christmas stockings with everyone's names posted 'round the walls . . . Don't look like such a bad place . . . Hallway like a school . . . nothin' dirty . . . no papers on the floor . . . more like a school type of thing . . . gonna be ready when the guys say, 'Yo, what's up? Where you from?' . . .*

The C-wing boys were sitting quietly on the couch practicing their after-school "success skills" with officer John Wiggins.

"*. . . Nobody say nuttin' yet . . . Nobody get up when they see me*

*walked in . . . I just sittin' at the desk . . . How to call my mom . . .
Where she is . . ."*

When Ray Ruiz started speaking Spanish to the boy, Ricardo felt his
terror draining away—snatches of phrases settling into a brain that
wouldn't concentrate—

". . . Don't be scared . . ."

". . . Everything gonna be all right . . ."

". . . Go to court tomorrow . . ."

It was a routine that Ruiz, a Vietnam vet and a father of five of his
own, had perfected to put the boys at ease. When he detected a Puerto
Rican accent, he always switched to speaking Spanish. Ruiz himself
had grown up in Camden and could make small talk about the town.

Officer John Wiggins logged in the boy's clothing on Ricardo's
clothing sheet: white La-Gloria sneakers, blue Adidas sweat pants,
white Nike T-shirt, green triple fat goose-down jacket.

The boy was settling down. If Ricardo had expected a stir when he
came in—the jumpings and fights for the new man in the wing—the
freshman—nobody moved. He was just another resident. Two-by-two
the boys were taking their turn in front of a chart of "success skills."
Role plays. The boys were working on *How to ask permission.*

John Wiggins went down the admission checklist with the boy and
assigned him to Room 198. One built-in bed. Two long windows. A
waist-high counter that spanned the wall. The colors of the doors in
C-wing alternate blue and grape. Ricardo's door was grape. He called it
"pink." Beyond the boundary fence outside he could see the woods.

He knelt beside his bed and sobbed. "I swear to God. I never done
drugs. Jail is for bad, bad people. Not me. I swear to God, not me.
Incredible! Incredible. Turnin' myself in . . . I ain't never thought I
was gonna get locked up. Ain't never got locked up before . . . I ain't
never think bein' in the wrong place at the wrong time . . ."

On a small scrap of paper he had written his mother's name and his
uncle's telephone number. Every time he looked at his mother's
name, he began to sob again.

"I didn't pull no trigger. I didn't have no gun in my hand." Between
sobs he imagined he heard Marielle, his girlfriend, begging him in the
eerie phosphorescent glare of the street light. "Don't go out the house,
Ricardo. Stay here in the house with me." "Me . . . walkin' down the
street . . ."—he could see it all again—"There go my mom yellin' out
the window . . . I shoulda listened . . . while there was a chance . . .
ain't no more chances now . . ."

Behavior log

11/28—Admitted Ricardo Fontanez. Room 198. Resident in for
murder and can't get in touch with his mother. Crying spells. *John
Wiggins*

If Ricardo Fontanez had never had a father, he was about to get one—in Leo Gold, the social worker who fathered the boys in C-wing.

Leo Gold had a father.

On summer Saturdays when he was a child, Leo, Jr., and Leo, Sr., frolicked with Duke, their German shepherd, in the rye fields and the wheat fields of a farm nearby in rural Gloucester County. Father and son. On Friday nights—like clockwork—they did the family grocery shopping at the Paulsboro A & P. ". . . Better meat there," his father used to say. Shopping for groceries. Hair cuts. It was always Leo, Sr., and Leo, Jr., together. On Sunday mornings the family trooped off to church together then returned to the kitchen and watched their father cook pancakes for Sunday breakfast. Sunday breakfasts lasted all morning in the Gold household—blueberry or strawberry pancakes—Botto's Italian sausage flattened and shaped into squares. And maybe homemade biscuits. "Two-and-a-half-hour breakfasts," Leo would always laugh about his father's weekly ritual. The girls teased him about how long it took him to prepare the meal.

No drips and drops of father . . . like most Americans got . . . Leo Gold got the whole ocean: front seat in the family car . . . next to his dad . . . always—since he could remember—with Duke, the family dog, sitting in between . . . always.

If Leo, Sr., went somewhere, Leo, Jr., went, too. Of five children in the Gold family, Leo was the only son.

It wasn't so much that Leo Gold's parents talked values. They *lived* them. Leo's father managed a store across the street from the Catholic grammar school they attended, so he checked in every lunch hour on his children's activities at school. School was a top priority: "As long as you give it your best," his father would say, "put out 100 percent. . . ." He didn't demand A's. But Leo and his four sisters pushed to get A's.

Leo could remember when he and his sister Nancy came home from second grade after winning the spelling bee. Successes . . . good report cards . . . the whole family trooping out to dinner to celebrate.

For every game Leo ever played in—he was a star in basketball for St. James High School in Carney's Point—it could be two hundred miles away—his parents were always there.

"Just seeing him there . . . ," Leo said. His father coming over, patting him on the back . . . "Good game, son." Leo never forgot the feeling. Twenty years later the memories still transferring their encouragement to every part of his life, almost like a jet-assisted take-off—like for every child well-loved at home . . . a head start.

At every game, the boy always checked in with his dad at halftime. Not a lot of talk. More a feeling: "How'm I doin', Dad?"

"Doin' great. Keep it up."

In his father, Leo had his own private coach. A man who never let him quit. The message was always the same: *You're too good to be ordinary.* Leo believed it.

Leo Gold, Sr., did not spank. If the boy strayed off course, his father always brought him back gently without bruising him . . . like the night his father was waiting up when Leo came in "extremely too late" . . . Leo expecting to be crucified but instead getting concern—not anger. That was the end of it . . . that was the way it was between Leo and his dad, instruction from a man who loved him.

A colleague of Freud was right. "What we cure with is love."

><i>•</i><>•<i>•</i>O<i>•</i>•<><i>•</i><

Medical Logbook—Ricardo Fontanez:

November 30—Resident states he will not eat while he is here. Girlfriend is pregnant. *Mary Nuzzo, R.N.*
December 4— Weight–126, gain 2 1/2 lbs.
December 13—States he didn't do anything wrong. Resident states that he would hang himself if he is found guilty. *Mary Nuzzo, R.N.*
December 15—Came to nurse's office obviously distraught. Feels his legal situation is hopeless. Having trouble sleeping at night. Says he doesn't care any more.
December 20—Poor appetite.
December 22—Is in need of regular individual counseling to offer support. He feels all alone at times. *Dr. Ortanez*

Leo Gold was used to tough guys sitting across from him in his office. "Gritting"—the street-talk look-to-kill. Tough guys who had spent their entire adolescent life in the corrections system. Places with names like Skillman, Jamesburg, Bordentown—all of them training schools for boys doing time. The toughest ones were invariably boys whose intellectual recreation was challenging the world. Proving their manhood to the world . . . proving that he "ain't no sissy."

Challenging Leo. "Mother f____r, you will get f____d up . . . word is born. You will get f____d up." "Word is born" was the street talk oath that had started generations ago as *my word is bond.*

"If you didn't know him, you would think he was insulting you." Leo always got a twinkle in his eye, talking to me about his boys. "It could be he was your friend . . . tough guy . . . do 200 push-ups a day . . . there cursing you out. You say to him, 'Get in line, LaMore.' He say, 'I'm in line, P___y. Don't worry about it.' " Leo knew his boys had to save face . . . feel like they had the upper hand. Appearances. Big show. Ask LaMore to go to his room for a timeout, he would say, "You m____r f____n' p___y, I'm goin' in because I'm tired, not because you tellin' me. Don't come near . . . 'cause I can close my own door. I'm doin' this, right?—because I'm doin' it—not because you tellin' me."

Anytime a new resident was admitted it was a challenge to an old

boy's kingdom, and Leo knew just what to expect. "You better get that
m____r f___n' p___y outa the wing, Leo. He think he's bad. He think
he's tough. I show him he's tough."

The old head was no longer king of the hill. Leo understood. Safe in
Leo's office, the boy would start to shake. "I can't take it," and slam
his fist on the table.

Leo always corrected his boys . . . told them he couldn't let them
act that way. The boy would sit, gritting at him, challenging him with
his eyes. Leo never buckled under the intimidation. Leo spent the
most time of all with his toughest boys, the ones with the most
serious charges.

"I know what you're trying to do, looking at me as though you want
to bite my ear off"—and the boy would laugh—a boy who knew
nothing but throwing things . . . nothing but kicking . . . punching . . .
"That does not faze me," Leo would say to the boy. "I'm here to teach
you the right way to do something. I deal with you straightforward.
You deal with me the same way. I will not permit that." Leo was good
at saying "I will .ot permit that." He knew that respect was all the
boy felt he had. Leo gave respect. And his boys gave Leo respect.

Leo's philosophy with his boys was uncomplicated: Respect them.
Respond immediately to their behavior. Most teenagers have no
waiting-power.

Leo would instruct the officers in C-wing at the weekly unit
meeting. "Correct them—right away. Get the boy back on track." Leo
used words like *respect* and *care* and *interest*. "When it comes crunch
time—time for you to tell them to do something, they take a look at
you . . . 'He wants me to do something—it must be the right thing to
do. This person is protecting my well-being.' Take a little extra time
. . . meet their needs . . . make them feel emotionally safe—their
whole relationship is different with you. They never forget you."

That was it. Leo's boys never forgot him. They remembered what
Leo had taught them how to do, like an hour of private lessons on how
to do lay-ups with the basketball . . . a hundred . . . two hundred . . .
three hundred times in the gym while everyone else was eating supper
and no one was around to see their mistakes while they learned.

One person can mean the difference between success and failure in
a boy's life. One person—even for late bloomers. Leo knew. Leo
watched Ricardo Fontanez in the gym—a thin, wiry, well-built
sixteen-year-old . . . the karate kick on the heavy bag, so swift, so
limber . . . promising athlete on his hands . . . Maybe weight training
to connect with this one . . .

Ricardo could barely bench press 110 pounds. Leo stood with the
boy in the weight room . . . "Bench press is just like doing push-ups.
Every day increase them by one a day until you do fifty at a clip.
You're going to increase ten pounds every week." Leo knew that if his
boys had an adult working out with them, they accomplished more.

Leo and Ricardo and five or six of his boys handling each machine: Bench press . . . dips . . . pull-down exercises . . . chest exercises . . . arm curls on the bench press . . . military press . . . sit down on the bench press and press the weights over his head . . . dip bar . . . and push-ups.

Actually, the room that the boys called the weight room was a gym storage room designed for holding bats and balls and volleyball nets. Long ago, bench presses and pulleys, the sit-up board and the pectoral deck had pushed out everything else. The single air vent in the vaulted ceiling struggled to carry off the hot sweat and breath of grunting bodies. Boys huffed and puffed the routines.

Officers on both daytime shifts started lifting weights with the boys. In his bedroom, Ricardo charted his daily sets—pulls and lifts he had finished each day for chest, arms, legs. Leo taught him to keep a proud record of his growth. On his chart, Ricardo penciled his starting press: 110 pounds.

In most places like the Youth Center, tension builds between officers and social workers. *Us-against-them.* Officers wear the badge of the tough guys . . . order . . . control . . . preaching expectations and giving time-outs . . . Most places, social workers are the teddy bear, rat-on-the-officers, and talk-to-mamma brigade. *Them-against-us.* "Them" is kids and the social workers lumped together. Officers live with this not-so-blurry feeling that social workers don't quite understand control.

Not at the Youth Center. At the Youth Center, every social worker had been an officer first. Leo had been an officer for five years; Leo was a first-class athlete and no one's teddy bear.

Officers were always referring their boys to Leo. Problem? . . . Call Leo. That's how Leo had first seen Ricardo . . . Officer Juan Colon standing there telling him this boy named Ricardo . . . back from court . . . crying . . . very upset . . . Officers often had trouble with tears.

Ricardo, sixteen years old, could manage math and reading designed for a ten-year-old. Not even school was a distraction from his pain. At first, Ricardo huddled, crying, in a study carrel every day in Signe Solem's classroom.

Miss Signe's power never hit you with a thump. In fact, she'd never even admit to having a plan of action—a strategy with tough kids. She'd be gliding around the classroom like a gold-haired elf—and all of a sudden—the boys never quite knew how—she'd have them wrapped around her little finger doing math or reading that they had never—ever—done for any teacher in their whole lives before. Miss Signe listened a lot. Ricardo with his eyes averted told her softly about the burns on his hands—why his skin had the burn marks on them: The night when this dude shot the gun on the corner of Nineteenth and Carmen streets, Ricardo had held his hands up to his face . . . flames from the gun flying off and burning him. He would cry again. "I didn't do it." And then Miss Signe would listen while Ricardo talked about his girlfriend Marielle. Marielle was going to have his baby.

Maybe it was the Liz Claiborne dresses Miss Signe wore every day—colors and flowers that made her look like a lady—never like some girlfriend or someone you'd want to talk cheap to—or disrespect. Maybe it was the unexpected question that started her class every school day at nine o'clock so that even the officer in the room got hooked with the discussion, making kids think, look at all sides of a question:

If you came across some personal letters written to your fifteen-year-old daughter by her boyfriend, would you read them?
When was the last time your father told you he loves you?
Your mother?
How would it change your life if you discovered today that your natural mother had been a prostitute who had died during childbirth?
If your girlfriend developed a serious allergy to the pet you have had and loved for ten years, what would you do?

A bunch of street kids hunched over math or reading assignments for the day—fierce competitions raging, competing for once with words and ideas instead of fists, outstretched hands or fingers jabbing to get their idea across. A lot of times the kids didn't want to stop with just one question. Signe Solem—five-feet-six inches tall, golden hair reaching below her waist—one minute she could be answering a question about what if someone wants to commit suicide and then next minute she'd be telling her very own story about the day her best friend killed herself—and how Signe felt. And no one would want to stop listening to Miss Signe talk. Because you could see on Miss Signe's face and hear in her voice that teachers could hurt, too.

Signe knew about wickedness. One day when she was twelve years old and her parents had gone to the Army-Navy game across the river in Philadelphia, she drove her mother's 1976 station wagon five blocks into a side street and hit a truck parked out from the curb. She was a kid with braces on her teeth and hair in yellow pigtails. When the police arrived at her home, Signe had camouflaged her face with grown-up make-up. For punishment, she had to appear with her father before the juvenile conference committee in the town and then sit with sixteen-year-old boys with long hair to watch a gory movie about drunk drivers.

There really wasn't any appropriate movie made just for twelve-year-old girls with pigtails who drove their mother's station wagon illegally on a Saturday afternoon, so the blood-and-drunken-driving movie had to be it. And it worked. Maybe that horror attracted her to kids in trouble. She had never planned to teach bad kids. In fact, she never saw her kids that way. She protested at words like *bad* and *rough*—like *bad* kids, *rough* kids, but once she got her first taste of teaching at the Youth Center, she never wanted to work with any other kind of youngster.

Signe could be listening to a Camden teen gospel choir singing a concert in the Youth Center gym and remind you that these youngsters came from the very same streets as our boys. "And you know what's the difference?" she would ask. "A parent, an aunt, a teacher." And that's what she intended to be—the one who made the difference. She'd get letters from her boys after they had left, saying she was the best teacher they had ever had and maybe they would never have gotten in trouble in the first place if they had had a teacher like her from the start.

Teachers had waiting lists of boys who wanted to stay for the hour of special tutoring after school.

The miracle part was Ricardo. He was always first in line to work with Miss Signe in her after-school class. He began taking his multiplication tables back to C-wing to memorize in his bedroom—a boy who had never done homework in his life. And every time the whole school teamed up for mock trials in the classroom—The Schoolhouse-Robbery Case, The Apartment-House Murder Case, The Unwed-Father-Wants-Custody-of-His-Baby Case—Ricardo couldn't wait for his part. He played a juryman, the prosecutor, the defendant, the bailiff. And when it came his turn to be the judge—everyone always wanted to be the judge—Ricardo, just to be peacemaker, let someone else have the job.

Ricardo had become peacemaker, standing up to new boys who might want to cause a fuss in Miss Signe's classroom, telling boys in C-wing to chill out. Ricardo was Signe's Spanish interpreter when she needed to give instructions to a Puerto Rican kid. Ricardo began tutoring other students in math.

Ricardo's baby was born in the summer. From the beige telephone above the officer's desk in C-wing, the officers phoned him through to the hospital so he could hear the monitor on his baby—*dee-dee* . . . *dee-dee* . . . *dee-dee* . . . And Ricardo cried. He was sixteen. The nurses kept asking Marielle, Ricardo's girlfriend, where the baby's father was—running out in the hospital corridors to find the man to let him see his baby. So Marielle—who was very shy and didn't really want to say it—had to tell them that Ricardo was locked up. And Ricardo cried all over again when he heard about it.

By this time the Youth Center school had been honored as "outstanding education program in the nation for juvenile corrections," and there was always a stream of visitors coming to see what made it work. Of course, I knew why: It was Sonnie DeCencio and her team of teachers. On any day, Sonnie might be just back from Washington or South Dakota or Kentucky from a session on teaching corrections teachers how to make a classroom come alive—success for youngsters who had believed they were going nowhere. Sonnie and her teachers believed in helping children to climb in little inching steps. It was a measure of Sonnie's own success—what she and her teachers gave to the kids. They gave to the students in their classrooms the gift someone had given to them: Someone sat you down and told you that you were going to succeed. You knew it in the way they looked at you, talked to you—the kind of work they gave you. The belief rubbed off.

Everyone knew about living up to your labels: You labeled the rats in the maze, and the "dumb rats" never made it through the maze. The "smart rats" did. Every teacher knew you pick up "smart rats" differently from the "dumb rats," talk to them differently. So the "dumb rats" never succeeded. Sonnie and her teachers weren't going to treat any kids like "dumb rats" and stand back and watch them fall apart, watch them turn angry and violent. Failure and going nowhere does that to a kid. They give up easily. Sonnie and her teachers gave kids the feeling that they were going somewhere, made them re-imagine their fu ires.

Sonnie stood at my desk year after year with academic profiles of the students: in every classroom teenagers old enough to be in high school who could not read, could hardly write; the average student in the Youth Center classrooms was reading and doing math four years behind other teenagers of his age. For every teenager in the Youth Center classrooms who was reading at his proper grade level or above, there were four who were reading below. In the cafeteria during school hours, a nonreader always got a tutor all to himself, away from curious eyes and easy distractions. In America, where thirty million Americans are illiterate, the Youth Center got the struggling readers. In a land where every school day more than two thousand teenagers drop out, the Youth Center school got the dropouts.

Ricardo was a dropout. When he arrived, he was a struggling reader.

Ricardo didn't mind telling anybody, "Miss Signe care about me, keeps me after school a lot to keep teaching me after class."

It was Miss Signe who cried when Ricardo was waived to adult court to face trial as an adult. What kind of legal system lets a psychologist test a Spanish-speaking kid with an IQ test in English? she raged. Something was wrong here. Of course, the boy came out looking retarded! There wasn't a retarded bone in the boy's body! And what kind of defense lawyer never answers how many telephone calls from a boy's teacher that she wants to testify for the boy in court? And what kind of defense lawyer, Ricardo wanted to know, tells a boy if his family comes up with $4000, it would take him just one month to get the boy home—and when the family comes up with $4000, the boy's still not home. And then the lawyer says if the boy gives him some more money he can get him home after his waiver hearing. And when the boy tells him "Don't B.S. me, be up straight with me, tell me the truth," the big lawyer—who's never been locked up a day in his life—says "Don't be mad at me . . ." after months and months of B.S.-ing. And what kind of defense lawyer, in the name of holy justice, sits next to a teenage defendant at a waiver hearing, asking the boy, "What do you want me to say next?" Like who was the kid on trial and who was the lawyer—in the name of all things fair!—getting paid how many thousand dollars?

You could buy your way out of trouble with a clever lawyer and expensive psychiatrists. But they were out of the reach of the poor whites and blacks and Hispanics that crowded America's lockups.

Miss Signe cried. And Leo was so angry at how poorly the boy had been represented by his lawyer at the waiver hearing, the only word he could summon from his mouth was, "Pathetic!" And Ricardo decided that if he was "possibly retarded" as the psychologist had told the judge, he simply wasn't going to do any more work in Miss Signe's classroom. And Miss Signe sat the boy down and said to him, "You don't do it for the system, Ricardo. You do it for yourself." And Ricardo knew that she was right.

>─┼─◆─○─◆─┼─◄

The hush. The lively activity. The respect. The rainbow colors. Walls splashed from top to bottom with childlike effort and success. I find myself reminding visitors—always astonished—that these were once school dropouts, school troublemakers. Most of them are teenagers who long ago gave up on school. School gave up on them.

Daniel, seventeen, and Rick, sixteen, are the tour guides today for college students now scribbling notes for a project for a college class. Rick attends a large suburban high school; Daniel, a high school in Camden.

"I thought the Youth Center s'pose to be the bad part, bein' away from you' home, but it's really the good part.

"The streets is the bad part. Since I been in here, three of my friends has been killed. I been here a month and a half. If I was out there wiff them, I coulda been killed."

"Feeling safe? . . . able to concentrate on school?"

"Yeh, since the kids don't have a fear of gettin' hurt." The boy's brother arrived a while ago with a bullet imbedded against his rib. Touching the bullet under the skin and wiggling it against the bone was the show-and-tell in B-wing during his stay.

The Youth Center gets almost instant conversions in its classrooms. Once a newly admitted youngster gets adjusted to new surroundings, new faces, new schedules, a comforting reality settles in—he's safe. No worrying about a rival posse coming to battle for his turf. No worrying about being hit by ricocheting bullets meant for someone else. No worrying about someone pulling a gun on him. Or seeing his friend or cousin killed on the sidewalk. These are the everyday—unexaggerated—realities of Youth Center teenagers. Schools are an arms race where 100,000 American youngsters will head off to school today carrying a weapon, where it is easier for a youngster to get a gun than a driver's license, where for every gun in school there are seven knives.

Hernando shows me a scar under his eye where he was hit in the face with a bottle at his school. Without blinking, he has just finished telling me about the day that he and his friends were playing hookey from school to fish . . . boys led by the stench to a rotting body of a man in the brush behind Pyne Poynt Middle School—he tells the story without alarm, as if finding bodies were commonplace in his part of town. Like the day someone found a body on top of East Camden Middle School. On this day, George describes a shoot-out by the lockers in his school. Food fights in the cafeteria. "So much food flyin' . . . hot dogs . . . sandwiches. . . . If you put your hand up, you can catch a soda," he says.

Feeling safe—survival—is the first requisite for learning.

THE DAY THE BULLETS HIT THE SCHOOL BUS
by RED DOG, age 15

John Rudd was the one the bullet hit, above his ear. Choir concert at Hatch Middle School. We was singing "Getting to Know You."

Morgan Village choir, guest singers in the Hatch auditorium. Gettin on the school bus to ride home.

Boys on the corner, carryin bats. Sticks. Guns. I dived under the bus seat when the bullets hit. BOOM BOOM BOOM. Shot maybe 16 times. 9mm, I guess.

Bus driver pulled away so fast. Left half the kids still on the sidewalk. I quit the choir.

In my small and quiet suburb, I always feel safe. I want to assume that everybody does. These children don't. I see children from the war zone of the city, "shell-shocked" like veterans of wartime combat, wounded spirits unable to shake off depression, unable to make new lives. I see it in teenagers whose shock regresses them to their childhood—grown bodies unconsciously reaching for the safety of a womb—teenagers sucking their thumbs, wetting their beds, sometimes refusing to speak. I see it in teenagers attacking an unsafe world. Victims becoming the victimizers. Why were we surprised? Why?

Children mirror the worst behavior of adult models.

>–+‹›–·–0–‹–+–‹

I pick out the phrases as Rick and Daniel lead the visitors around the classrooms: ". . . Teach on an individual basis . . ." ". . . Just care an awful lot . . ." "If I need help, she'll come to me before she does anything else . . ."

"Miss Cathy is a very nice friendly person. She will do anything—you know—to help you learn . . ." "Stretch our mind little bit . . ."

Rick is smiling. ". . . Like spring in cartoon land here. Everything's just happy . . . 'n easygoing. Everybody's . . ."

"I've learned things here I—they didn't even attempt to teach me in public school," says Daniel.

"And the way the teachers teach here is—like—fun. Like a big game."

"Fun?"

"Yes."

"Like what?"

"Incentives."

"What incentives?"

"Candy." Rick laughs. "You work, you get candy. By working . . . Miss Mary Ann, she calls it Vitamin C. C for candy. Vitamin C pill . . . it's really candy . . . so we can stay healthy . . . do our work."

"And GQ awards," says Daniel. *GQ* stands for the Gentleman's Quarterly award for being polite and cooperative in school. The weekly GQ tally is posted in the school hallway. Boys posted their GQ certificates in their bedrooms.

"And first place in newspaper-reading contests," Daniel adds.

"On the outside, it's hard. Awards eliminate we who don't understand. Everybody in the world should have a chance. Out there I was tryin' my best, but there wasn't no one there to teach me.

"Like when I first came here, I couldn't ever, never in my life read a newspaper. Miss Cathy help me out so much in reading. I never read a newspaper in my life. Today, I got first place on the newspaper-reading contest."

The boy can't get it out of his mind.

"First-place winning contest. I was shocked at myself."

A memory sometimes peeped up in my brain from the past—a world away, in a Japanese concentration camp, my own teachers creating a comfortably predictable world for their students—a sense of safety in a bloody war. My teachers in Weihsien Concentration Camp gave us peace and order in the midst of war. Here I was, my arms stretched across generations to bring that peace and order to children in another war. What could I give to children where a quarter of America's major urban school districts now use metal detectors? Where children even in small-town America practice "drop drills" and DBS (drive-by shooting) drills, hitting the dirt when gunfire erupts?

The gift was *order*. In the classrooms you could hear a pin drop. Teenagers thrived in the structure.

"It's like everything changes when you get from off the streets. Completely. Attitude change. Behavior change," Daniel looks up at the visitors. "Everything you go about changes. The streets should be like the Youth Center. I know it sound kinda strange, when I came here, I was on the third-grade math level . . . month and a half. . . . I'm leaving here on the eighth- and ninth-grade math level."

"Since I've gotten in here, I'm gonna be unstoppable." Rick glows. "Finish high school. Go to college."

The visitors stand—looking at street toughs completely absorbed in school. Happy. Productive. Respectful. "I guess you've got a secret."

I think for a moment. "Children who succeed stop being unruly."

So what keeps them coming to a Youth Center classroom?

It isn't a secret formula.

It's small, it's safe, it's friendly, and it's run by a caring—and very patient—staff. Everyone knows everyone else, just like a big extended family. Youth Center teachers dispense values and the most powerful motivator of them all: high expectations.

>─┤◆├─O─┤◆├─◀

Four first-place certificates for newspaper reading plaster Mark's bedroom wall in C-wing. One Student of the Week award. Posted to catch attention head-on when visitors open his door. This is an honor room, and Mark expects visitors frequently. He nudges me to sneak my attention from the visitor admiring the awards. "You coming to the spelling bee tomorrow?"

I nod. "You going to win?"

The youngster starts acting shy and modest and happy all at the same time—like a teenage girl when someone tells her that she's pretty. Ricardo and Mark have been roommates for the last month, two Spanish-speaking boys from competing street gangs, Ricardo from a close-knit family clan and Mark from Twenty-fourth Street Black Posse.

"He's goin' to win the spelling bee for sure," Ricardo tells me. "I been drillin' him every night in our room. Backwards and forwards. All the words."

Ricardo and Mark meet in a blur of high fives in the middle of their bedroom.

Later in the day as I loop by his classroom, I find Cathy Fraser, his teacher, drilling Mark.

"Banana."

Claudio, coloring a jack-o'-lantern at the next table, interrupts—
"'b-a-n-a-n-n-a." Claudio winks.

"Be your own man, Mark. Stick to your guns." I frown at Claudio's game of let's-trip-him-up.

"b-a-n-a-n-a."

"Acronym."

"a-c-r-o-n-y-m." I want to hug him. But it can wait.

Spelling bee day dawns with brilliant Indian summer sunshine. Leaves on the euonymus hedge along the parking lot are turning red. Chrysanthemums bloom yellow and rust and pink along the sidewalk. And in the lunchroom, Ricardo from C-wing assures me that he's put $10 on his roommate, Mark. A sure bet to win the spelling bee, he says. "I been drillin' him every night."

At 1:00 P.M., Room 123 is jammed, a scramble of excitement. Extra chairs are full. Boys overflow on top of the study carrel desks. Brenda Reid and teacher aides sit on the ventilator by the window. Head teacher, Sonnie DeCencio, with video camera on her shoulder stands ready to record it all.

"Everyone in the spelling bee, please stand up behind the tables," Miss Cathy says, trying to make order out of the excitement. Youngsters who have been drilling for days in small classes of five or six, are suddenly overwhelmed by a standing-room-only crowd.

"We gotta stand the whole time?" Mark groans as five boys move to the line. "My legs ain't gonna hang the whole period."

"Where are the rest of you that signed up?" asks Miss Mary Ann, her eyes searching across the room. Suddenly stagefright has hit with a vengeance. Contestants are hiding their faces in their hands, huddling around classroom tables, trying not to be noticed.

"Danton, I'm disappointed in you," says Miss Mary Ann, looking at a youngster who earns "A" for effort from her every single day.

Danton slowly stands and joins the spelling line. The room bursts into encouraging cheers. These are not students that sign up for spelling bees anywhere else. From time to time my boys here tell me about "nerds" who actually carry books to school in Camden— imagine books instead of beepers!—scoff at the "nerds" who actually listen to their teachers in the public schools.

"It don't bother me if I lose," says Mark, who has now moved over near Ricardo, his roommate, for moral support. He sits down on the edge of a study carrel, wearing his light blue-and-white North Carolina Tar Heels hat, the peak pulled down over his right shoulder.

The spelling line is a joyful mix of America's racial, ethnic, and neighborhood roots. Danton, Gordon, Claudio, and Mark have come up through Camden schools. Stanley and Rick are from down-county suburbs. Colors and geography don't seem to matter in this contest. The real competition is the partisan cheering for B- and C-wings. Three from each.

Miss Cathy quiets the room to give the rules. "Say the word. Spell the word. Say the word. You get two chances to spell the word right. Ready? Okay?" She pauses to let the instructions sink in. "Danton, *echo*.

"Echo. a-k-u-l-e, Echo."

"Try one more time."

Danton speak slowly. "a-k-u-l-e." I get the feeling that Danton is trying to get out of the competition fast. Miss Cathy shakes her head. Danton sits down.

Jetty.

Claudio frowns. He is wearing his new black Philadelphia 76ers basketball cap with the tag still hanging from the side—his proud badge that he has earned honors. "Jetty. j-e-d-d-y. Jetty."

Miss Cathy shakes her head, crisps her pronunciation. *Jetty.*

He tries again. "Jetty. j-e-t-t-y. Jetty."

Wearing his black California Angels shirt, Gordon looks unsure that he wants to be in the competition at all. He wipes out on *immune.*

Stanley aces it: "i-m-m-u-n-e, and C-wing cheers.

"Claudio, *helicopter*

"Helicopter. h-e-l-i-c-o-p-t-e-r. Helicopter."

The B-wing sits down. That's two out from B-wing.

"Rick?"

"Helicopter. h-e-l-i-c-o-p-t-e-r. Helicopter." Clearly, Rick is B-wing's last chance. when he breezes through *embryo* and *skeleton,* B-wing partisans applaud wildly. The line is down to three: Rick from B, Stanley and Daniel from C.

"Mark, *aerobic.*

"Aerobic. a-e-r-o-b-i-c. Aerobic."

"I got twenty dollars on my man," Ricardo is beaming in the corner, adding another ten dollars for each word that Mark gets right. *Quotient.*

The room hushes on a word that half of the group has never even heard before. Stanley thinks hard. "Quotient. q-u-o-t-i-e-n-t. Quotient."

Somebody interrupts the applause: "The other two's sayin' 'I'm glad *he* got it right.'" Stanley is smiling bigger now as he warms to his success.

The three breeze through *laminate* and *anatomy* and *tranquil* and *vaccine.*

"Stanley, *diamond.*

"Diamond. d-i-a-m-o-n-d. Diamond."

"He's getting all the easy ones," Mark complains across the room to Miss Cathy.

By the time Mark scores on *fishery,* Ricardo is gambler-happy: "I got fifty dollars on this man!" Somebody mumbles about gambling with food stamps, and the room breaks up. Miss Cathy has to wait for the room to quiet down.

Snarl.

Rick thinks for a minute. "Snarl. s-n-a..." He pauses and ends with an

rl" sound gurgling from his tongue and his lips, and the room howls
with a chorus of laughter. Rick smiles his halfway smile.

"Say it again," he asks.

Snarl.

"'s-n-a-r-o-w-l.'"

"He's out! He's out!" Mark waves his arms. "'s-n-a-r-l. He's out!' B-
wing's last best chance dies as Rick sits down.

I can't help thinking about what the Camden police sergeant said to
me last week when his Youth Taskforce officers toured these rooms:
"This class would be the envy of any school in America."

The two C-wing boys stand side by side. Seventeen-year-old Mark,
muscular and five feet four from the city—with just a hint of a
mustache—and fourteen-year-old Stanley from the suburbs, six feet of
gangly teenager topped by a blond crew cut.

Stanley scores on *juvenile.* Mark scores on *kindergarten.*

"Stanley, *macaroni.*"

"Macaroni: m-a-c-o-r-o-n-i. Macaroni."

"Try it one more time," Miss Cathy tries pulling it out of him.
He goes more slowly. "M-a-c-o-r-o-n-i."

Mark leaps for the celing. "I won! I won!"

"Yo, you got to spell it, man," someone from B-wing shouts at him.

"M-a-c-a-r-o-n-i. Gimme *any* word." Mark is caught between a sob
and a shout. A devilish somethimes-I-amaze-myself look crosses the
boys face. The classroom shudders with sound. *Razzamatazz.* r-a-z-z-
a-m-a-t-a-z-z. *Pedicure.* Any word." Part of him weeps in disbelief, and
part of him tries to scream hosannas. Mark plunges over to hug
Ricardo, his roommate and spelling coach. For how many weeks has
Ricardo been drilling him in their room at bedtime? "I can spell them
all backward or forward. I'm goin' off." He dances around the room,
clasping two proud hands over his head. "If I can spell them right
when *Ricardo* says them to me, you know I can spell them right when
Miss Cathy says them to me.

English is not Ricardo's native language.

Sitting there in this crowded, bubbling classroom, watching these
master teachers inspire their teenagers with new dreams, watching
them wrap their students with affection, watching these workers of
miracles make boys and girls reach ever beyond where they think they
can reach, I am struck by the limitless potential here. I dream of
success like this shared by every child. Shared whether a child is born
to poor white Appalachians in this nation or to wealthy New Yorkers,
to poor blacks and Hispanics in all the Camdens of America, or to the
rich in America's Princetons and Cherry Hills. All our children
deserve to be heirs of America's promise.

16

MISCHIEF NIGHT

Smoke blankets the city tonight, muffling the beat of helicopters hovering overhead dispatched from the state police and Army National Guard. The stench is a city on fire. Sirens—like air raid warnings—wail over Camden.

Bricks crash through windows. Hell sets the city ablaze. Mischief Night. Devil's Night. October 30. York Street is burning from a gasoline bomb thrown in a row of skeleton buildings. Half a block in flames. Ghost houses.

Once-elegant rococo wreaths and swags in bas relief above lovely bay windows upstairs tell a story about proud American householders who built these homes a century ago. The Germans. The Irish. The English. Home owners competing, neighbor with neighbor, to out-decorate the rest. Carved wooden turrets top each roof. Once-cozy row houses—tonight they're belching fire. In better days, York Street boasted of itself as prime real estate not far from the waterfront. No more. These days the local missionary priest calls it "a garbage-strewn, needle-infested hellhole."

Seven row houses blaze at Sixth and York, flames leaping like fireballs, melting plastic windows on cars parked along the street. Children screaming. Firefighters arriving at the blaze find the closest fire hydrant—broken. Police officers hold back dazed home-owners bent on racing into hell to save humble treasures of a lifetime.

It's hard to imagine: Dilapidated tenements squeezed between rotted timbers and tottering bricks of abandoned houses along this stretch rent for $450 to $500 a month. The street dies like the burning rubble of a bombing blitz.

Up the street, teenagers gather in battle lines, cordoning off grocery stores. Teenagers armed with eggs and potatoes. This is North Camden just up from State Street. They used to call State Street "Lawyers Row." Proud brick homes for doctors and lawyers who abandoned North Camden years ago, fleeing the aroma of decay. Now it stands—the husk of something, a skeleton, a graffiti-smeared eyesore inhabited by squatters, scavengers, and teenage posses. Draw a map of this neighborhood. Stick it with pins to mark the hottest drug corners. You'll count fourteen—fourteen of Camden's most thriving business enterprises these days. Drugs.

Tonight, a fire bomb. Two. Ten. Fifty. Teenagers in the city call them "cocktails," thrown by prowling vandals. One hundred-fifty fires set in businesses, houses, cars, trash piles. Eighty-six buildings in the city ablaze.

Across town on Haddon Avenue, Krazy Discount Store is burning, its charred ribs cloaked by the airborne soot of a city in flames. Until tonight, a Korean merchant sold cookies, detergent, stockings, and greeting cards here. Korean merchants own more than one hundred-twenty businesses in the city—jewelry, fast food, discount stores. Koreans are targets. In his album, *Death Certificate*, the popular twenty-something rapper, Ice Cube, suggests burning down Korean-owned stores.

"'s a shame," a police officer says to nobody in particular. "I used to get my sunglasses here at Krazy's. Cheap. Got no respect for nothin'."

"You got kids hanging out, bored, with nothing to do, and all of a sudden, fire trucks, cops, TV crews are pulling up," says Sergeant LeRoy Palmer. "It's exciting, and pretty soon they get that fever. People who hadn't even thought of setting a fire are starting them just to keep the excitement going."

Tonight it's Mischief Night fun: Taunt the police. Revile your neighbors. Pelt your homeboys with handfuls of eggs. At Second and Main streets a gang of thirty teenagers rules the street.

Brandy Green, seventeen, looks over his shoulder at the crowd growing behind him. "Da-a-ag," he says. "Where all these people come from?" Swarming like an angry beehive getting bigger. Blacker. Uglier as it swells through the street. Boys high from smoking marijuana joints, passed from mouth to mouth. Drinking beer. A rented U-Haul truck, loaded with teenagers hiding behind hockey masks, squeals down the street—posse members hurling eggs and bricks and bottles.

The Youth Center boys are full of stories of Mischief Night, past and present—"Mystery Night," Joseph calls it. Joseph has spent all of his eighteen years in Camden, and Brandy, most of his life. Safe in my office, much later, I am full of questions. "On Mischief Night, does anybody have a gun?"

"You don't know. . . ." That's the terror of the city. Guns. You never know. ". . . like somebody gets really mad . . . gets hurt in the other group . . . they gonna start shootin' . . ."

"Didn't your mom ever tell you to stay in on Mischief Night?"

"Not really," Brandy says. "*I* tell my mom to stay in."

"You tell your *mom* to stay in? . . ."

"Yeh, so she won't get hurt," Brandy says. "An' I say, 'Mom, if you need something from the store, I go the store for you now 'cause the store gonna close . . .' so my mom won't go out . . . get hit with a egg . . . that would make a lotta people wanna go get the guns."

Hitting someone's mother with an egg could start a war in Camden. "Yeh. Get yo' mom to stay in. . . ."

"I tell *my* mom to stay in," Joseph says. "My mom tell me— 'Mystery Night. Don't go outside." He shakes his head quietly. "I'm goin' outside anyway." I love the gentleness of these boys when we're talking real. Real talk. Real feelings. Like holding something fragile in our hands. A boy who sits talking with me for the very first time always seems surprised that his words and feelings interest me. Here in this room, the bluff and swagger melt away. *Gentle* is left.

Corner stores in Camden close early on Mischief Night. Some close the whole day, lock tight the iron grates across the windows and the doors.

"They got this Chinese store on 25th Street. . . . Guys buy the eggs in the morning because they know the stores close early on Mischief Night, like all stores close. . . ."

"O−o−o−oh . . . so you go early Mischief Day . . . to get the eggs because you don't want all the eggs to be bought up. Gonna close early because of the troubles?"

"Mm-hm. . . ."

"So people expect troubles." I find myself making statements now instead of asking questions. A given. Camden folk *expect* trouble.

"Yeh."

"In other words, the store owners. Would somebody bomb a store?"

"Yes." Brandy looks at me as if I should know.

"They *would?*"

"Yes."

"They would bomb a store?"

"Anything. Sometimes they would beat up the owners. Like . . . somebody would walk in . . . try to pay for somethin' . . . while other boys are in the back of the store stealin' the eggs."

Joseph interrupts. "I'm walking home, and I see some guy throw a cocktail into a 'bandoned house, and the cocktail blewed up. The whole house was on fire. Teenagers. Cramer Hill . . . on my street.

"Throw it against the building, and it's like a flash of flame wherever the gas hits?" I ask.

"Yeh." The cocktail, Joseph says, "hit a crack house . . . old, abandoned house . . . all beat-up like . . . and people break in and then use it for a crack house. . . ."

Brandy wants to be sure that I know what a crack house is. "When somebody buy their drugs and they have nowhere to go, 'cause they don't wanna go home 'so they don't want their family to see that they doin' drugs, they go to the crack house and do their stuff there." A shooting, snorting, smoking gallery for addicts.

"So it isn't that somebody lives in this house . . ."

"Nah . . ."

"So . . . a place where people do drugs . . ."

"And sell drugs there, too," Joseph adds. Hideaway and hangout for drug sellers.

"How many crack houses are in your neighborhood, Joseph?" The boy pauses to count.

"Five."

I don't even try to hide my amazement. "Five crack houses in your neighborhood?"

"Yeh. The one that got burned down. Another two houses got fixed up. Two people live in the houses. . . ."

I look at this boy who can hardly read. Eighteen years old. Spilling out the recipe for a "cocktail" fire bomb. And I see it all. Every day of his eighteen years he has spent—growing up around crack houses. With the dregs and vermin of the land.

"Wait a minute . . ." I stop him. "Five crack houses on . . . one block?"

"Different blockses."

"Within a square radius of how many blocks?"

"One . . . two blocks. . . ."

I put my face in my hands and groan. *It's the children*, I say to myself, *who are paying the price*. On Mischief Night their rage is turned inside-out on their city.

"They burned down . . . all of them burned down . . . specially by teenagers. Fires on Mystery Night, that's their day. Kids beat up old men or adults . . . or get soap . . . rub it on cars . . . mess up the cars . . . flat tires. . . . That's Mystery Night . . . burn houses . . ."

Brandy breaks in. "Get a hammer . . . break all the cars' windows . . ."

"Break car windows?"

"Mm-hm."

"Somebody who did a bad thing to you?"

"No. Just anybody's car. . . ."

"Anybody's car?"

Both boys answer. "Anybody's car."

"My car?"

Brandy nods. "Yes. Your car."

"So then they just go with a hammer . . ."

". . . and they smash the windows. Car ridin' down the street, they pick up a brick. . . . You know, throw bricks at the car and if the guy or somebody who's in the car try to get out . . . like he get out and say 'Why you gonna break my car?' . . . they try to jump 'im. . . ."

"Throw a brick at 'im . . ."

"The idea is to hurt someone?" Nothing helps me to understand.

"The idea is to go out . . . go all out . . ."

"To go all out?"

"Go all out."

Wilding, I think to myself.

"It be bad on Mystery Night, 'specially after dark. Mystery Night is *their* time. . . ." Joseph runs his fingers up the close-cropped sides of his head into a mop of curls on his crown. His neighborhood was one of the hardest hit in the burning. "The teenagers . . . that's *their* fun. That's when they get the crazy person out of them. Ain't nobody can't do nothin' 'bout it. . . ."

I listen to a value system turned upside down. To me, the terror of the streets is a frightening risk. To them it's a thrill. The thrill of challenging death is what keeps some boys committing crimes. For others the major joy of crime is the thrill of challenging death on every shift. Guns, fire bombs, drug wars—you could be going out to die.

"Any house in your neighborhood get a brick thrown through the window?"

"The crack house. . . ."

"Cocktail?" I ask. "Burn down?"

"To the ground. . . ."

>—⬦—○—⬦—<

In the 1920s and '30s, Camden was divided into ethnic cells: English, Irish, and Scottish shipyard workers lived in Fairview and Morgan Village. Most of the Jewish professional and business people settled in Parkside. Poles, who had started settling in the city around 1870, joined newly arriving Italians in clashing with blacks as the newcomers competed for their jobs. South Camden became known as Little Italy. Whitman Park, predominantly Polish, was nicknamed Polacktown; indeed, Polish was the first language in the Whitman Park Schools. North Camden and Cramer Hill were an ethnic mix of working classes.

Camden boomed as a cultural center. In 1844, Walt Whitman, they called him "America's poet," bought the only house he ever owned—Number 328 Mickle Street—for $1,750. Camden was his kind of town—a poet who liked buckwheat cakes, beefsteak, oysters, and strong coffee; who liked to drink directly from his water pitcher or bottle of sherry or rum—America's bard of the working man. Walt Whitman chose "a raddled two-story house in a working-class neighborhood," where trains rumbling along the Camden and Amboy Railroad shook the house, where factory whistles and shipping along the Delaware reminded him day and night of the bustle of the city, where southwest breezes wafted choking fumes across the river from a fertilizer-processing plant on the Pennsylvania shore.[4]

"Include all the hells and damns," Whitman told his confidant who was taking notes on the poet's life. "Whatever you do, do not prettify

---

[4]Justin Kaplan, *Walt Whitman: A Life*, 14.

me." Whitman and Camden matched—proud of their *hells* and *damns*.

With all those literary figures coming all the way from Europe to visit Whitman, some folks even said that Camden would become "America's Stratford."[5]

Camden, New Jersey, stood proud in the land. It manufactured everything from pens to battleships for America. Not just the resting place of Walt Whitman in Harleigh Cemetery, it was also the home of "Jersey Joe" Walcott, national heavyweight-boxing champion.

Quakers had so wanted the land in the early 1700s that they bartered with fishhooks, kettles, bells, combs, Jews' harps, needles, brandy, and guns to purchase an Indian deed to the territory.[6]

They named it for the ferry that shuttled fruits, vegetables, dairy products, and livestock across the Delaware River to Philadelphia. Cooper's Ferry flourished. When the first locomotive came to Camden in 1834, cheap, efficient transportation connected the town to population centers like New York.

Immigrants and freedmen poured in. With the railroad and its prime location on the river, the city flourished as a manufacturing center by the time of the Civil War. Esterbrook Steel Pen Company was thriving at the foot of Cooper Street. Ship-repair shops and ship-building establishments dotted the waterfront. The city boasted the only nickel-refining business in the country.

Among its 125 industries were cloth factories and woolen mills. A man named Joseph Campbell started a modest canning factory in the city to process the rich harvests of the fertile New Jersey countryside; it was the beginnings of the world-famous Campbell's Soup.

By 1880, Camden had boomed to become the forty-fourth largest city in the United States, a countrified city where hogs and livestock roamed the unpaved streets. Like those in the rest of the country, laborers were beginning to protest low wages, twelve- to fourteen-hour days, and children under fourteen working in the factories.

Booster committees erected large signs along the railroad tracks in the twentieth century to announce the benefits of Camden as a prime site for corporations. The shipyards came, building everything from fireboats to battleships, schooners, luxury yachts, and warships. Europeans poured in to find manufacturing jobs. Strange-speaking aliens crowded Camden's streetcars, sidewalks, and schools.

Camden boasted that it had everything: When the whole nation panicked with the dread of typhoid in every well, local committees bottled jars of Camden water with the label, "Camden's Pure Artesian Water. . . . There is no typhoid fever." It competed with Philadelphia

---

[5]*Camden Post*, March 30, 1892, 1.

[6]Jeffrey M. Dorwart and Philip English Mackey, *Camden County, New Jersey, 1616–1976: A Narrative History*, 11.

across the Delaware River. Gatley and Hurley's department store on Broadway boasted, "We clothe the entire family for 33% less than Philadelphia."[7]

Until the end of the First World War, the electric streetcar was the city's primary transportation. For a nickel, Camden and Philadelphia picnickers could ride the Camden-Haddonfield trolley route that connected the Federal Street Ferry through Camden's Parkside and Harleigh Cemetery to neighboring towns. Folks from even the remote towns in the area took the trolley to Camden City to shop in its department stores and dine in its restaurants. The trolley was popular—even with its bumpy ride and uncomfortable cane benches—because mud on the roads was often shoetop deep, churned up by heavy wagons struggling through the mire to get their loads of tomatoes from the outlying Jersey farmlands to the Campbell's factory in the city.

The trolley tracks were eventually pulled up during World War II and used for much-needed scrap steel. Camden's became the first motorized fire department in America, replacing horse-drawn fire apparatus with fire trucks from American LaFrance. When horseless carriages finally replaced farm wagons, truckloads of tomatoes lined up bumper to bumper from the Campbell's plant, extending across the city as far back as Westville.

Automobiles arriving on city roads added new problems. Collisions between motorcars and horses in Camden City became so frequent that the city horse ambulance carried away disabled animals every day. The county prosecutor, an avowed enemy of horseless carriages, stationed constables on the White Horse Pike to shoot out tires of those who refused to stop their vehicles.

Roller skating on newly paved roadways became the rage. Skaters knocked down people and tied up traffic, until outraged townsfolk forced the city to pass an ordinance banning tandem skating, hitching rides to trucks, wagons, or streetcars.[8]

Dance halls so multiplied—featuring steps called the Turkey Trot, the Grizzly Bear, and the Bunny Hug—that a letter to the editor in a Camden newspaper in 1912 claimed that the dances "had an injurious effect upon the morals of our girls and young men."[9]

By 1925, New York Shipbuilding Company's work force had reached 17,500, shipyard employees living in neat row houses along streets named Milton, Burns, and Byron, called affectionately "Poets' Row." Construction of a giant bridge was underway to span the Delaware. Factories on both sides of the Delaware belched pollution

---

[7]Ibid, 169.

[8]Ibid, 179–180.

[9]*Camden Post-Telegram*, Jan. 18, 1912, 6.

into the air and water so that for the first time anyone could remember, fishermen along the river failed to catch any shad.

Car ferries could no longer keep up with the flood of motor vehicles in the city. Improved roads connecting Camden to the seashore made traffic jams even worse. Long lines of autos backed up on city streets. In 1926, President Calvin Coolidge dedicated a thirty-seven-million-dollar suspension bridge that stretched 9,570 feet across the Delaware River between Philadelphia and Camden. The Benjamin Franklin Bridge was an engineering marvel that was supposed to solve the city's traffic problems. But demolition that made way for the span and its accessways wiped out lovely homes that had once formed the city's society hill. It razed factories, businesses, and homes that had been lucrative tax ratables. The bridge cut the city in half, north to south, isolating the gracious homes of North Camden and starting the decline that led to the death of a once-gracious neighborhood. In one lifespan, the bridge put a hangman's noose around the jewel of North Camden and turned it into a hell zone called The Danger Zone.

The bridge was to have made Camden the hub of a giant metropolis. Instead, the city lost money and business and people. Travelers heading from New Jersey to Philadelphia had once ventured through the heart of old Camden. They now sped through, stopping only long enough to pay the twenty-five cent toll. Vacationers bound for the sun and sand of Atlantic City and the Jersey shore fouled the air with exhaust fumes. Eighteen million vehicles crossed the bridge during the first eight months of 1947. Five-hour tie-ups along the roadways beyond the bridge became common.

In the suburbs, first-generation immigrants found a new frontier: fresh air and grass and developments with swimming pools, athletic clubs, a mating ground for their young. It was a dream of something better than the street-corner hangouts of the city. Developers like Bob Scarborough sold 2000 two-story New England salt-box houses called *The Sturbridge*, with windows all around the house only eighteen inches off the floor. Parents with their children from crowded row houses of the city looked out of those windows and saw the future.

But if people were moving out of the city, a flood of others was pouring in. By 1950, Camden City had boomed to 124,555. It is hard to remember now, but until the 1960s, northern cities like Camden were beacons of hope for blacks fleeing the rigid segregation of the Jim-Crow South. Blacks fled north when the mechanical cotton-picker stole their jobs. Puerto Ricans headed for the mainland when the sugar plantations collapsed. They replaced European immigrants in factories and low-paying service industries.

The Delaware River, a waterway that Camden shared with the Port of Philadelphia, had once been the launchway for some of the nation's mightiest ships: a riverboat named *Robert Fulton*, battleships with names like *Oklahoma*, *Michigan*, *Utah*, and *South Dakota*, the

aircraft carrier *Saratoga*. U.S. Marines had guarded the Camden
shipyards during construction of the huge dreadnought *Idaho*. But by
the end of World War II, John Gunther's *Inside USA* called the river
"the largest, vilest, and foulest fresh-water port in the world; its water
is so tainted that, literally, it damages the steel walls of ships. Every
day, some 350 million gallons of raw sewage pour into the rivers that
are the city's only source of water supply."[10]

On a September morning in 1949, an obscure pharmacy-school
dropout, stalked among his neighbors at River and 32nd in East
Camden and methodically shot to death thirteen people and wounded
three others in a span of only twelve minutes. Howard Unruh was the
first of what was to become a long and bloody line of American mass
murderers. He set the national record for the bloodiest murder by one
person. On the day of the tragedy, police found Unruh's Bible in his
bedroom, open to the verse in Matthew: ". . . and these are the
beginning of tragedy."

A proud city began to crumble with its industries. New York Ship,
which had built 500 major vessels including submarines, closed in
1967. Esterbrook Pen Company that had turned out 600,000 pens a
day was torn down in 1970 to make a parking lot. On polished desks
in Washington, presidents had used Esterbrook pens to sign new laws.
Middle-class whites fled the city to thousands of new suburban homes
in towns with names like Cherry Hill, Voorhees, Gloucester Township. Success was *escape*. Blacks, Latinos, and poor whites were left.

The factory jobs that had made it possible for unskilled men and
women to climb out of poverty were gone. Across America, those in
"the great left-out"—no matter what their age, no matter what their
hopes—were out of luck. The decline of manufacturing jobs had done
as much as discrimination to trap the poor in the prison of poverty.

By 1969, FBI crime figures said Camden City ranked in the top ten
worst urban crime areas in the nation. By 1970, four thousand false
fire-alarms became a barometer of the ghetto's anger. Crime hurried
the flight from the city. The theaters were gone. The roller-skating
rink was gone. The bowling alley was gone. The department stores
were gone. For a youth population of more than 30,000, the city had
virtually nothing to keep its young people off the streets. No
entertainment—but two hundred bars.

In many parts of town residents could go weeks without encounter-
ing anyone, black or white, who was a middle-class achiever. During
1990, Camden had more crime per capita than New York or Los
Angeles and twice as much as Philadelphia. Drug gangs had swelled to
almost fifty.

---

[10]John Gunther, *Inside USA*, 606–7.

>—+—◆—○—◆—+—◁

At the peak of this Mischief Night in Camden, the torch-and-burn boys are setting fires at the rate of one a minute.

Five hundred firemen are out, called in from every fire department in the county. Called across the river from Philadelphia. Desperate summonings from neighboring counties.

Just up the pike, Chief Frank Lonsdale at the county fire-communications command post in Lindenwold warns his troops. Watch out for ambushes. "These kids set traps for the firemen. They set fire to vacant houses, pile trash in the living rooms, and set their fires—pull out floorboards then cover the hole with oilcloth so the fireman falls through." Be prepared for urban guerrilla warfare. At Fifth and Bailey—The Danger Zone—firefighters dodge a hail of rocks and bottles thrown by teenagers on the rooftops.

Camden has 4000 vacant or abandoned houses. Tinderboxes. Six weeks ago, the folks who know about such things predicted all of this. Angry neighbors shouted down the mayor: *Tear down abandoned houses. Board them up.*

But where was the money? Taxpayers elsewhere around the state were already paying two-thirds of what it cost to operate the city.

Flying with the ashes in the wind are ugly whispers. Hints. Gossip that the city itself is burning down the town to save the cost of demolition.

"Sometimes they let the kids do it . . . to demolish the old houses," Brandy says.

Burning ashes ride the wind tonight. Lindenwold crackles an SOS on the airwaves to summon five 8000-gallon water-tanker trucks. The city has run out of water.

A patrolman reports churn-'em-and-burn-'em gangs hurling Molotov cocktails at patrol cars.

A ride through hell. A night of $300,000-worth of rage—the rage of angry youth that will push even the Arab-Israeli peace talks out of morning headlines in the *Courier Post*. October 31: "IT'S LIKE BEIRUT OUT THERE." Next to the article appears a picture of Bessie Trader standing in the doorway of her burned-out home on York Street. She had lived there for twenty-seven years.

>—+—◆—○—◆—+—◁

Winsor Cooper could remember the first time it happened—when he spoke, when he seized a room, when God connected with the hearts through Winsor Cooper's voice—like a voice from God. It would all rush back to him. The faces of the teenagers. The preacher's sons. The Mount Zion Methodist Church on the White Horse Pike . . . the words that God had given him the night how many months before when the mighty hand of God pressed down upon his chest . . . his chest crushed hard against his back . . . the hand lifting him up from the bed to his feet. He had remembered it a thousand times. He had heard the word of God in the night: *Stand still and see the salvation of the Lord.*

With smoke blanketing Camden on this Mischief Night, under handmade Hallowe'en masks hanging on the polished brick walls thirteen older boys squeeze together *shhushhhing* the girls, and the younger boys crowded together in rows of chairs along the Youth Center cafeteria's serving counter across the room. On any normal day a giant Hallowe'en-decorated birthday cake with orange frosting would be the center of everyone's attention. Or maybe Officer Al Thomas's steel drums from the Virgin Islands. But not tonight.

The cafeteria is crowded tonight for a surprise birthday party—love fest—for the Reverend Winsor Cooper. Seventy-second birthday.

Posted as a lookout, all six-feet-six-inches of shift commander John Golaszewski signal that the Reverend Cooper is approaching down the hall. The *shhhushhh-ing* and the giggles stop. *Surprise!*

The Reverend Cooper's mouth pops open with all his usual drama. The dazzling Cooper smile with the one missing tooth in the front. Mrs. Cooper, carrying her tape-recorder music box, beaming as John leads them to seats of honor by the window, flanked by adoring youngsters.

Wednesday night is the Reverend Cooper's night. The Reverend Winsor Cooper, a seventeen-year legend at the Youth Center.

Far away from the wailing fire sirens in the city and beating rotors of helicopters overhead, the gentle twang of steel drums from the island leads a roomful of adoring teenagers in the hymn.

> *Amazing grace, how sweet the sound,*
> *That saved a wretch like me,*
> *I once was lost but now I'm found,*
> *Was blind but now I see.*

No other time in all the year would we bring together in this cafeteria every youngster in the place. Not ever. Three-Two posse against the Sons of Malcom X. Rose Street Boys against the Parkside Mob. Boys from the street, often locked in deadly competition. I look around the crowded room. Boys who have killed. Youngsters who tote guns. Boys who sell drugs. Girls who sell their bodies—children all bonded with adoration for a gray-haired man with a sparkle in his eye and a shine upon his face. Tonight these children are bound to Christians around the world with the music and words of an ancient hymn.

> *Through many dangers, toils, and snares*
> *I have already come.*
> *'Twas grace that brought me safe thus far,*
> *And grace will lead me home.*

When the Reverend and Mrs. Cooper came as volunteers seventeen years ago, no one expected them to last. Most people don't. Even good-hearted people who want to touch the world with their love and goodness get worn down after six months. Or even less. They dream of changing the bad boy with a miracle of love. And then the boy says "f__k" and "s__t" once too often . . . won't sit still to be loved . . . looks out at every stranger with eyes that never trust. Or the boy who can't read—this boy whom they're tutoring each week in the classroom—doesn't get an instant cure to be a superstar reader. The college student. The man from the Lions Club. The lady from the Junior Women's Club. The volunteers melt away.

These children are used to people who give up on them. The Reverend and Mrs. Cooper never gave up.

Gabriel takes me aside one day to show me his New Testament tucked under his pillow. The Reverend and Mrs. Cooper have just taken a tour of his residence unit. "Every time I walk in there to his service, he always say, 'That's my *main* man, Gabriel. That's my Gabriel. That's my right hand.' Everytime I walk in, he always call out my name. 'Gabriel. Gabriel.'"

Week after week, Mrs. Cooper, once a salaried church organist and school teacher, brings her music box and leads youngsters in songs that let them jump and clap and laugh. She helps them find the Bible verses on the page. And the Reverend Cooper talks about good and evil, God and the Devil, with stories every boy understands. Evil stalking boys and girls, "seeking whom he may devour." In the Reverend Cooper's stories, Evil is friends who lead you with them down the wrong path. Evil is the urge to shoplift. The tug to use drugs. The "babes on the street."

The language is so simple, the pictures so clear, the Reverend Cooper nudges everyone else off the schedule on Wednesday nights. There was the year that Alcoholics Anonymous had to shift out of its slot on the Wednesday night schedule because even the teenage alcoholics wanted to go to church.

The Youth Center packs its daily schedule with *requireds* and *electives*. School and recreation are required. So are health and vocational speakers. Electives—aren't. No one has to go to religious services at the Youth Center—Muslim, Roman Catholic, Protestant—but the Reverend Cooper has always attracted half the residents. Wednesday night is the Reverend Cooper's Night. When he talks about the Devil tempting a teenager to smoke a marijuana joint, he pinches his thumb and index finger to his lips and demonstrates until around the crowded circle of the church table everybody laughs and nudges his neighbor because the Reverend Cooper makes it look so real. When he talks about the Devil's tempting a boy to shoplift, he struts in his dapper tan suit around the table, looking all so innocently ahead, while snatching an imaginary tape cassette with his hand and stuffing it under his coat. The boys all know that the Reverend Cooper knows the scene.

God walks through all his stories—the One who put His hand on the Reverend Cooper's chest while he was in bed as a young man long, long ago. The hand lifted him off his bed, he tells the wide-eyed boys. The party man. The boxer. The athlete. The trumpet player. The one who liked to go to the bars. Winsor Cooper was all of them.

Gabriel can tell me every word. "The Reverend Cooper told us about the old time when he used to be playing the trumpet. . . ." Every boy has mastered a Reverend Cooper imitation, strutting and playing his trumpet. "He never used to be in the Word of God . . . just into parties, just like us juveniles right now. He was always into the trumpet havin' a nice time, lookin' at people drinkin' wine and havin' a nice time, doin' negative stuff, havin' parties. Until one day he was sleepin', an God came and put His hands on his chest and the Reverend Cooper tried to get up, but he couldn't. But the hands pulled him up and put him in the air and then just laid him back on his bed."

I listen in wonder—a boy from streets as bad as any in Sodom and Gomorrah telling me almost word-for-word all of the Reverend Cooper's stories.

"God was askin' him to leave all the negative stuff, the trumpet, havin' parties, and it was time for him to start preachin' and believin' in God and learnin' the Word of God so he could speak to people 'bout God—let the word out 'bout God. He changed a lot. Left all the negative stuff.

"He make us happy. Reverend Cooper makes us want to believe more and more about God and accept Jesus Christ as our personal Savior. So when he talk to us, he just talk to us about how fast he changed—that's the way we could do it the same way—have God make an immediate change.

"It been a few years he been talking about God. *It's wonderful*.

"Let the word out 'bout God." There's a soft glow to the boy's voice, this boy who is charged with shooting a man to death on North 24th Street.

"Reverend Cooper is alive like. Makin' funny. Make us laugh. Make us proud. He talk about God. Things that is negative that God don't want us to do—stuff like that. Tell us a lotta stories about God.

"Everybody believe him."

That was it. The Reverend Cooper could tell a boy about God putting His hand on a boy's chest and lifting him up. Just like on this night of a surprise birthday party for a seventy-two-year-old man. The lead-off verse tonight is John 3:16. "Who'll read it out loud?"

Ricardo Fontanez raises his hand. Across the room, youngsters rustle the pages of the pink New Testaments. Mrs. Cooper always brings a bagful of paperback Bibles, enough for everyone.

For God so loved the world ...

"Can't hear." Ricardo glares at the older boys across the room as the hum of the refrigerator motor in the kitchen muffles his voice. *For God so loved the world, that He gave His only begotten son that whosoever believeth in Him should not perish, but have everlasting life.*

"Wonderful. *Wonnn*-derful!" The Reverend Cooper punctuates all his conversations with repeated exclamations: "Beautiful. *Beau*-ti-ful!" The Reverend Cooper's praises always come in doubles.

As he does every Wednesday night, the group prays the prayer that ends every one of the Reverend Cooper's services: *Lord, forgive me for my sins.*

Children's voices echo him around the room. "Lord, forgive me for my sins."

As always on Wednesday nights, the amens are very loud. On this birthday night, every youngster—all twenty-three of them—wants a picture taken with the Reverend Cooper. Gabriel and the Reverend Cooper hug so tight, the arms wrap almost twice around each other, the bright blue sweatshirt crushing the blue suit and the red silk tie. The boy's tousled curls bury themselves in the man's shoulder, a boy's body reaching for a father he hasn't seen since he was a child. The boy won't let go. *When was the last time a man hugged any one of these boys?* I think to myself. The long lineup for hugs tells me its own story. The arms that hug tonight are black and white and brown. Gentleness and violence packaged together: Sometimes these arms and hands kill. Sometimes they hug.

The Reverend Cooper reaches for a pile of homemade birthday cards all full of childlike spellings: *Happy brithday ... my friend in Crist.* C-wing has made a card of yellow construction paper so giant that Mrs. Cooper has to help hold it up to read the names. Ricardo has made a card with praying hand and spelled out the words, "With Jesus in jail."

In B-wing, two of the boys have been practicing a popular song—like two sons waiting for a father's praise: Corey and Terrance pull up their white plastic chairs to the Reverend Cooper's knee and start to sing "It's so hard to say good-bye to yesterday." The old man's eyes begin to sparkle, his hand reaches out to touch a shoulder, and his mouth puckers up in the Cooper "O–o–o–o ...." that blesses every child who offers him personal treasures.

I look around the cafeteria at children eating spice cake with orange frosting from paper plates and know that the Reverend Cooper and his wife will leave an overflow from this Mischief Night. Tomorrow when I do my Clean-and-Tidy inspection of each room, Danton's sheet will be pulled tight with a cross formed by a small New Testament and tracts. Ricardo will bow his head and thank God before he eats his breakfast. Tucked next to his pillow, Gabriel will have his New Testament to reach and kiss before he falls asleep.

17

'57 CHEVY OR
SPACE SHUTTLE

Mario Pinardo looks up at the clock
on the classroom wall. "By 11:15 this morning, you're gonna have in
your head the keys to unlock success. I stumbled on this secret, when
I was thirty-seven years old."

In the Youth Center classroom on a summer morning, boys crowd
in a giant circle around the room. Wilson's heart tattoo ripples along
the bulges of his bicep, a red heart banded with a green sash lettered
M-A-R-G-A-R-I-T-A. Harry flaunts his honors status, perched on his
head a red Chicago Bulls athletic cap embroidered with white horns.
Purple sneakers—the newest rage. The sweat of skating roller hockey
bonds the group—in the sweltering heat of the gym, yellow sticks
against blue sticks, or the sweat of flag football in the fenced-in grass
together. In a strange way, we have made them brothers—these boys
who compete on the grubby drug corners of the street.

There's a sacred bond to this Thursday-morning class. Real talk.
Real feelings—all protected by agreed-upon rules: No spilling outside
the classroom what someone else has said. No busting on each other.
No interrupting anybody else. Respect.

Renee Pinardo has been wrapping teenagers with love ever since
Something turned her life around at a religious retreat half a lifetime
ago. She was a runaway girl, awash in drugs, a school dropout,
suddenly feeling herself washed over with love. That moment was
like God's dropping a pebble in the pond and watching the ripples
spread to touch shores that no one could even see.

In the miracle that followed, Renee started reaching out to
youngsters like herself in teen drop-in centers called The Bridge. By
the time the ripples reached the Youth Center, Renee and The Bridge
were touching 14,000 teens a year. On Thursday in the summer Youth
Center classroom, this former runaway, former rebellious teenager,
reaches into the no-man's-land of adolescent feelings and gets answers
no one else can ever get.

"We all know that your first priority in life is to get outa here.
Right? No one wants to make this their home. Right? Today, let's
look for a *dream*, a *wish*, or a *want* of your life. Think about your own

life. Remember your presentation skills. Sit up nice and straight. Heads up high." Squiggly teens sit still for Renee.

"Who's first?"

Lauren waves a hand. On the street, his habit costs him $150-a-day, smoking marijuana laced with cocaine. He arrived at the Youth Center early one morning with marijuana weed matted in his hair. This is a boy who has never known his father. His mother is a drug addict. I sit trying to guess what the boy will say today. A want. A wish. A dream.

"My parents better than what they are," he says. Yesterday, Lauren was wishing that the judge would send him someplace where he could get help with his addiction. Today, he aches for a family.

"To be an auto mechanic." Harry has bounced in and out of the Youth Center since he was twelve years old. His lavender sweatshirt hangs over faded dungarees.

"Stay outa trouble." Shawn told me this week about the war zone he goes through each day to get to his school and back, through battling posses armed with guns and bats, and pit bulls ready for the after-school crowd at his middle school.

"To graduate high school. Have my grandmom there watching."

"My dad, my cousin, come back in my life." Jesse got the news just yesterday—his cousin hanged himself in jail. Today he can only whisper. I lean forward to hear.

"Get outa here."

Jimmy looks across at me. "—To run this center." Every single time that Jimmy makes a wish, he tells me he's going to run this center.

If Jimmy ran the Youth Center, the menu each day would be black olives for lunch and pickles for dinner with maybe a side order of cheese steaks. Some days he makes a special effort to show me that he's taken one chip of lettuce—maybe two—from the salad bar—a response to my motherly nagging that boys eat something green. I used to say, "Didn't your mother tell you to eat something green every day?" Sometimes I don't.

Many of the boys don't have mothers. Jimmy doesn't. His father is an alcoholic. At thirteen, Jimmy is an imp that likes to play the trumpet I keep hidden under my bathroom sink, a battered treasure left over from my own childhood.

The parade of speakers in the Youth Center's summer classes aims at a catalog of tragedies: The county medical examiner holds the boys spellbound with words about bodies at the county morgue—the beautiful—cold—young bodies—dead from bullet wounds. The young man in his twenties—dying of AIDS. BEBASHI—Blacks

Educating Blacks About Sexual Health Issues. The lady from Narcotics Anonymous talking about her struggle in and out of addiction.

Substance abuse hits most at America's well-heeled middle class, so the guest is a suburban white. James Thornton, senior investigator from the prosecutor's office—owner of a Black Belt in karate, two dalmations, a karate school—grabbing their psyches by the back of the neck and talking street talk: "You play games with the law when you don't even know the rules."

Renee Pinardo says the class today is about setting goals, how to make dreams come true. She has brought a guest now sitting relaxed on the desk, his feet dangling above the floor, a blue sport shirt open at the neck. Mario Pinardo, her husband, teaches people how to succeed, she says. How to use their minds. He teaches doctors, Olympic athletes. Around the room, the backs sit up a little straighter. An important guest.

To a roomful of thirteen boys, shuffling their Nikes and Champions and Vikings on the floor—laces stylishly untied around their hightops—Mario Pinardo paints visions of dirt bikes and '57 Chevys and space shuttles. He moves his gaze around the room. Through years of teen discussions at The Bridge and workshops on motivation, he has learned to read body language—who crosses his arms to resist, who exposes his undefended chest in a sign of trust, who taps bored fingers on the arm of the chair. Lauren leans forward in his seat. He has stopped tugging on his hair.

"I'm gonna give you the keys to unlock success. I stumbled on this secret when I was thirteen years old," he says.

Mario Pinardo doesn't believe in blaming someone else for everything you do—imperfect parents, rotten schools, and shabby neighborhoods. The "victim trap." Always. Blame someone else. The summer classes concentrate on strength. The old-fashioned notion of personal responsibility.

Mario Pinardo looks up at the clock. "Let's get into how to use your imagination. Imagination," he says. "The key to success."

Lauren's head tilts sideways, his mouth open, leaning toward Mario. "I was very depressed." Mario says. "Thirteen years old." Lauren is thirteen.

"Every single thing that I thought was important to me . . . well, I was the opposite. Dumbest kid in the class. Worst grades. Shortest kid in the class. Fattest kid in the class. I stuttered. Had dorky clothes. And when I wanted to talk to chicks—do all the fun stuff, I wouldn't get picked. Get into sports, I wouldn't be picked to play any of the sports. Get cut from the team."

The boys are planted squarely in the pins and needles of adolescence. They are hooked.

"I was always the last person to be chosen on a team. If I wanted to talk to the chicks—like . . . nowhere. I got more and more depressed.

"One day I got so depressed, I sat down and I made a list. My list read, *What Do I Want To Change About Myself?* I remember the first thing was: I wanted to lose forty pounds. I didn't put anything down about grades because I didn't know I could change that. I knew I could change what I weighed, and I knew I could change the clothes I wore.

"Then I continued to write down the *Things I Want To Get For Myself.*

"The things I wanted to get for myself, like a new stereo. I wanted to get a dirt bike. Then I started to get real creative. Wanted to travel to Florida. I wanted to get my pilot's license. Fly airplanes. Take karate. I was thirteen years old."

The eyes are glued on Mario. "By the time I was fifteen years old, I accomplished every single thing on my list.

"Not that I was a superhuman kid or anything, but what I did was I wrote down what I wanted. Then I would write down how I was going to get it. And I got a notebook like this."

Mario holds up an ordinary school notebook. "I called my notebook *MY PLAN OF ACTION.* And I would take one page and put down *DIRT BIKE* at the top of the page. And I put down all the places I would ride when I went out riding. And I put down research on how much it would cost. I got pictures of them and got a *MOTORCYCLE* magazine. And then I set a goal and saved up so much money. It took me like a year and a half. I saved up $450.

"On my fourteenth birthday, we drove down to a Yamaha shop, and we picked a brand-new Yamaha dirt bike. We put it in my brother-in-law's Volkswagen bus and rolled it into my house in the front room. For two days I slept with that bugger, with my hand on the foot pedal—took my sleeping bag next to it. I had accomplished something.

"For the next two years I rode the heck out of that thing. Put a thousand miles on it. I was an animal on that thing. Took my friends out on it . . . chicks out on it. . . .

"Remember we talked about imagination? My plan of action had made a picture in my head. Imagination is creating an opportunity before it exists. Creating a way to make it exist.

"I didn't know it, but I had stumbled across the keys to success. I created an opportunity on paper—before it existed. And on paper, I started to create ways to make it exist."

There's good news and there's bad news, Mario says. "The good news is every one of us has a computer as good as a space shuttle or even better up here in our head." Mario points to his brain. "The bad news is . . . most people think they're driving '57 Chevys. That's bad news, ain't it?"

There is a pained look of reality sinking in.

"Now what if they wanted to play a joke on the space shuttle and said, 'Look, guys. Instead of telling the space shuttle it's a space shuttle, programming it to take off and go around the world and land back on earth again, let's play a joke on it. Let's program the space shuttle and tell it it's a '57 Chevy.' Is it gonna argue with the people?"

"No." A chorus—almost childish enthusiasm that might normally come from a roomful of eight-year-olds.

"No. 'Cause they're saying it's a '57 Chevy. I'm gonna be a '57 Chevy. They put it up on the launching pad. They push the launch pad. Where does it go?

"Nowhere.

"It may head off to a movie down the street. But it sure ain't gonna blast off and circle the world and come back again. Right? A space shuttle good enough to go around the world and you're only driving it up the block.

"If you take what I'm saying . . . listen to what I say, apply what I say, I guarantee it will change your life . . . not just now, but forever. What happens in your life, you're gonna have greater control over.

"How many of you, if you could tap into this power, would use it?" The sneakers have stopped shuffling. Every hand goes up.

"When I would stop writing . . . that thirteen-year-old kid . . . dreaming about a dirt bike . . . if I didn't know what else to write on my page . . . well, that space shuttle up here in my head was going a hundred miles an hour to figure out what else I could write on my dream list. Priming my imagination. It was going around. And I was thinking out more information. Like if I needed more money, the space shuttle in my mind would figure out ways to make money. Figure out ways to get what I needed to get.

"Success starts with *you*. There are plenty of people that have opportunity around them—and people around that actually want to help them to be successful. . . . They could go to school, they could do whatever they want, but they're still not successful."

The man is hitting close to home.

". . . use their mind like a '57 Chevy. No matter how much help they are getting, they are not gonna be successful.

"Then there are people in the situation where no one wants to help them, and they end up being the most successful people. They end up doing astronomical things with their life—as far as their ability can take them. People can help. And you do want to get people to help you.

"But, again, the responsibility—we *have* to take it.

"The reason most people aren't successful is that they never knew they could be successful."

Hope rushes in as Mario talks.

"Until you know you can be successful—you don't think about

what kind of success you want to have—and the power. You can't get someplace that you don't even know exists."

Faces fill with dreams.

"The power exists in your imagination. And it exists in abundance. Write down your dream. Write it down. Until you write what you want, you don't know what you want."

Like most of the boys, Foster wants shortcuts. At fourteen, he weighs 215 pounds and finds himself the butt of jokes about his weight. "But isn't it the same—keeping it in your mind, instead of writing it all down?"

"If you can't write it down, you're not done thinking about it," Mario says. "*In your mind* is not enough. Most of us can't even add two four-digit numbers in our head. Yet we can, if we write the numbers down. If we can't even add two four-digit numbers in our head, how are we going to accomplish our goals in our head? If you write it down, you'll do it. If you don't write it down, you might not ever do it.

"Write it down: *What* you want. *When* you want it. *Why* you want it. That powers your imagination. Gets that creativity going."

He lets silence suffuse the room.

Out in the hallway the intercom summons the shift commander away from his own fascination with the scene before him in the room. Summer classes always attract a bevy of curious officers listening just inside the classroom door—AIDS, addiction, dead bodies in the morgue. Today the attraction is a road map for success for boys who have been at the Youth Center, most of them, one or two times before. Mario's eyes again search the faces around him, halt again on Lauren.

"We call it, *Writing your own book so you don't become a character in someone else's script*. Sometimes we get in trouble because someone gets us to be a character in their script. They put us in that character. And then we got in trouble. If you have your own book you're writing, you don't have time to be a character in someone else's script. The book that you're writing is the book of what *you* want. What *you* want to be."

I look at Wilson—church, family, everything in place—a boy arrested in a police raid on a vacant house on 24th Street. Guns. Ninja suit and mask.

The boy is listening to Mario. "Someone comes to you and says I need a go-fer—need someone to do my dirty work, and I'm gonna pay this much money. You say, 'Wait a minute. I can't accomplish what's in my book, if I'm gonna be a character in your book.'

"If you've made a mistake, remember this: Failure is your opportunity to begin again—more intelligently.

"In this book, you become the author of the novel of your own life."

In the hush of the classroom, the boys struggle to pull dreams out of their heads. Put them on paper. I have seen this struggle so many times before—boys who have never, ever, known hope. Most boys like these don't even dream of getting out.

Personal experience is their only security. Success is a drug lord. The money is too good, and the alternatives are too few.

Change is terror.

Jackson looks up at Renee for help. The paper asks him to write, What is it about your life right now that makes you want to change? He struggles with the words. "'Cause I don't like how I am now."

But Jackson knows the dream. In large printed letters he writes: STAY OUT OF TROUBLE. TO MAKE IT IN SCHOOL.

I can't keep my own feelings at bay. The boy has dodged bullets hitting his school bus. He tells me about "Thursday and Friday fight days" outside his school. The boy calls me "my main lady." His mother is dead.

His hand moves slowly down the page. Why don't you have it now? I watch his pencil moving. *Didn't try hard enough.*

What will you have to do to make your dream come true? The boy's pencil moves slowly: *Make myself beleave I can do it.*

Across the room, Nickee keeps secrets. Tiny, scrimped letters hiding on the page. He comes from the bombed-out, burned-out, glass-strewn ruins of North Camden. The only home he has ever known. Twelve of his friends have died since he was in junior high. At seventeen, Nickee himself is marked for death. A boy on the drug-war hit list. Sons of Malcolm X against the world. The world against the Sons of Malcom X.

What would you like to change about your life?
Selling drugs.
What dream would you like for your life?
To keep living.

CONSEQUENCES

Julio props his chin in his hands as he talks to me across my desk about the Youth Center school. "That old lady in the classroom—the one I call Grandmom—she taught me how to write my name."

The boy gets a faraway look. "You know how it is when your mom runs off," he says. "Runnin' loose."

At seventeen, Julio has been "running loose" since he was nine years old.

When the voice on the radio tells me that thirteen-and-a-half-million American children are poor, the number doesn't hit me until I try to imagine thirteen-and-a-half-million Julios. Poverty isn't ever a number at the Youth Center. It's a child that arrives in the night with the underwear rotting on his bottom and the socks disintegrating on his feet. Poverty is a stench—of urine and sweat and unwashed clothes. This is a boy who can't list a place when we ask him for the address to mark onto the record card. A boy who asks himself the most basic questions every night: Where am I gonna sleep? He sleeps in cars.

Poverty is Emmadine, at fifteen, who has never—ever—been in a car. She hunches her body awkwardly, in terror as you ask her to get in; she has never stepped into a car.

Any mother knows that children freeze before they starve. Stark choice: Heat the home? Or feed the children? At the Youth Center they often arrive hungry. Long ago I added a reminder question to our admission checklist: Have you offered this child something to eat? Can a youngster who's hungry concentrate on arithmetic? Learn to write his name?

Julio's mother, a drug addict and a prostitute, abandoned her fourteen children eight years ago. Julio prefers to believe that she died. The boy says he can walk around the city with his eyes closed— "empty houses, abandoned buildings, abandoned cars. The lady at the cheese-steak store used to feed me every day until I started trappin' (selling drugs). After that I could support myself without beggin'.

"I didn't know how to spell or write or read. Grandmom, there"—

he points to Thelma Shevlin, our foster-grandmother, photocopying schoolwork in the room next door—"she told me, 'Well, you gonna learn now because I'm here and I'm gonna teach you.' She help me out a lot. I'll never forget her."

Here, the boy doesn't have to worry about where his next meal comes from. He takes a paper from my desk and writes his name in an uncertain scrawl—*Julio*. We put his story—and his shaky handwritten signature—on the front page of *WHAT'S HAPPENING*.

Success changes behavior better than anything else I know. I once heard a psychologist say that terror is marked on our bones. I think that success is, too.

Success is always a landmark memory. I took a memory trip to China a year or so ago . . . me . . . standing outside a door of an ancient building, half a world away, the rotted paint peeling from the door at the end of the long, familiar corridor.

It's funny what you remember about a concentration camp that ate three years of your life. The door to my dormitory in Weihsien Concentration Camp. Padlocked shut. I begged them—BEGGED them—to find the key to let me in. When they finally unlocked the door, I stood on one special spot. And I started to weep.

Not weeping about barbed wire and guard dogs but about the years of feeling like the dunce, the misfit in the class and the dormitory. The terrors of looking at *b* and thinking it was *d* . . . the terror of failing—again . . . I learned to dread. I'd be running across the quad, flushed, healthy, a tumble of blue-eyed frolic, and then I'd remember: Oh, please, God, NO! "Mental arithmetic" today . . . my mind blank as I stood in the front of the class, Miss Stark dictating the numbers I had to add in my head—failing in front of everyone. My tongue dry. Failure choking my brain.

And now the tears streamed down my face as I stood on that spot on the concrete floor of that crumbling room . . . another memory . . . twelve years old I guess I was. My teacher reading aloud the end-of-the-marking-period averages for all our classes. My adding them up. And adding . . . again . . . again—Mary, AGAIN—to be sure. And there it was. Top average in the whole Chefoo School. Not top of the class. Top of the very whole school.

My daughter, Alice, held me as the tears washed my cheeks . . . remembering . . . on that trip. She seemed to understand. She took a picture. Mary and the starting point that changed her life. I was not dumb. NOT DUMB! That was the moment. From that time on, I knew that I always wanted to reach for the top.

Ben reaches over and pats my arm at the lunch table where I'm telling my story to boys and girls from A-wing.

People didn't believe you could motivate "these boys." They were wrong. The daily Clean-and-Tidy inspection taught me more about "using psychology" than anything else. It was its own parable about the taste of success.

When I was growing up, "using psychology" was the way to get results. My sister Kathleen would promise to let me take her blue satin dress to college, and I'd be nice to her for a whole week. Dad would make a nice fuss about how I'd made the kitchen sink sparkle *and* say something like "Mary, Sweetheart!" and I'd scrub the sink *and* the stove the next time around.

Renaldo taps me on the shoulder one morning—very politely—as the boys line up at the door for school. He holds up a yellow Post-it sticker lettered with red grease pencil and my printing: "Good job," it says. He has taken it from his bedroom door.

"Boring words," he says. "Not with it."

"Oh, yes?" I try to look wide-eyed.

"I give you a list of new words—hip words for our doors. We like stuff like *chillin, fat,* an' *decent.*"

Great, hulking street boys improving my vocabulary . . . English teacher and all. Some days the boys can be shaggy and loveable, with Saint Bernard charm.

"Gather round, guys. Renaldo says he wants to improve my choice of words. Vocabulary." Twitters chirp along the line. Nods.

"These words, you guys, these words you're giving me, you know I have to check them out. Did I ever tell you the story about the time the guys got me in trouble because they gave me a dirty word?" The school line breaks. Teenage giants, street urchins crowd in to listen. For this conversation today, school will have to wait.

"Kids always want to tell me a word—like today—something new for their door—on their happy-face sticker for the day. Get a new word . . . use it a lot. One day, inspecting the bathroom in the girls' wing, I hear this little voice from the dayroom, squeaky and upset, saying, 'Who put them nasty words on my door?'

"I stopped dead to listen.

"'What's wrong with that?' I heard Miss Charlene say. 'Mrs. Previte put that on your door.'

"'Them words be nasty,' she said. I heard the girl's voice pause . . . 'Wouldn't even say the words out loud.'"

The boys look at each other as I talk. John nudges Renaldo. Half-cocked smile.

"I come out of the bathroom and look at the Clean-and-Tidy sticker on her door. 'What does "fat jammies" mean?' I ask her."

The boys began to snort. John falls to the floor and rolls under the bench, holding his sides.

"Fat jammies" is the street code for parts of the body that the boys know I don't talk about.

The next day Renaldo takes me aside with his list of new words written in pencil on yellow paper with blue lines. I can see that the boy is taking me under his wing. "These words will be okay, for sure." He hands me his list:

You got it goin' on
That's dope (it means great)
decent
chillin
fat (it means nice)
the real deal
Okay family

I keep my "approved" list growing, taped to the brown file cabinet near my desk for a quick refresher just before I made my daily Clean-and-Tidy rounds.

A nudge in the classroom here and a suggestion in the hallway there—always with a new word—keeps my approval ratings high.

It was my assistant, Greg Lyons, whose idea inspired the daily Clean-and-Tidy competition how many years ago. . . . Messy bedrooms, beds always rumpled like a kid who hadn't washed or combed for a week, soap scum streaking the bathroom from dozens of showers a day, dust fluffies playing on the floors. Why not let the units compete for a weekly prize? Daily inspection. A Clean-and-Tidy score sheet. A stay-up-late-Friday-night video and special snack for a prize.

There was another bonus to the project. An administrator can get buried in paperwork, preoccupied with grown-up meetings—endless, important projects—and never see a kid. If classrooms were my first-stop visit every morning, the Clean-and-Tidy would now be my daily excuse to look inside each bedroom. You can tell a lot about a boy or girl by the way he makes his bed or she decorates her bedroom . . . what's happening in their hearts.

For kick-off day—Day One—I knew I'd have to leave my mark to show the boys I had been around inspecting . . . instant feedback for the Now-or-Never boys. No way the troops would wait until the end of the week to find out how they had done. So for kick-off day, pink or yellow or blue Post-it stickers were a perfect solution. For every bedroom that passed inspection on Day One, I stuck a Post-it on the door. I drew a round, happy face marked on with magic marker. Smiley faces. And words like *PROUD, NEAT, SUPER STAR, BEAU-TIFUL, WONDERFUL, WOW!* My mix of cheering section and very proper English.

For teenagers, the most unspeakable punishment is having to wait. Day One. Pastel stickers created instant winners.

Halfway through Day Two, social worker Leo Gold was at my desk.

Leo was Unit Manager of the wing for younger boys. His were the thirteen- to sixteen-year-olds, still in the hormonal no-man's-land of junior high school. In C-wing, the boy that in the morning dreams in the weight room of building his muscles like a grown-up man, by nighttime may be curled up in a fetal ball on his bed and sucking his thumb like a toddler.

When he has something serious on his mind, Leo has a way of walking in to sit in the blue chair across from my desk: "My boys want to know where today's stickers are."

"Stickers?" Stickers, I had figured, were just to get it started. Just for Day One. To let the boys know I had been around.

Leo leaned over my desk as though all fifteen of his boys were right behind him. "Muh—boys—want—to—know—where—their—stickers—are," he said.

Stickers *every* day?

And that's how stickers grew on doors—every day. Some of the boys collected them like baseball cards. Sometimes we suffered sticker thieves. They papered their doors with Post-its marked with a smiley face and a word in red grease pencil. Lined them up in rows on their walls or doors.

"You want to see my stickers?" They'd pull over a visitor to admire their display. Lamont had snagged a visiting member of the local Board of Education: "GLORIOUS. I LOVE TO INSPECT THIS ROOM. See this? THIS ROOM IS A MODEL FOR EVERYONE TO COPY—that's my favorite." He would read down the list of words above each smiley face.

Tell a boy on Monday that his room is magnificent, and he will reward you on Tuesday and Wednesday and Thursday and Friday with not just one magnificent room—but also bedrooms, bathrooms, and refrigerators. Strange how a boy clings to a few Post-it stickers that help change his vision of himself.

Even haircuts. This is the week that Jamar in C-wing gave a very shaggy Danton a fashionable flattop box cut with an ear-to-ear fade. It doesn't matter who comes into the building—Board of Trustees, interns, police—Jamar is the officers' trophy for big-deal introductions: "This is Jamar, the best hair stylist in the Youth Center. You should see the box cut he just gave Danton." Before my eyes I watch a shy youngster transformed into a boy glowing with pride. Next he sprouts confidence. I can't stop Jamar from cutting hair. After 3:00 P.M. shift change, after supper, boys line up at Jamar's makeshift barber chair next to the Ping-Pong table.

At our house, we called it "using psychology."

>─┤◆>─○─<◆├─<

The officer looks me straight in the eye. "They're pigs, Mrs. Previte. Pigs."

B-wing has been a disaster for weeks. The older boys.

Silence.

"Well, motivate them. Show them how."

"You can't motivate pigs."

And sure enough, they are.

Not long after that, the officer is injured in a work-related injury. Officers who call the boys "pigs" often are.

In his place, Officer Vernon Boyd is assigned to B-wing in the mornings. Vernon isn't a talker. And when he smiles, only half of his face humps up.

But suddenly the loser—B-wing—is winning Clean-and-Tidy every day. Six weeks they go in a stretch, winning the weekly Friday-night video and special snack. Beds in B-wing are like something out of the Marine Corps. Picture-perfect-like *House Beautiful*. The bars of soap are lined up along the sinks every day, squared off as if someone has measured the inches between them. In the refrigerator, even the half-pint red-and-white milk cartons look as if they have been lined up perfectly for roll call. A-wing and C-wing can't come close.

Occasionally, I wander into B-wing among the boys when no one sees me coming. Sometimes I hear Vernon preaching black pride. "You can be anything you want to be if you set your mind to it," I hear him say. "Anything."

I ponder it. In just a matter of days a collection of boys has changed. "Pigs" turn into winners before my eyes. Vernon passes out pride with the combs and toothbrushes in the morning.

Michael, one of Vernon's B-wing boys, sits talking to me on the sink-down couch in my office one afternoon. "When I be finished doing my time, I want to come back here." The boy finishes quietly. ". . . An' be an officer," he says, "just like Vern."

This morning gives me time enough only for a "lick-and-a-promise" inspection for Clean-and-Tidy. The boys are all in their class-rooms. Today I will skip unlocking closet doors to look for neatly folded underwear and towels . . . skip the daily search for dust fluffies under the benches. I may even skip my daily sparkle test of every urinal.

"Have you checked the toilets, Boss?" Shift commander John Golaszewski's voice comes from the B-wing drinking fountain behind me.

I'm hurrying.

John has a way of bending his six-feet, six-and-a-half inches over me until I pay extremely close attention. John has always been bonded to his boys in B-wing, perhaps because of the Monday nights he returns on his off-duty time to lead a religious service, to talk to anyone who wants to hear about Jesus. No boy ever challenges John. It may be the six-feet, six-and-a-half-inch part of him. It may be the Jesus part of him. It may be the love part of him. More than any other member of the staff, John goes to the Hall of Justice in Camden to testify in court to the judge about the good behavior of his boys.

"You checked the toilets yet?" He insists. I can see today Big John is not giving up.

I round the corner of the tan privacy dividers and look down at the B-wing toilets. Iridescent white tape stretches tightly over freshly swabbed toilet bowls. Giant letters—SANITIZED—neatly lettered on the tape.

I shriek.

My arms stretch high around John's neck, then I race for the intercom in my office. John's boys will be listening, I know.

"May I have your attention, please." The voice sounds very proper, very businesslike, very urgent: "May I have your attention, please. B-wing boys, report back to your unit. B-wing boys, please report back to your unit."

Great big hulking man-boys, grinning like kids troop in . . . head straight for their toilets . . . checking out the tape and lettering all over again. A few high-fives smack overhead.

In the "using psychology" textbook in my head, SANITIZED toilets deserve an Academy Award. For the next half hour, I lead guided tours of the B-wing toilets. A snaking line of C-wing boys and A-wing girls and teachers, rec staff, secretaries. Even the cooks.

Someday when I pull out the treasures from my treasure box of memories, very close to the top will be sixteen grown-up, grinning, teenage boys with their freshly swabbed toilets banded with iridescent tape marked: SANITIZED.

>⊷⊶•O•⊷⊶⊰

The corrections sergeant in the blue uniform—navy slacks with a long stripe down the leg—ushers the Youth Center boys into Riverfront State Prison's Cell #2.

"Okay, you guys. Listen up. I want these I.D. cards chest-high." He barks off their names and hands each boy a yellow visitor badge to clip to his chest. As if to make the message clear that security is Priority Number One in this bastille, he pat-searches the boys again behind ceiling-high chain-link fence before ushering them in to the Fresh-Start conference room. Three adult inmates in khaki prison suits and tan boots sit waiting in a circle of chairs.

"I know you guys went through some stuff to get in here." José, a twenty-two-year-old, state-prison inmate from Paterson, New Jersey, starts talking about his life. "I want you to relax. This isn't Scared Straight." The inmates pass hard candy around the circle, and the five Youth Center boys settle into their chairs.

Fresh Start introductions mince no words. "I wasn't carin' s__t about nothin'. . . . I shot the guy in the back with a sawed-off shotgun."

Ricardo flinches. It is his own story, told by a young Latino man who looks like him—except the boyish playfulness is gone. José is Puerto Rican. Darrell is black, a twenty-four-year-old from neighboring Lawnside in Camden County. Tom, fifty-four, is white, born in the Lower East Side of New York City. Darrell says he was trying to get back at his father, ". . . Didn't express myself . . . held my feelin's in . . . didn't care about nothin'." He looks at the five young boys across the circle. "I built a wall around myself . . . didn't let anyone in. It's a good thing to talk to someone," he says quietly, almost with regret. "I was locked up for armed robbery."

"Before I talk to you . . ." Tom wants a conversation. "Do you guys think before you act?"

Almost without thinking, Ricardo says yes.

"My father punched the dog s__t out of me trying to toughen me up . . . baseball bats. . . . On the streets I got a sense of belonging . . . colors . . . turf . . . girls. . . ." Tom is clearly the leader of the group. "I was very, very angry . . . poor. . . . I blamed my father and mother for bringing me into a world like this." Tom's candor about his family surprises the boys. We all take a loyalty oath when we are children. The rules and reminders in a thousand messages that "family business" is sacred, inviolable, and private. Fresh Start sets aside those rules.

Tom bares the beatings and the abuse and tells a story of membership in social clubs and gangs and posses. His search for a substitute for a family. A way to escape the pain. "At fourteen years old I put a needle in my arm."

Ricardo bends over at the mention of posses and rests his chin on his folded hands.

"I stabbed a guy in the mess hall in front of one thousand to establish myself. I don't care what they say, nothing in jail rehabilitates you. I became an alcoholic in the prison. I did six years in prison and when I was released, I was a walking time-bomb . . . stick-ups, robberies, drinking. . . . I shot and killed two cops. I don't even have a living memory of it. I was sentenced to death . . . spent nine years in solitary on Death Row." The boys sit frozen in their seats. And I do, too—knowing again that *other fingers are on the trigger when an abused boy kills.*

People who know about these things will tell you that children who witness violence among parents, by parents, are likely to use weapons themselves. Shoot . . . stab . . . hit . . . kick—instant violence becomes their response to almost any conflict. Desensitized to violence. Blocking out the horror. Grown-ups teach children the lessons of violence all too well.

José lets Tom's story—twenty-eight years in prison—sink in before he speaks. Tom went to prison before these boys were born. What do they think goes on in prison? Tom wants to know.

"Drugs. Sex. Fights," says Ricardo.

"Ask any questions you like."

"What do you do here?"

"Wait. We'll tell you. First we want to hear from you. What do you think it's really like?"

"Overcrowded."

"Rape."

Aaron shakes his head as though he's already decided to change his ways. "I think what I do."

Ricardo, who will soon be eighteen, looks at José. "They put you here when you was eighteen?"

"Eighteen."

Heath shudders at a knife shaped like a cross, as the inmates pass large photographs around the circle. "Those are things they find in here? They make their own shanks?" he asks.

"Just wait till everyone has a chance to see."

"This bed wouldn't pass Clean-and-Tidy. . . ."

"And that's one of the nicer ones, too."

Tom shows a picture of a corrections officer with a gun. "That's a picture from Rahway. What is this guy's job?" Everyone in New Jersey knows about Rahway State Prison.

"Shoot."

"His job is to shoot you. It's not a joke. Guys have been killed . . . crippled. . . . It's not a TV commercial. It's your mother's tears. The end of your life."

The boys finger a picture of a prison kitchen. "Imagine yourself in these pictures . . . one year . . . five years . . . ten. . . . They's people that ain't clean . . . not care about your health . . . put their finger up their nose . . . scratch between their legs . . . go to the toilet and not wash their hands and fix your food. It doesn't matter the name of the place: It's Prison, U.S.A."

"What you think is gonna happen if you refuse to go in the cell here?" Tom doesn't wait for an answer. "There gonna be more blue here than the Atlantic Ocean. You have no power. There's no tough guys in jail."

José has a bit of an accent as he speaks. "We always thought we had a master plan—how we'd not get caught . . . getting my 'rep' up . . . cars, jewelry, ridin' round with all the girls." On his lap, his outstretched fingers touch at fingertips. "You don't get used to this s__t . . . no such thing as privacy. In the dormitory . . . is the most dangerous setting in the prison. . . . When you go to sleep, your a_s is up. You bump someone, step on someone . . ." He leaves the rest of the story to their imagination.

"You might get killed over a wedding ring, a religious chain . . ."

"But where are the guards?"

"Only two guards for a hundred prisoners."

Tom looks at Danton. "You look like a guy that carries weapons on the streets. What you carry?"

"Knives."

"What you see in this picture?"

"Ice picks ... machete ... gun ... cross ... knife ..."

"Guys are not in here for lickin' stamps. The cops was bringing this dude here to get his prison clothes. ..." Tom pinches the fabric of his khakis. "... These gorgeous clothes we're wearing. These masked prisoners jumped out and stabbed the guy to death ... didn't even get his prison clothes yet. ..."

Ricardo grabs for a candy.

"There's no friends in here ... even in your crew. Twenty-eight years I've spent in New Jersey prisons. No friends ..."

José breaks in, a face squeezed dry of joy—or any other sign of feeling. "The judge turns off your lights." He points to his head and his heart. "There's something missing."

"We're part of the walking dead." Tom pulls the boys back into the conversation: "What is it you lose when you come to prison?"

"Lose your freedom. Gotta ask to go to the bathroom."

Tom nods. "Whatever they give, they can take away. Lose any choice."

"Lose your life, can't be with your family." Damon dreams family because he really hardly has one, but what he has is all he's got.

"Your girl," says Ricardo, who by this time is trying to imagine being without Marielle for twenty-eight years. "You can't be close to her ... someone else having fun with her ... losing love."

"Your girl ... she ain't your girl no more when you're locked up in here."

"Love and affection. That's a real loss, man."

"To do what I want to do."

"Privacy."

"We all have to have our number on our shirts."

"You guys get haircuts here?" At the Youth Center, Ricardo always makes sure to keep trimmed.

Tom laughs. "Plumbers and bricklayers do the haircuts."

"Seems like you lose all your rights—right to feel safe when you lie down to sleep. ..."

"I saw a guy killed for stealing half a tube of toothpaste. But I tell you, suicide is the number-one killer in jails. Not a knife."

"Any of you guys ever get raped?" Ricardo asks.

"They don't care if you're Bruce Lee," Tom says. "The big dope dealers are the ones with the big a_s h___s—the ones they're gonna take ..."

Tom points to his two young partners with obvious affection. "I look at these two men and have to keep from crying. They never got a chance before they got here. I killed those cops, I gave up chances for life. We want you to have chances. We didn't think. *You're* getting a chance with one foot in jail ... *getting a chance*. ...

"When I was locked in the death house was when reality struck me. I gave my whole life away. We are not a movie. Our lives have been destroyed by the things we chose to do."

Tom pauses before he moves on—trying to turn walls into doors for these boys. He wants the word chose to sink in. *Chose*. People get to prison by their choices. "What goal do you want to accomplish in the next six months?" He waits for an answer.

Aaron shuffles his sneakers. "Haven't set any."

"Didn't give myself any."

Ricardo speaks quietly. "I want to go to trial and get out. Get a job. Get my G.E.D. Be with my girl."

"Get out of Jamesburg." Jamesburg is the state training school for boys—always overcrowded.

Ricardo has been shaken by his morning at Fresh Start. "If it take makin' burgers at Burger King, you got to do it."

I look at the prisoner number on Tom's shirt as he talks: Someone who used to be a man, now Prisoner #4-1608. "I used to think working for minimum wage it was punk s__t," he says. "Almost guarantee if you don't have no goals, you gonna wind up in jail."

What hits a bunch of kids in the Fresh-Start circle? Losses—that's what hits. "To play with my dog ..." The grown man in the prison khakis with a number on his pocket bursts into tears, sobs catching even the grown men by surprise. ... Play with my dog ...

Losing ordinary joy ... choices ... dignity ... self-respect ... having fun ... going where you want to go. Men in hell shout warnings to young boys stumbling on the wrong path. No one moves.

A very quiet group of boys walks back through massive security doors, past chain-link fence and into the Youth Center van secured in the sally port. The sky around Riverfront Prison is rimmed with razor ribbon, towered guard posts, and officers with guns. "Gotta set a goal for myself," says Aaron. "Don't go back to selling drugs ... go to school ... set a goal ... don't wanna end up here."

>⁃⧫⦁⬥⧫⦁⧀

Vincent Aspirez, fourteen years old, had tried to kill himself a time or two before.

But that was before.

Certainly nothing the Youth Center knew about a boy who didn't speak English.

Swallowing detergent out on the ocean when they caught him as a stowaway on a boat, trying to get away from the Dominican Republic. Nobody knew how many times he had tried until he finally made it to America. Vincent Aspirez. Maybe Vincent Reyes. Nobody knew for sure. The admission papers from the Camden police listed AKA (also

known as) Vincent Reyes. No known address. A checklist of answers—unknown . . . unknown . . . unknown . . . After it was all over,
someone said "seems to be" living with a woman in the city who had
picked him up off the street and taken him home. He wouldn't say
who or where. You never knew if a thing like that was sexual or
motherly. Fourteen-year-old boy. On the streets, you never knew for
sure. Surviving by silence. A ghost. Illegal aliens were often like that.
Dodging the immigration snoops. The boy said there were three
sisters somewhere in America. He didn't know where.

All you ever had on a boy like this was "seems to be . . ." Until a
thing like this—when it was way too late—and then when the kid
was dead or mangled or who knows what out there, someone would
figure it out.

And there the boy was, crouched on the highest red rafter of the
gym, spitting, crying, throwing dust balls from the ledge . . . threatening—in Spanish—to jump.

"The ear"—that's what Ray Ruiz always called it. That sixth sense.
Ray was a shift commander on the 3-to-11 shift. "Expect the
unexpected—always . . . always!" Ray would tell new recruits.
"Always"—the way Ray said it—always sounded urgent. "When it's
quiet, somepin's wrong. When it's loud, it might be coverin' up
somepin' else. Status-quo changes . . . somepin' is wrong. Always
monitor." You developed "the ear," Ray Ruiz would say. B-wing is
noisy. Yes, you know B-wing is noisy. Older boys. B-wing comes back
from the cafeteria, walks into the wing and does not make noise, you
know they messed up.

Someone wasn't listening to "the ear." Towel wrapped around the
boy's neck earlier in the day. Now, 6:50 on a Sunday night. No
Spanish-speaking staff around. An officer—chasing only two steps too
far behind—a boy shimmying up the rafters of the gym. And, no, the
officer was not going to climb the wires. The boy was threatening to
jump if anyone came near.

It was Ricardo who volunteered to go after the kid. Ricardo was the
"big brother" in C-wing. Some people even called him "junior staff"
because he had been there so long. Giving out clean socks and
underwear to new boys . . . knowing just the size to pick. He had
gotten so good at it, sometimes a new kid would come up to
Ricardo—his muscles now all bulged to make him look like a grown-
up . . . five-feet-eight . . . maybe 190 pounds. A kid would ask Ricardo
permission to use the phone, and Ricardo would laugh and tell the kid
that he wasn't an officer. Sometimes it was hard to tell because Youth
Center officers didn't wear uniforms.

Ricardo was telling everyone that Aspirez up on the rafters said he
was going to stay up there until his court date—and no one knew
exactly when that would be . . . and no one had a ladder that tall . . . so
it was Ricardo . . . maybe a comforting big brother could do it if

anybody could ... volunteering to climb up—7:15 on a Sunday night—squatting like a hunchback, stooped with his knees bent on the thin, red rafter and his back braced against the white insulation of the ceiling, inching toward this boy who was crying and spitting and throwing ten years' worth of dust fluffies from the rafter onto the hard tile floor, twenty-five feet below. Wanting to die ... no friends ... tired of his life ... missed his brothers and sisters, he said ... no girlfriend ... him ... the only one that could support his mom back in the Dominican Republic—fourteen years old ... charged with possession of a shotgun ... supporting his mom back home ... a man of care so long before his time ...

It was sad about these kids from the streets. . . . And "Get the Bible, Ricardo. Read to me before I jump." . . . Yep, it was sad ... a fourteen-year-old stowaway—boat person—who couldn't speak English—up on a rafter in New Jersey wanting a bit of a religious ceremony before he died ... looking down at wimpy, 3 x 8, blue exercise mats set out twenty-five feet below to cushion his jump. . . .

Aspirez liked Ricardo. The boy was hanging by one hand. Then one foot. Then lying down on the rafter. Hanging. Swinging. Dangling. People gasping down there ... twenty-five feet below. It was crazy up there. Everything moving in s-l-o-o-o-o-w motion. Please, please, God, don't let him jump. Then Ricardo began giving the boy Leo Gold's speech. He heard it every day after school in Leo's office. . . . Just because you're locked up, it doesn't mean your life is over, and anyway, think of what your family is going to feel if you was dead. Stuff like that, a boyish mix of strong and gentle, and the boy said he wanted to be handcuffed together to Ricardo on the rafter, and Ricardo didn't think that was such a good idea ... in case the boy jumped. . . . Finally, Ricardo made a deal: "I'll take one step along the rafter, and you take one step. I'll take one step ... and you take one step ..." kind of the way Leo did with him ... leading the way.

And so Ricardo took one step and the boy took one step behind him all the way down. Ricardo then Aspirez, the young boy following Ricardo's footsteps. Someone to follow. And at Ricardo's count to three, they jumped the last few feet together. And Ricardo gently put the handcuffs on the boy and sat him down on the floor in case he'd decide to try the whole thing all over again. And Trish, the nurse, gave the boy a cup of water to drink. And the lady from the crisis hotline came.

At the award ceremony, everyone famous from the Youth Center almost to California was stretched across the Guard of Honor line to shake hands with Ricardo—some of the female officers and teachers even gave him hugs—yes—under that very same suicide-tempting, red rafter in the gym—Camden Police Chief Bobby Pugh, (who gave an "I-came-from-the-same-place-you-came-from" speech right then and there on the Guard of Honor line) and his lieutenant . . . Detective Lenny Hall who had first brought Ricardo to the Youth Center, chairman of the Board of Trustees, Ricardo's teacher, Ricardo's mother and brother, his girlfriend, Marielle, and their baby, and half a dozen little nephews and nieces, and all the staff. And Ricardo was feeling deliriously happy on the inside but acting all straight and sober on the outside because he was still a guy from the streets—with all the boys watching—and no self-respecting man from the streets would be caught dead, smiling sissy for a camera.

Some people didn't think much of the idea of giving Ricardo an award ceremony, but they were the ones who didn't know what happens to a place like this when a kid kills himself. The newspapers. The do-gooders. The embarrassed politicians. I still had the yellow newspaper clippings from 1973 when George Dunbar, fourteen years old, hanged himself.

The giant award plaque with an American eagle, wings stretched wide across the blue, quoted from the Bible. Ricardo liked that part: *Greater love hath no man than this that a man lay down his life for his friend.* And Ricardo didn't know whether to give the plaque to his mother or to his girlfriend, Marielle—and ended up giving it to his mother.

And then he had cake and juice with his family in the conference room and blew out candles and took more pictures—because it also was his daughter, Maria's, first birthday.

>–+‹›–O–‹›+‹

Behavior logbook:

August 3—Ricardo has shown us what little boys can grow up to become. The Youth Center should be proud of such accomplishment. Ricardo is doing exceptionally well. *Janet*

>–+‹›–O–‹›+‹

Tommy pulls me over to his table nearest the Great Bear watercooler.

Then, like a summer storm, his face clouds. "Gordon went away." There is a very big pause. He is talking about Gordon who has just been sentenced for murder. Storm clouds can gather fast at the Youth Center. I see eyes turning to me from all four tables in the cafeteria. "He got thirty years?" Tommy asks.

"Thirty and fifteen." All talking stops. Even the serving line quiets. Everyone here knows the code: Thirty and fifteen. A maximum thirty-year sentence. At least fifteen years to serve in prison before parole. Gordon is sixteen. He'll be more than thirty years old when he gets out of prison. Everyone listens.

Gordon has been our "senior citizen" in B-wing. Youngsters who are accused of killing someone almost always stay the longest waiting for trial. Court hearings. Tracking down witnesses. Lawyer conferences. The hearing to try them as adults instead of children. Plea bargains. Delays and more delays. The trial. Sentencing. It can take months. Even years.

Gordon came to us—every inch a gentleman—charged with murder. There was a veil over his voice, a veil over his face. He had a sad smile all the time—like a veil over his entire being. Gordon, the gracious. Gordon, the polite. Gordon, the student. I used to measure him with the mother side of my heart: You would want your daughter to bring home a boy like this. During his seven months as one of my boys, I never saw Gordon's temper. Not even once.

But on the bricks, a street fight over being *dissed*. Disrespected in front of some girls.

Just one blow—to even the score.

Two days later the victim died.

"Gordon was nice." Tommy is looking up into my face, pulling on my hand as I stand beside him, looking for reassurance that I cannot give. The center's thirteen- and fourteen-year-olds have one foot planted tenuously in childhood and one in a world too grown-up for a child. Through my hand, I can feel a youngster reaching for the comfort of a mother. I am talking to a child.

I rest my hand gently on Tommy's back. "Gordon is nice," I say softly. "Nice. And polite. A good student. A sophomore at Woodrow Wilson." The boy puts his fork down. I look down into two big, unblinking eyes looking up into mine. "Shall I tell you a story?"

"When I was fourteen years old—a long, long time ago—I bumped my hand on a buzz saw—the kind with a big round blade . . . spins 'round . . . really fast. You know the kind? An accident. I didn't mean to do it . . . don't even know how it happened."

I feel Tommy shiver under my hand.

"And I was nice. Fourteen. And nice. And polite. Nice-and-polite doesn't protect us. And everybody liked me. And now look how old I am. And still I have just one hand—something I did when I was fourteen."

Silence.

Having one hand isn't something people talk about. Notice, maybe. Look. But—except from the very young—polite silence. A miracle happens when we allow our wounds to show. Tough boys turn gentle. I hear the hush. A common pain wraps us together. Gordon is gone. They listen—wide-eyed—as if reaching for comfort from a wounded healer, almost afraid to miss a word.

Personal responsibility and consequences—do we ever really get this message across? We shape them for a week, a month, a year. They think that consequences happen to someone else. Anna and Billy die.

Leche dies. Gadget. The magical thinking of a child—always someone else.

Ricardo agonizes in the safety of my office—his voice barely a whisper. "I ain't never pulled that trigger. But I knew there was a gun. Should I go to trial? Face a jury? They could find me not guilty. Let me go home." A long pause. "Or they could find me guilty and send me away for thirty years. My baby would be grown and married by the time I ever got out.

"Or I could accept a plea bargain. No trial. Take a sentence of maybe seven years. Maybe less. Maybe more.

"When you got a gun in your hand, and you got money, and you got a girl, a beautiful girl, you got cars, you got gold—you don't think about what's gonna happen to you. All you gonna think is, I gonna get my respect one way or another. A lotta people think pullin' a gun is like eatin' a lollipop or somethin', you know. Like they pull the trigger—and there goes half their lifes. A gun make you feel completely powerful."

I think about how guns have become the cool thing to have—like beepers and flashy cars. Having guns leads to using guns. Guns turn petty disputes into killings, petty pranks into tragedy.

A thousand boys and girls a year in this place seduced by dangerous fashions, a get-over world. The pay-off. The con.

At the Youth Center, we teach consequences. Every part of the building preaches consequences.

Each time Ricardo heads for our classrooms, he passes the Youth Center's Hall of Fame: Mounted on giant stars and posted proud are the photographs of the Youth Center's honor residents. His photograph. The color picture is only half the story. The other half is the special privileges he has earned: Wear your own clothes, instead of Youth Center sweat pants; make an extra phone call to a friend; stay up later at night instead of 8:00 P.M. bedtime.

>—·◇·—O—◇·—·<

Leo spent half of his time listening to kids and half of his time trying to undo all the deadly lessons they had learned on the streets. It was a career of catch-up fathering.

"If someone try to stare me down or somethin' . . . if I don't try to stare him back," Ricardo said, "the rest of the residents in here gonna think I'm a punk." It was like Ricardo was reaching for the adult guidance he had missed. Substitutes. Like kids from blown-up families reaching for the security blanket of the television; their favorite shows about healthy families. Leo knew. He could talk to a thousand boys and get the same answer for what had led them to commit crimes. "I wanted them to know that I was no sissy. Nobody's punk. I had to prove that I was a man."

Leo taught Ricardo step by step. It was undoing the lessons of mothers who had taught their boys, "He hits you, you hit back." Might makes right. It was undoing the lessons of violent television heroes who had become their fathers. Undoing the lessons with deadly consequences—better to kill than to be labeled a punk.

Ricardo had advanced to doing algebra in the classroom. Literacy experts say it takes fifty to a hundred class hours to jump one grade level in reading-and-writing proficiency. Ricardo had jumped more than three grade levels.

After nearly two years at the Youth Center, Ricardo and his newest roommate, Gabriel, had transformed their room into their home—the honor room looking out on the woods beyond the fence. Twenty-one pin-up pictures covered every inch of wall above their beds. Next to his radio, Ricardo had a pouch on the shelf behind the bed filled with family pictures, his girlfriend, Marielle, and their baby, Maria. A rubber band bundled together a stack of letters from Marielle, mostly marked with a heart on the envelopes, next to the yellow pad where he charted his daily sets of pulls and lifts in the weight room. Ricardo kept his paperback New Testament on the shelf; Gabriel always had his New Testament tucked next to his pillow for more easy reaching in the night—like reaching for teddy-bear comfort. The sheets were always stretched tight, setting the proper example so C-wing would win the weekly Clean-and-Tidy competition.

The letter to his lawyer—on top of everything else—was the giveaway for what was on the boy's mind.

Ricardo's future put him into a funk. Ricardo got scared every time he talked to his lawyer. He had hired a new one, a man who talked to Ricardo straight up about facing the biggest decision of his life: To go to trial, or agree to a plea bargain.

All this because of why? Ricardo would ask. "Hangin' with a bad crew. They always say 'That's my boy, that's my friend, we down together. . . .' Ain't nobody down together when you come to jail. The only thing you are when you go to jail is a number. That's all." The homeboys didn't send him letters or money . . . didn't come to visit. The boy's voice now sounded like a tape player in slow motion as he agonized over his decision. In New Jersey, a teenager fourteen years of age or over can be tried as an adult for a serious crime. Ricardo had been fifteen years old the night the man was shot. He had never changed his story: He had gone to the street to "fight a fair one." He was not the one who fired a gun.

Ricardo accepted the plea bargain. The charge of murder would be dropped to aggravated manslaughter with a sentence of twenty years, seven of these without parole. The official record would show that he did not pull the trigger.

"It's hopeless, Leo. . . . Everything I'm doing for nothing—gone up so many grade levels, I'm bench pressing and doing good, but where's it get me? I'm still gonna do all this time. It's not gonna help me."

Leo would tell him that a strong person does not give in. "Right now, if you give in, the correctional system will eat you up. You either get everything out of this—or—if you get institutionalized . . ." Leo would explain to him, ". . . get hopeless . . . you don't care . . . people with that type attitude never get out."

Leo talked a lot about a father's responsibility. "If you don't care about anything, Ricardo, you need to care about that daughter. Now you brought someone into this world, you have a responsibility. If you really care about her, you'll give one hundred percent every day. Anytime things get bad in your head, just put a picture of her in your mind." He looked at Ricardo sitting with his hands cupping his chin. "Is that worth working for?"

Ricardo got a big smile, and tears trickled down his cheeks. After that, Leo would hear him in the hallway talking to the boys. "I'm workin' for my daughter."

Teaching fatherless boys the responsibility of being a man was a never-ending challenge. What models did they have? Television, the culture of the poor, exposed children to brutality and violence. Their world resolved disputes with bloodshed, exalted families without men. Leo could preach manly responsibility for month after month and wonder if anything he said was getting through—these boys who only had tough-guy models on the street, in the movies, on television, and then—boom—Ricardo would do something tender like send a sympathy card to Bob Ranjo, whose wife had just died. Bob was a supervising officer and all the other boys in C-wing were saying, Why would you bother to send a card to an officer? And when Bob came back to work after burying his wife, he said he'd never forget that card and for Ricardo to let him know if ever he could be of any help. Leo would know from things like that.

He was getting through. And, yes, it did matter whether or not you could turn around a boy charged with murder who was facing big time in prison, because no kid was locked up forever and you wanted to tether him to something and someone decent—school and family and church. Leo believed in hope. Hope made pathways in the brain. You could teach hope . . . a kid talking to himself about succeeding. Leo liked to call it positive self-talk . . . thinking about goals . . . breaking big goals into small goals a boy could reach.

The officers in C-wing started teasing Leo. "Hey, your son needs to talk to you."

>─◄◆►─O─◄◆►─◄

Marielle was crying during evening visiting hour when she asked Ricardo to marry her before he went to prison. If Ricardo's "little crew" had abandoned him during his two years at the Youth Center, Marielle had not. She had mothered Ricardo when he was a child, alone in Puerto Rico, his mother in the hospital. And he had fathered Marielle in Camden when her mother had returned to Puerto Rico. For ten years they had anchored each other. Teddy bears, trips to Atlantic City, celebrating each other's birthday parties.

Strange how you could be surrounded by a crowd of visitors in a youth center cafeteria, where sounds bounced off the orange ceiling and walls of speckled tile, but there you were—alone—you and your man—making promises and dreams to love, honor, keep each other—a few days before your man was going to prison ... Marielle whispering Spanish promises to wait for Ricardo, and Ricardo whispering ... wanting to get off the street, away from the cars and girls. And there was Maria, their baby, eighteen months old, needing a proper father and mother. "If you gonna have a future, you gotta work hard," Ricardo said.

It would be hard.

The wedding was in the gymnasium on a cold January night two days before Ricardo's sentencing in adult court. Ricardo was eighteen. Marielle had just turned twenty. The boys didn't have a clue about weddings—except that Ricardo was going to be nervous in a black tuxedo, and Marielle was going to wear white.

Ricardo, who couldn't decide whom to pick for his best man because so many of the officers had helped him grow into a man, finally decided on Leo. And Marielle insisted that I be her matron of honor. It was Officers Gwen Walters and Laurie Scott who had taken Ricardo aside a few days before and whispered to him that he needed to learn to dance—dignified—for his wedding dance with Marielle. And so, to the music of the radio in Ricardo's bedroom, officers Gwen and Laurie had taught him how to dance—gentle and polite and not too sexy—for his first dance with Marielle after she became his wife. And that was going to be hard because when you hadn't been touching your girl for two years ... and the main thing everyone wanted to know—asked in a thousand ways—Was I going to let Marielle, uh, stay the whole night with Ricardo after the wedding? and I said no.

Bob Ranjo, always a very dignified shift commander, spent most of the day making his special recipe of spicy chicken wings—160 of them—for the wedding buffet in the gym. After his wife died, Bob had never forgotten the sympathy card that Ricardo sent him. Ricardo, in a royal-blue T-shirt and sweatpants, pacing my office floor and wanting me to assemble the handful of residents he had invited to his wedding—"I feel nervous, man."

And shift commander John Golaszewski's coming in to feel Ricardo's feet: "Just checking to see if you're getting cold feet, Ricardo. . . ."

"I can't have them buggin' out and embarrassing my bride." The
way Ricardo saw it, Marielle deserved everything. . . . "She never had
another man in her life . . . never cheated on me . . . stuck by me . . .
made me the only man in her life . . . wrote to me two or three times a
week . . . a guy can't never find a girl like her. . . ." Ricardo and
Marielle and baby Maria were going to be a family. And someday there
would be a Ricardo, Jr. So we summoned the boys into my office two
hours before the wedding—even the ones on the keep-apart list—and
they sandwiched their hands with Ricardo in a sweaty and solemn
heap in the middle of the room—like football players pledging
solidarity before the game—and vowed they wouldn't bug out. And
they dressed so nice—Gabriel in a mustard shirt and tie, Stan in a suit
and tie, Edward with a Penn State sweatshirt on, Rick with a black
sweatshirt, Orlando in jeans and a black T-shirt.

No one in the world could have told they were anything but a very
proud group of high-school friends. The women on the staff who knew
about weddings spent the day transforming the gymnasium into a
wonderland of blue and pink—hundreds of construction paper swags
and bows circling the walls, the basketball backboard and hoop
suddenly soft with pink and blue crepe-paper ribbons and wedding
bells, and over against the wall the arch of pink and blue balloons
where Ricardo and Marielle would make their vows.

It wasn't just a wedding, I knew. This was a celebration of a family
of people—officers and teachers and social workers—who had taken a
boy for two years and shaped him as their own, shaped him with the
homely rituals and memories that make a decent human being—
Officer Gwen Walters bringing Ricardo a birthday cake on his
eighteenth birthday, his teacher Miss Cathy taking pictures of his
baby's first birthday party, the men who had formed his exercise team
in the weight room.

While Officer Richard Clark took pictures on the video camera,
Officer Al Thomas from the Virgin Islands, played the wedding march
on his steel drums, and the minister married Ricardo and Marielle
with a ceremony all spoken softly in Spanish.

Seated in candlelight with all the guests, the boys ate Bob Ranjo's
chicken wings and Puerto Rican food and looked in awestruck wonder
at ceremonies they knew nothing about . . . Ricardo putting bistilla
into Marielle's mouth and Marielle putting bistilla into Ricardo's
mouth . . . The lovely Marielle throwing her white bouquet over her
shoulders to the girls . . . Ricardo sitting his bride on his knee,
removing the blue garter from her leg and throwing it over his
shoulder to the boys . . . and everyone throwing confetti and eating
the tiered wedding cake . . . and none of the boys had any idea what
any of these ceremonies meant—but fell in love with weddings—
licking their sticky fingers from chicken wings and spare ribs and

shaking their heads in wonder about one of their own promising to love one girl till death do us part . . .

Two days later, in a courtroom reserved for adults, a chain of us held the boy like a human lifeline holding the boy's hand against the waves of his past that were pulling him away. Too grown-up and yet so much a child, Ricardo was sentenced to prison.

Across the courtroom, uniformed sheriff's officers escorted the boy away—before we could even say good-bye.

Bob Ranjo, six-feet, three inches of officer and no-nonsense, strode into the hall and wept.

ACORNS

I motion for Juan to sit next to me in the blue bucket chair beside my desk and start as I always do. "Everybody has hundreds of stories inside." We sit knee-to-knee. "What kind of story do you want to write? Happy? Sad? Proud? Scared?"

"Violence," he says. And Juan, fourteen, writes a story about "Those Killer Parties in Polacktown."

Who stole the child's world of "Twinkle, Twinkle Little Star" and turned it into *Killer Bullets* and *Blood Revenge*? And who was going to change it back?

WHAT'S HAPPENING has become the sound of a child's voice crying above the din. Killings and rape and drugs. The sound of bullets whizzing in the night.

December is memorable this year. In the two weeks before Christmas—peace on earth, goodwill—I get three youngsters charged with murder.

Puerta Rick, age seventeen, writes the December cover story.

WHEN THEY TELL YOU YOUR BOY GETS KILLED, YOU WANTA KILL

My boy Mike. Fifteen years old. Shot with a .38—three times in the chest. Dead on the sidewalk.

I stood on that very same spot and waited. Where he got killed. Next to the dried up blood spots. Me an Leon—strapped. You don't know who to look for. You sit. And wait. And wait.

'Til somebody make a move.

They got Leon two nights later. Shot with a .22. One time in the head.

I didn't wait quite long enough.

I listen to youngsters who have killed. Youngsters who have escaped death.

The leading cause of death for teenage boys in America is gunshot wounds. A *growth* industry—coffins for the young. I'm sitting next to this boy, knee-to-knee, and he has a hole in his face. A bullet hole.

HOW I STARTED SELLIN DRUGS
by The True Hustler, age 17

My mom cryin—worryin about the 'lectric bein turned off cause she couldn't pay for it. Got to buy school clothes for three kids an she can't buy a lot. Always cry.

When my dad left—3:00 o'clock in the mornin—I never forgot— woke me up—said he had to go—told me I had to be the man in the house.

How does an 11-year-old support his family? Sell Kool-Aid to the drug dealers in front of my house. Cup of Kool-Aid for $1.

An then this guy one day in front of my house, Hey, Little Bo, go sell this bag to that guy in the car. I'll give you $10. An that's how I started sellin drugs.

P.S. No matter what my mom went through, I still think she the best mother in the world.

The horror isn't just for boys.

BLOOD IN THE MIRROR
by T.T., age 15

Door closed to my bedroom. Nighttime. Me in bed. Thirteen years old.

Door slammed open against the wall and my mom came in. High.

Gets real mean when she get high.

Call me bitch. Slut. Whore. Punch me in my face. Threw me from the bed to the floor. Punch me in my face again. Pull me up to the mirror. "Look at you! Look at you now!"

Blood all over my face. All over the floor.

T.T. is a child who needs to touch. Whenever she finds softness— but that is rare—she snuggles. She hugs.

When she has written one story on the page, she asks me if she can write another.

DREAMS GOING UP LIKE SMOKE

I used to watch my dad do drugs. Smokin his pipe. Rock of cocaine on the screen. Light up with a match or a lighter.

I wished he wouldn't.
But what could I do? Thirteen years old.
Talk to him. Hug him.
He said he couldn't stop.

When T.T. finishes telling me her story, she gets up from nestling beside me in the blue bucket chair and walks to the door.

"They wouldn't tell me how she died," she says.

I turn slowly and type the sentence on the page.

To decorate T.T.'s page, Miguel draws a bloody face looking out of a mirror in a blood-splotched room. Three days later T.T. cuts her wrists with a piece of molding from the floor. We rush her to the Crisis Center.

For almost a generation I have listened, almost always feeling more than the children whose voices are whispering next to me. Their voices sound so dispassionate—a voice floating—not even attached to an injured child. As I listen, I feel shock and rage and sorrow and love and shame—perhaps because of my own curiosity. Should I rage or weep? Pretend it doesn't matter?

Violence and abuse send shock and rage and terror scurrying into hiding in the nooks and crannies of a child's soul. Sometimes the feelings never resurface. No feeling—not even joy—whole parts of a being that cannot feel—a child's creative way to protect himself from reexperiencing the horror. Psychiatrists call it "creative survival." At the Youth Center we see the rage speaking in other voices—depression, headaches, wetting beds, sucking thumbs—little voices saying, Can you see me? Can you *listen*?

The blue bucket chair is a safe place for teenage voices.

I *listen*.

The stories from the youngest hit me hardest. Twelve. Thirteen. Fourteen years old. Stories of a child's world—a child's ideas—what I reach for—innocence—hardly ever comes from their mouths any more—not like when we started *WHAT'S HAPPENING* twenty years ago: Burying a puppy under the swings in the backyard. Birthday cake and blowing out candles and Jennie kissed me.

WHAT'S WRONG WITH SAMMY
by SAMMY, age 13

My father keep sayin, *I don't know what's wrong with Sammy. Don't know what's wrong with Sammy.*

Me on the bed, screamin and cryin, bleedin from the ribs where he hit me with a pipe.

My father throwin up from being drunk all night. I go to school and tell them I don't want to go to gym today. Don't want them to see this open cut on my rib.

An the principal of Pablo Casals School pulls my shirt up and sees the cut.

An my father keep sayin, *I don't know what's wrong with Sammy. Don't know what's wrong with him. I try the best for him.*

Sammy's father is a preacher.

⊱┈◈┈○┈◈┈⊰

RAPE ON A SATURDAY NIGHT
by SAMANTHA, age 14

It was the winter. About seven o'clock on a Saturday night when my little brother came home crying. He came into my bedroom—sort of little brother to big sister. It was always that way. He was raped by a teenage guy. And my brother was 9. Crying like it was pouring down rain.

I watch the boy in Mary Ann Zeiser's classroom shaping the eyebrows with plaster of paris and gauze over a giant purple balloon for his Hallowe'en mask. Darrell never says very much. A young boy with a hunch, like an old man's back. When I look at his eyes, I see suspicion and mistrust peeping suspiciously from the deep, a forbidden cave. You never know what's inside the boy.

Darrell's trademark is sucking his thumb. He tugs on me to admire the newest pin-ups in his immaculate bedroom, pulling on me to let him write a story for *WHAT'S HAPPENING.*

After we buried my cousin Steve in Evergreen Cemetery . . . the next day we went lookin for the person.

Me. My cousin. And friends. Three cars deep. Everybody had a gun. Me with a 9 millimeter. Four packages of bullets.

When a drive-by kills your cousin. Fifteen years old. Him dyin in your arms by the bridge, all you think of is paybacks.

Someone else is gonna die.

No 15-year-old should die with a .38 bullet in his chest. For nothin.

Darrell, age sixteen, insists on the wording of his headline: REAL NIGGAS DON'T DIE FOR NOTHIN'

Where are the memories of jumping rope and riding bikes and decorating Christmas cookies? My pages are full of children who never made it through their childhood. I top his page with giant letters: BLOOD REVENGE. Beside me the boy is sucking his thumb.

My friends will ask, What did you do today? I will tell them that Jason, fifteen, wrote to me today with a very wobbly pen on white paper with blue lines:

Dear Mrs. Previte,

MY MAIN LADY. You was like a mother to me. I miss you. I been roller-skating. Crabbing. I found three girls.

By telephone, Stanley tells me he is making A's and B's in his gifted and talented class, that he lost the election to be student representative of his high school sophomore class, that he wants to start a summer volleyball league in his neighborhood.

I will tell them that Lauren, fifteen, sat in the blue bucket chair beside me today. Lauren says he wishes I was his mom. I'm strict with him, he says, and he needs that. He says that he hasn't had a drink or any drugs for eight months. Sober. Lauren's mom is an addict—crack cocaine. He never knew his dad.

Sometimes what you do in a day is less important than what you undo.

I will tell my friends that I wrote to Teema, age thirteen, today and sent her a snapshot I took of her before she left. Good-bye smiles. And hope.

A day of little miracles.

Sometimes in a place like this you get to thinking, You know I'm tired and I want to stop. And then you see the note from Robert, posted on the office bulletin board: "They just made me a department manager at Boscov's at the mall." A boy who belongs to no one.

Nothing is impossible: My father taught me the words of Jesus: Faith moves mountains (Matthew 17:20). I grew up in a deeply religious family and have no doubt that I do what I do because of that spiritual grounding.

Who are the healers who manage to turn people around? Not pinched-hearted bureaucrats. Not paper-pushers. Not people with proud diplomas framed on their walls. Not people competing for power. Not size, not funding, not buildings make the difference—soul touching soul. The one who won't give up.

One day out of the blue, the light goes on. The boy sitting across from social worker Robbie Reid says he wants to get the tattoo of the killer gang erased from his left shoulder.

You grab a youngster by the heart—like Jacob wrestling with the angel in the ancient story—and shout it to him till your words bounce back from heaven: *I will not let you go until you bless me.* And you don't let go. Not even when Ricardo goes to prison. Or Saleed. Because these boys and girls—almost every one of them will be back. They— and every one of their friends. Back in our cities and on our streets.

Childhood and youth are the time to plant the seeds that bring success.

I found my parable one day, not in the words of Jesus but in *Organic Gardening* magazine. Two paragraphs—about acorns.

On my morning run, I pocketed a handful of acorns from the road. When I arrived at the Youth Center, I went to classroom 126 and told my newfound story to the boys before they opened their reading workbooks for the day. Some had never seen an acorn—had no idea what an acorn is. I showed them from the handful in my pocket. Brown like the sand. Pointed. Some, unprotected. Some still cozied tight in their acorn cups. I told them a story.

The young traveler on the mountainside of the Alps was puzzled at what looked from a distance like a lonely old shepherd wandering among puny sheep and goats. As the old man walked among them, he poked the sunbaked mountain with his shepherd's crook, dropping something small—hardly noticeable—into the ground. Perhaps an old man's game to while away the hours.

"What are you doing, Old Man?" the traveler asked.

The shepherd paused—as if the traveler should surely know.

"I am changing the shape of my mountain."

He scoffed. He shook his head. Perhaps the shepherd had not heard. Who can change the shape of a mountain?

Curious now, the young man drew up close. As he watched, the old man pierced the barren mountainside with his shepherd's crook. Then with an aging hand, he reached into a battered bucket on his arm and plucked from it an acorn and dropped it into the hole and covered it gently with his foot. One acorn. Then another. Again. And again.

"What is that you're doing?" the young man asked again.

As if looking through a dream, the shepherd paused.

"I am changing the shape of my mountain."

Sadly—slowly—the traveler walked away. For he knew what everybody knows: You cannot change the shape of a mountain.

Then the young man himself grew old and dreamed of retracing the long-ago travels of his youth.

The map in his hand told him he had reached the mountain. Yet nothing seemed the same. Where once he had seen a barren, sunbaked, godforsaken mountain, he now saw mighty oaks. Villages nestled, shaded by leafy branches. Children played on country paths. Birds nested safe among the leaves. Soft clouds drifted overhead.

And then the man remembered the old shepherd who believed he could change the shape of his mountain.

I kept a few acorns forever in the pocket of my jacket after that. Wherever I went, I talked about changing my mountain. One acorn at a time.

I could hold the wonder of a child in my hands. One day. One month. One year.

But Candy was dead. And Cody. And Russell. Anna and Billy. And Jason—the details too gruesome to tell. Teens under pressure—peer values, poverty, family violence, absentee parents, educational failure, drugs.

Of how many million children in America, I could touch only a thousand boys and girls a year. Solving the problems of America by giving success to teenagers in my Youth Center was like solving the problems of America's violence by beefing up trauma response in the hospital emergency room.

It was strange how the tragedies hit me. I found myself cradling my daughter, Alice, in my arms—even when she was grown—feeling the silk of her hair safe under my fingers—holding her tightly and thanking God—and her—for a child that had blossomed into someone beautiful. With each new tragedy, I looked out my window to my neighborhood up the street. For more than twenty years at times like the Fourth of July I had been in charge of the children's games. And even after twenty years—I knew that I could not stop.

Building childhood memories for the children on my own street was not enough—creating memories and traditions—I could not stop. It was my small part of joining with a neighborhood to anchor our streetful of children to families and neighbors—anchoring them to something good and gentle. And when a child on my street grew up and telephoned me to borrow my crumpled list of games, I knew I was looking out on a mountain where one of my acorns was growing across town—someplace else—mothers and daughters stumbling in three-legged races, teenagers stomping balloons at their ankles, toddlers scrambling for peanuts, old men groaning in tug-o'-war against their sons. Touching someone else's children. Making new memories.

When I looked for answers, I thought of the Chinese proverb: *If everyone sweeps his own yard, soon the whole world will be clean.*

I started sweeping my Youth Center world—with each new issue of *WHAT'S HAPPENING.* I typed the children's words as a wake-up call—from boys who had killed, girls who had run away from home:

BLOOD REVENGE
THE DAY THEY SHOT THE SCHOOL BUS

I KNOW I WILL DIE OUT THERE
PICKING OUT THE WRITING ON MY TOMBSTONE

By the time I pulled the papers out to remember, some of the young writers were already dead—youngsters shot in the head. Shot in the chest. Face blown away.

When I looked for answers, the answers—small and powerful, like acorns—came from the children:

A MOM IS SPOSE TO TELL YOU NO
TOO LATE TO START ACTING LIKE A DAD
DEAR MOM: I FOUND SOMEONE TO LISTEN

I wanted so desperately for it all to be a fantasy. It was not.

In the last ten years the number of youngsters ages ten through seventeen arrested for murder has almost doubled nationwide, not just in the cities. The report on my desk says that large numbers of American youth admit that they steal, they lie, they cheat at school, at work, at home.

People in the grown-up world out there talk about selfishness. Me-first. Individualism. Ego. Looking out for Number One. Feeling good about yourself. Is that the connection? Me-first parents and kids who cheat?

Feel good. American students score lowest achievement scores on a math test administered internationally but feel more confident of their math skills than any other group tested. Who taught us that whatever makes us feel good is okay? Endorsing any choice that makes us "feel good about ourselves"? "Moral decisions" based on *feelings*? I listen to children who feel good because they have *killed*.

In a first national survey of this kind, the Harris poll asked Americans in 1987 if problems facing American children are more severe than when they were growing up. Three out of four Americans said yes.

If I wanted to find answers for a complicated world, I found them from my boys and girls. I asked them. And they gave me simple messages: *Give me a childhood. Give me parents. Give me time.* I call them messages from my mountain.

Message Number 1: *Spend time with me.* Bind me close to you with memories I can never forget.

WEEKEND DAD
by VINSON, age 17

Most of the time, a dad be havin time for you only on weekends. Only time a mom have time when the family be going out to the mall. So who you thinkin a kid learn from most of the time? Who else is gonna be there for them?

When I put Vinson's first story next to the second, I found out who had become the boy's substitute father. The streets were his family. Drug dealers patted the boy on the back:

FAME

If you be feelin little and unimportant, dealin with drugs can make you big and popular.

Drugs help you buy an image. Fancy clothes. Gold. Chains. Rings. Gucci watch. Calvin Klein jeans with a silk shirt. You rent a limo and a chauffeur to take you to the show at the high school.

Limo pulls up on the block. Dark-tinted windows trimmed in gold. And you get out. Everybody notices. Suddenly you're the talk-of-the-town.

Before that you was just the average person on the block.

With children we get no second chance. "The adult time zone allows for delay, distraction, pushing away," says Richard Louv. "If not this year, next year; that's when we'll do it. . . . 'Be patient,' they say—'these things take time.' But no such luxury exists in the children's time zone because children annoyingly grow up. By the time their parents do have time for them, many kids don't have time for their parents."[1]

Gordon had trailed me across the older boys' residence unit one day, pointing to Troy's story in *WHAT'S HAPPENING*: "Too Late To Start Acting Like a Dad"—

"I have a story—just like that."

TOO LATE
by GORDON, age 16

I didn't really hear from my dad UNTIL I got in trouble. Then he start calling, writing. To give advice.

It was too late.

Gordon was awaiting his sentencing for murder. Thirty years.

One boy's story—three sentences long—an American tragedy.

I have never seen Gordon's dad. But my heart has questions for him:

Dear Dad. At the end of your day, what matters most? Your flourishing career—or the minutes you stole from your son?

Dear Dad. At the end of your day, what matters most? Those

---

[1]Richard Louv, *Childhood's Future.* Boston: Houghton Mifflin, 1990, 19.

delicious, memorable moments with the latest romance in your life—
or the memories you never gave your son?

Dear Dad, your son is right. It *is* too late.

Grown-ups can wait, delay, distract, and push away.

But not your son. Your son grows up. By the time you *do* have time
for him, he's already bonded to boys on the corner, drinking buddies,
the mall rats, the wrong girl. By the time you *do* have time for him,
he's already thumbing his nose at school.

So who *has* shaped your child?

Someone taught your son what it is to be a man—that a Real Man
settles every slight with fists or with The Club or with a gun.

And, Daddy, were you there to teach him another way? The average
American working parent spends thirty seconds a day in meaningful
conversation with his or her children. The *average*—thirty seconds a
day.

Daddy, you spent not even that. This boy beside me—Gordon—
has a giant hole in him where a father should have been.

Building a conscience in your child takes more than thirty seconds
a day. So does teaching him to love his God, respect for fellowman—
especially when the television set is on seven hours a day in the
average home.

I shall hold Gordon's hand today and write a letter to all the fathers
of America: Dear Dad, you want to change America? Pull out the
stopwatch in your home. Time yourself. How much time do you
spend each day just *talking* to your child? Building memories?
Anchoring him with family traditions? Showing him how to be a
father—just like you?

Double that time. Triple it. Quadruple it. And watch what happens.
Time together builds memories. Time together builds values. Time
together builds families. Time together builds family traditions. Time
is *love*.

Dear Dad, Dear Mom, your son calls out to you: *Spend time with
me. Bind me close to you with memories that I can never forget.*

I heard the "too late" message too often. "No one would listen to
me at home, Elizabeth told me one day. Elizabeth's mom was an
Avon lady in Baltimore. Her father drove a truck. Nice, middle-class
family. "So I started hanging around with older people—who would
listen. They were bikers and street people, too. But when I cried, they
gave me tissues. They were good to me, and I thought they could do
no wrong. They took drugs. So I did, too. At eight years old."

As I always did, I tried to pull family memories from this girl. How
did they play? When did they talk? What traditions tied them
together? She thought for a while—like lowering a bucket into an
empty well—and remembered once putting tinsel on the Christmas
tree. But that was all. No traditions anchoring her to a family. No

wonder she was anchored to the motorcycle gangs, caught on a rural highway with a trunkful of drugs.

What happens to a world that doesn't put its children in an honored place, that doesn't care, that allows its bedrock values to crumble? Girls like Elizabeth told me—boys like Gordon—America's children—boys and girls who had been through the holocaust in childhood and adolescence. Children who sat looking at me with vacant eyes. They were children who had no past and probably no future. You could put a gun in their hands and say, "Shoot," and they would shoot—*bang, bang, bang.* Why should they care?

People ask me, How can these children do these things? Have they no conscience?

Conscience is learned from fathers and mothers. It is learned from communities and churches and synagogues and mosques. What happens to a child who is touched by none of these? When the school gymnasiums are locked up and closed to youngsters at night—afraid of lawsuits—and churches can't get insurance if they let the kids play inside?

When the average working couple spends four minutes a day in meaningful conversation with each other, and the average working parent spends thirty seconds a day in meaningful conversation with his or her children, who is cupping the heart of a child in their hands those other hours?[2]

MY MOM'S GOT THIS BOYFRIEND
by TEEMA, age 13

My mom got this boyfriend.
He come live in our house. Sleep in her bed.
An then she ain't have no more time for me.

The cry of the children—*Spend time with me.* The gift of time has to start the minute a child is born—the first day, the first year—hands touching the velvet of a child's skin and stroking her hair, the hour-by-hour echoing back his baby *ooohs* and *ahs.* Hands and eyes and lips that tell a child he is precious. It wasn't just my children giving me this message. It was pediatricians and criminologists: Bonding with a baby in the first year of life is like falling in love. They all said it one way or another: If a child doesn't get it in infancy, he'll never get it later on. A child growing up with a sense of "It doesn't matter what I do" shows with every action that he expects to fail. Like Saleed—no

---

[2]*Priority Management Systems, Agenda for the 1990s; An International Business Lifestyle Survey* (Irving, Calif.: Priority Management System, 1989).

father. No mother. Eating from garbage cans. Like Elizabeth—a father
and a mother who never anchored her with memories or traditions.
We can predict: These are youngsters who will fail in school, disrupt
the classrooms, invent their own rules that make them teenage
terrorists. They will get our attention.

If a child is to bond to a parent, substitute parents won't work. A
child doesn't bond in thirty seconds a day. *Spend time with me,* the
children shouted to me.

When *Woman's Day* asked three hundred of its readers what they
would do if they could turn back the clock and raise their children
over again, the lament heard most often was "not enough time spent
with [their] children." Most (95 percent) would opt for as much time
or more, just as they wish, overwhelmingly, that their children "had
spent the same or more time with grandparents, other members of
their families, and, most poignantly (61 percent) with their fathers."

Topping the list of regrets were: not taking more vacations, not
going to church as a family more, attending movies and sporting
events more, and visiting relatives more often.[3]

Without family memories and traditions, what tethers a child to
the anchor of the home? To whom do children turn when their
parents don't have time for them? Gangs, for one. Other children on
the edge. In America's cities, gangs give youngsters the feeling of
belonging and acceptance they crave. They turn to others—usually
not so gentle—to gangs, to cults, to drugs, to too-early sex partners to
find what they cannot find at home. They turn to computers and video
and television, an open window on an increasingly monstrous
world—those frightening *others* who shape our young.

We are bonded to a family by memories and family traditions.
These are the gifts we give our children. At a family reunion around
the Christmas fireplace, my brother John asks everyone to tell a
Christmas memory. Around the circle, one child after another drags
us back through how many years to the annual ride on the Magic Sled
to Santa land in my cedar closet across from the washing machine. At
our house the walls bulged at Christmastime with families getting
together after caroling for the children's ride on the Magic Sled to
Santa land. The Magic Sled, it turned out, was our rusting old Flexible
Flyer. As each blindfolded child climbed aboard, she was whisked
through the air on a turbulent ride, carried by two equally excited
lawyer daddies to the magic domain of a very freckled Santa Claus
whose ho-ho-hos always sounded suspiciously like Alice Ann's daddy.

Upstairs in the kitchen, fifteen or more wide-eyed children rolled
out barely edible gingerbread boys and girls from tubs of dough made
by elfin chefs stuccoed with dough and frosted with delight.

---

[3]Sherrye Henry, "A Report from Mothers: 'If I Could Do It Over Again,'" *Woman's
Day,* (April 19, 1988), 66–69.

These small moments, riding Magic Sleds, making pizza at grandma's house, jumping together in piles of yellow leaves when we raked the driveway, tucking the covers up around a child's chin at bedtime every night, skipping smooth stones on the rippling waters of the lake, cookies baking in the oven—who took away the tiny moments? Or did we give them up—swapped for sixteen-hour shifts? Bigger cars? Atlantic City? Sony CD players?

When you dig inside your heart to find a family, what you have is a bank of traditions and memories—tastes, smells, touches: throwing tinsel, one string at a time, onto the Christmas tree; lighting the Hanukkah candles in the window; building the snow fort together behind the house; first-day-of-school pancakes always in the shape of teddy bears; Easter morning brunch with the family at a big hotel—and, yes, even the memory of the Easter morning when Karyn threw up. Holding hands around the table when you blow the birthday candles out. Asking the blessing first before you eat. A good-night kiss and always singing, "Jesus, Tender Shepherd, Hear Me" before we close our eyes to sleep.

When my mother died in the village of Spring Arbor, Michigan, we sang her off to heaven, children and grandchildren around her bed, stroking her haloed hair. We gave to her the gift she had given first to us: her grown-up Taylor children singing in gentle harmony the tender lullaby she had always sung for us—whenever darkness fell and we closed our eyes in sleep.

> *Jesus, tender shepherd, hear me.*
> *Bless thy little lamb tonight.*
> *Through the darkness be thou near me.*
> *Keep me safe till morning light....*
>
> *Through this day thy hand hath led me,*
> *And I thank thee for thy care.*
> *Thou hast warmed and clothed and fed me,*
> *Listen to my evening prayer.*
>
> *Let my sins be all forgiven.*
> *Bless the friends I love so well.*
> *Take me when I die to heaven,*
> *Happy there with thee to dwell.*

It was her gift to us. A family memory. It was ours—at the end—to her.

Message Number 2: *Feed my spirit.*

The child standing beside me pulls up the sleeve to show me the needle tracks on her arm.

My fingers cover the wounds as if hiding the scars will make them go away. The girl is an addict. "Can you tell me, little one?" I wonder out loud. Why does a ten-year-old girl walk away from her family in

Camden, New Jersey, board a Trailway bus for Forty-second Street in New York City—the Port Authority Transit?

"Weren't you terrified?" Pimps prowl Forty-second Street looking for runaway children. Booming sex markets sell fresh, young bodies—boys and girls—for the wolves.

Torrie pulls herself tall in the chair, tosses her hair and changes before my eyes into a woman of the world. "I get off the bus and act real grown-up. Like I know exactly where to go." Ten years old. In a park she found a young girl crying. "Maybe I could have her job, she said." Newly fired from the topless go-go bar just up the street.

"They hire me." Torrie looks at me as though I ought to know. "You know how it is in New York. They don't care how old you are—as long as you look—you know—like a virgin. That's the way they say it . . . a go-go bar. All mans—black, white, fat, skinny—all different kinda mans—lookin' on me—puttin' tips in my panty strip.

"They get you all shoot up with drugs so you wouldn't care who's touchin' you or nothin'." She runs her fingers along the needle tracks on her arm.

"So you want to know why a ten-year-old girl starts workin' at a go-go bar—men payin' the manager to sleep with her?

"You get beat up so many times at home with the TV extension cord. Always hungry, raggedy, dirty. You get called 'freeloader' so many times at your own house. . . .

"At the go-go bar, they called me "Sweet Stuff.'"

I saw youngsters—like everybody else—reaching to be Somebody. If they couldn't be Somebody at home, they would go someplace else where they were—Somebody. Or Sweet Stuff.

Killed to be Somebody. I watched boys collect their press clippings. Taped to their walls. Frayed in their hands. In the religion of the street, they called it RESPECT.

Feeding a child's spirit starts very, very early. Touching, hugging, counting baby fingers and toes. It means noticing him and being at his events, being always in his life. It means her photos and drawings on the refrigerator. It means noticing out loud what he wears and how she looks, how he keeps his bedroom neat. It means a pat on the back or a squeeze on the hand or a hug for mowing the lawn or washing the car or helping to cook supper.

I heard the message—*Feed my spirit*—in a thousand different ways. It wasn't that the boy hadn't earned the Guard of Honor basketball signed by the Philadelphia 76ers.

Peepers had been on honors for four unbroken weeks—going to school, role playing how to listen, how to follow instructions, how to ask permission. The boy had been making his bed so perfect—like a display in a furniture store, like a magazine picture. It wasn't that he hadn't earned the honor—it was the way the older boys were trying to bring him down.

My assistant stood at my glass-topped desk wondering out loud about skipping the honor tradition for Peepers—just this once. Skip the Guard of Honor ceremony in the gymnasium—the whole place full of every boy and girl and staff and visitor . . . my telling the story all over again about what the honor meant . . . about climbing step-by-step to success . . . and calling out the boy's name in front of everybody . . . watching Peepers rising shyly up from his seat, walking across the gym in front of everyone, starting at one end of the Guard of Honor line . . . getting hugs and handshakes and high fives from the line that stretched with well-wishers all across the gym till he reached the end. Getting his basketball. Just this once, to skip the congratulations in front of everybody, flashing strobe lights for his Polaroid picture for the Hall of Fame, and getting his autographed 76ers basketball. The biggest deal of all the very big deals that the Youth Center created to reward success—the Guard of Honor ceremony.

"Couldn't we just this once just give the boy his basketball . . . no fuss . . . in your office? The guys are going to bust him, bring him down, if you give him the works out there."

The Guard of Honor ritual creates a happy contagion that nudges everyone in a positive direction.

I called Peepers in for a choice: "Guard of Honors in the gym? I know the guys are trying to bring you down," I explained, ". . . or basketball and pictures—just me and you in my office—no fuss from the boys?" A private ceremony.

". . . everybody noticing me in front of all them people . . ." he said.

". . . You mean none of that?"

Peepers shook his head from side to side—like—"Why would you even have to ask?" And when the strobe light stopped flashing to take his picture in front of the whole school in the gym, he wrote his story:

TOP PRIZE WINNER!
by PEEPERS, age 17

What does it feel like to get the top prize in the whole school? I'll tell you what it feel like.

You don't know whether to smile. Walkin up in front of everybody, your heart feel like it gonna jump outa your mouth. It make me noticeable.

Being bad can make you noticeable. But being good can make you noticeable too.

Getting the prize, it felt like the smile would never come offa my face.

All from bein nice.

Everybody lookin at ME.

And I didn't even wanta look.

First time! Sort of nervous.
But real proud.
I never won an award like that until today.
I been bad half my life. And now I just wanna start bein good.
And I makin a change.

Message Number 3: *Be the boss.*
The child plopped down in the blue bucket chair beside me carried his "spose to" list of family rules in his heart—like the Sermon on the Mount or the Ten Commandments. Something everybody ought to know.

A MOM SPOSE TO SAY NO
by EMERSON, age 14

It give you a feelin that your mom don't care about you, you goin to school at 8 o'clock in the mornin an not comin home til 4:30 in the mornin. She don't say nothin.
You sit down an think about it—that she don't care.
You do it the next night—she don't say nothin. Don't ask bout it.
So then you stay out all night. All day.
If you out for a while, you mom spose to ask: Where were you at? And how come you ain't call?
If she don't care, I can do what I want.
Lotta kids, their mom don't ask.

I don't know why it surprised me—hell-raisers settling almost gratefully into a world of rules and order we created. I knew it. Weak parents, weak teachers—troubled teens. Emerson had come to us from a frightening world of no rules—where youngsters ran the show, where no one was the boss. At the Youth Center when a youngster first arrived, there was often a tussle for a day or so to test the authority. Kids reached their toes out to test the ground to see how firm it was. And when the ground felt predictable and firm, they usually settled in. They felt safe.

Who said that those who speak of rules and discipline are kooks and fuddy-duddies? In a dangerous and disorderly world, children want someone to be in charge.

Families and schools need to be secure ports in personal storms, places of nurturing, warmth, and gentle humor. No child learns in the middle of chaos and disorder. Only after we gave them order, did they thrive. At the Youth Center the first great gift we gave the youngsters was order and discipline and safety.

I want to shout it to the wind. *Anchor them. Give them rules.*

Make them feel safe. Reasonable rules say, This is the way that I take care of you. Rules say, The world is predictable.

I look at two nice, white suburban boys—dreams of two mothers— dreams of sons and honor rolls, football and basketball, and tassled caps and robes for graduation. Your everyday American dad and mom giving their kids the ultimate gift: freedom to do what they want. Two boys—fourteen and sixteen—the gift of a whole summer alone at Wildwood on the Ocean. The Boardwalk. Beer. Girls. Sun. Sand dunes. Freedom. Breezes. Parents letting go of a kite string. Glorious freedom—to crash-land.

The police report says they returned from the summer—and, with a bat and a knife, attacked a man.

I say to myself, What happened in America that we thought freedom was the ultimate gift for children? Freedom from rules was supposed to be a sign of caring.

NEVER!

I want a whole list of rules. Rules say, *I care.*

I want you home at a certain time.

I want to know you're safe.

I want rules that say, You study or read for an hour at night.

I want a rule that says, You take your own dishes from the table. Clean your room. Do your share. No free lunch.

I want truth to be your banner. Never lies.

I want a rule that says, You treat other people the way you want to be treated. Respect and gentleness.

I want a rule of absolute honesty.

A rule that says, You don't have any sex until you're ready to take on the responsibility of caring for that baby.

I want to chisel a whole tablet of stone—family rules that can never be erased.

Do children really want parents and teachers to draw the line? Set limits?

Yes. Yes, absolutely, yes.

They'll fog you with "But Jimmy's mom lets him . . ."—but cut through the fog and you'll find that children know that *reasonable rules are a sign of love.* Haven't we all heard a child boast, "My daddy can beat up your daddy"?—reassuring himself of that strength. But first he needs that parent or teacher to earn the right to be boss.

"It's easy to see what prevents most children from becoming killers," says Deborah Prothrow-Stith, M.D., of Harvard University. "Those young people grow up in homes where they are taught to respect and value themselves. They can envision themselves succeed- ing politically, economically, socially. They learn that conflicts can be resolved without losing face and that violence is not a sanctioned way to deal with frustration."

Tony was facing charges before the Family Court.

I WANTED THEM TO BE THE BOSS
by TONY, age 17

When I grow up and have kids of my own, I would teach them the right way before they got too old.

I got away with a lot of things that I did. Sometimes my parents would correct me and sometimes they wouldn't. I wish they would have been the boss.

Message Number 4: *Be my model.*

"Where have you learned to be a man?" I ask the younger boys around our lunch table.

"Jamesburg." Jamesburg is the state training school for boys, four hundred delinquents strong.

"The streets."

When his turn comes, Adam wants to pass. But I'm curious about Adam. When I get him alone in the blue bucket seat by my desk, Adam gives me his answer.

DO WHAT I SAY. NOT WHAT I DO
by ADAM, 16

I seen my dad crushing up white powder in the kitchen, rock form, into coke. Measuring it with his eye and bagging it. Putting a Happy Face sticker on it. 'Bout 50 bags. Called it Smiley Face.

Then he tells me, Don't mess with drugs.

Youngsters look for—*want*—a higher power. Footprints to plant their feet in. Something to tell them that they fit in, that they belong. That higher power may be positive and lead them in the right direction—a father, a coach, a teacher, youth minister, scout leader. It may be negative and drag them down—drug dealers, older boys, criminals. Children supported by home and church and school can resist the negative higher power. Children who have only two of these legs supporting them will wobble. Those with none are headed for disaster.

Alice, my daughter, taught me a lesson one day. She was three years old, standing in a green corduroy jumper on a kitchen chair, helping to grind carrots for a carrot cake.

I watched . . . a child who had grown up with a mother with one hand . . .

I handed her an egg, to let her break it into the bowl. A child of three.

I saw her take the egg and break it open—with one hand.

>⋅↭⋅●⋅↫⋅◁

Two boys of mine faced each other in Courtroom 54 today. Isie and Gabriel.

Thirty-four years ago, a seventeen-year-old student of mine graduated from Camden High School: bright, full of mischief, full of life, full of promise, head filled with dreams. I called him "Isie." Isaiah Steinberg.

Today, another seventeen-year-old student of mine, an apple-cheeked child of the Youth Center, stood in Courtroom 54 to be sentenced for a shooting on the street. Bright, full of mischief, full of life, full of promise. I call him Gabriel. A curly-topped boy in handcuffs. The judge who sentenced Gabriel was Isaiah Steinberg. Two of my boys. Isie and Gabriel, in one courtroom. One in a black robe. One in dungarees. When it was over, back in Isie's private chambers I wept in the judge's arms.

"I knew what you were thinking," Isie said to me.

Gabriel left for prison today.

Yesterday Gabriel sat close beside me to say good-bye. A boy with apple-cheeks and curly hair, one buckle of his overalls dangling undone from his shoulder. The boy had been mine for nineteen months. Gabriel—charged with murder.

The story of Gabriel is a true story of a boy of America. Taped near his pillow so he can touch it while he sleeps is a picture of his brother dead in a coffin, a brother and a sister gunned down inside his home. A boy from nearby North Twenty-fourth Street.

Gabriel gave me my favorite gift this year. His good-bye conversation at my desk.

The boy leans forward to nestle closer. Very private. The birds' nest with the blue robin's egg perch on the bookshelf beside the wall. The empty turtle shell and a Play-doh fortress stand on the table behind the boy. Gabriel knows them all. He helped to make the paper lanterns hanging overhead.

"Did the Reverend and Mrs. Cooper say a good-bye prayer for you last night?" I ask the boy.

"Reverend Cooper held my face in his hands last night and said that the same God that I met here—take Him with me and let Him be my God forever. And that when I go to Yardville that I'm not alone and that I always got a friend—the one friend that always gonna be there with me is God." Yardville is a prison.

I feel the hands of the clock cutting me off from the boy.

"Who touched you, Gabriel . . . like a brother or father . . . inside this place, painting this new picture in your head?"

"In this building?"

"Uh-huh."

"Mrs. Previte touched me." The boy is speaking of me. Third person—as though it is too personal to say "you." "Mrs. Previte touched me."

I can hardly speak. And when I make the words come out, they are almost a whisper so as not to break the spell. "Mrs. Previte. What did she do?"

The voice is gentle, not touched with even one pause to reach for words. "Mrs. Previte taught me that my future doesn't have to be my past." His simple eloquence catches me by surprise.

". . . that I can get an education. She tell me about all the good things that could happen in the future. Make my life better than what I got it now."

The voice floats on—about all the people who have touched him in this place.

Gabriel points to Stevie's picture on the wall. Stevie, with light from the skylight putting a halo around his face. "Somebody drew that right there?"

"That's a photograph of one of my boys that went to college, his college honor-roll picture when he graduated from Camden County College."

"He was right here?"

"Yeh. See, when you graduate, Gabriel, don't think of keeping your picture from me. I want your picture for my wall. See how I keep it here where the sunshine shines on it. Stevie, his name is. One of the first boys when I first came here. You hear me?"

"Uh-huh."

"I mean that. I try to make a picture inside you, so you get a picture of yourself—talented, educated, full of wonderful information, reading. I can start the picture for you. But *you* have to make it happen. Don't be content to be little when you can be big. Don't be content to be a nobody when you are already somebody. You are already somebody wonderful. You hear me? Nod your head. You already are. But you can be even better. You are already up to the twelfth-grade level in reading. You can be up to the thirteenth, fourteenth, fifteenth. Keep growing. Get that dream in your mind of what you want to be."

I cannot say good-bye. "What did we give you, Gabriel?"

"You give me a lotta things. Love. That you care. You gave me a lot. Lotta help."

I find myself thinking out loud. "You can't expect a child to change overnight. Sometimes you have to wait til a child is ready to hear. Maybe I was able to give you something. Just a little thing."

"A big thing."

"There will be some day that you can give that gift to someone else. I put one gift in your hand—love, caring. . . . You're some day gonna do something lovely to somebody else . . . maybe give it to some other person. And I'll remember . . . I gave Gabriel a present. And now he's gonna give it to somebody else.

"*Child, I love you. And I want good things for you. I want you to see as much wonderful inside of yourself as I see inside of you. Let that vision be from me to you. From you to somebody else.*"

"It was a long night, if it were only a night. . . ."

The chimes were ringing the three quarters past eleven at that moment.

"Forgive me if I am not justified in what I ask," said Scrooge, looking intently at the Spirit's robe, *"but I see something strange and not belonging to yourself, protruding from your skirts. Is it a foot or a claw?'*

"It might be a claw, for the flesh there is upon it," was the Spirit's sorrowful reply. *"Look here."*

From the foldings of its robe, it brought two children; wretched, abject, frightful, hideous, miserable. They knelt down at its feet and clung upon the outside of its garment.

"Oh, Man! Look here. Look, look, down here!" exclaimed the Ghost.

They were a boy and a girl. Yellow, meagre, ragged, scowling, wolfish; but prostrate, too, in their humility. Where graceful youth should have filled their features out and touched them with its freshest tints, a stale and shriveled hand, like that of age, had pinched and twisted them and pulled them into shreds. Where angels might have sat enthroned, devils lurked, and glared out menacingly. No change, no degradation, no perversion of humanity, in any grade, through all the mysteries of wonderful creation, has monsters half so horrible and dread.

Scrooge started back, appalled. Having them shown to him in this way, he tried to say they were fine children, but the words choked themselves rather than be parties to a lie of such enormous magnitude.

"Spirit! Are they yours?" Scrooge could say no more.

"They are Man's," said the Spirit, looking down upon them. *"And they cling to me, appealing from their fathers. This boy is Ignorance. This girl is Want. Beware them both, and all of their degree, but most of all beware this boy, for on his brow I see that written which is Doom, unless the writing be erased. Deny it!"* cried the Spirit, stretching out its hand toward the city. *"Slander those who tell it ye! Admit it for your factious purposes, and make it worse! And abide the end!"*

"Have they no refuge or resource?" cried Scrooge.

"Are there no prisons?" said the Spirit, turning on him for the last time with his own words. *"Are there no workhouses? . . ."*

(from "The Second of the Three Spirits")
—*A CHRISTMAS CAROL* by Charles Dickens